Walt Whitman
and
19th-Century
Women Reformers

**FRANCIS CLOSE HALL
LEARNING CENTRE**

Swindon Road Cheltenham

Gloucestershire GL50 4AZ

Telephone: 01242 714600

UNIVERSITY OF
GLOUCESTERSHIRE
at Cheltenham and Gloucester

E

NORMAL LOAN

44706 03/05

Walt Whitman
and
19th-Century
Women Reformers

Sherry Ceniza

The University of Alabama Press
Tuscaloosa and London

∞

The paper on which this book is printed meets the minimum requirements of
American National Standard for Information Science-Permanence of Paper for
Printed Library Materials, ANSI Z39.48-1984.

Library of Congress Cataloging-in-Publication Data

Ceniza, Sherry, 1938–
Walt Whitman and 19th-century women reformers / Sherry Ceniza.
p.   cm.
Includes bibliographical references (p. 269) and index.
ISBN 0–8173–0893–8 (alk. paper)
1. Whitman, Walt, 1819–1892—Political and social views. 2. Women
and literature—United States—History—19th century. 3. Whitman,
Walt, 1819–1891—Friends and associates. 4. Feminism—United
States. 6. Women's rights in literature. 7. Social change in
literature. 8. Radicalism in literature. 9. Women in literature.
I. Title.
PS3242.W6C46   1998
811′.3—dc21   97–24621

British Cataloguing-in-Publication Data Available

Leaves of Grass *is essentially a woman's book: the women do not know it, but every now and then a woman shows that she knows it: it speaks out the necessities, its cry is the cry of the right and wrong of the woman sex—of the woman first of all, of the facts of creation first of all—of the feminine: speaks out loud: warns, encourages, persuades, points the way.*

—Walt Whitman

To Barton and Shawn

Contents

Acknowledgments

My book quotes extensively from letters and other unpublished sources. Abby Hills Price to Abby Kelley Foster, 7 August 1844, which I quote, is located in the Abigail Kelley Foster Papers, American Antiquarian Society, Worcester, Massachusetts. By courtesy of the Trustees of the Boston Public Library, passages from the following letters from the Anti Slavery Collections are quoted: Edmund Quincy to Caroline Weston, 17 September 1844; Abby Hills Price to Samuel May, 5 or 6 July [year not given]; Samuel May to Richard D. Webb, 24 September 1858. The Henry Scholey Saunders Collection of Walt Whitman, at Brown University Library, holds the letter from Augusta Larned to Harry S. Saunders, Ms. 81.5, dated 4 November 1915. Paulina S. Wright to Sidney Howard Gay, 4 April 1845, is quoted courtesy of the Rare Book and Manuscript Library, Columbia University, the Sidney Howard Gay Papers. I quote many letters from Paulina Wright Davis to Caroline Healey Dall and one from Harriet Fosby to Dall (1850–1855); I used the microfilm of the Caroline Healey Dall Papers and reproduce the quoted passsages courtesy of the Massachusetts Historical Society, which holds the originals. The many excerpts of Louisa Van Velsor Whitman's letters to Walt Whitman, held in the Trent Collection, are quoted courtesy of the Special Collections Library, Duke University. Also quoted is an excerpt from the Providence Physiological Society Records (MSS 649), the Manuscript Collection, Rhode Island Historical Society, Providence, Rhode Island. I used passages of letters from Mary Wright Johnson to Ellen Wright, 20 May 1857, and from Martha Coffin Wright to David Wright, 26 October 1856, from the Garrison Family Papers,

Sophia Smith Collection, Smith College. I also used a letter from Mary S. Gove Nichols to Paulina Wright Davis, 29 June 1875, and an undated manuscript of a speech given by Davis, titled "On the Renting of a Hall for Woman's Rights Meetings"; these manuscripts are held in the Paulina Kellogg Wright Davis Papers and are quoted here courtesy of the Special Collections, Vassar College Libraries.

The Charles Feinberg–Walt Whitman Collection and the Horace and Anne Montgomery Traubel Collection at the Library of Congress have contributed much to my book. From the Yale Collection of American Literature, Beinecke Rare Book and Manuscript Library, Yale University, come a letter from Abby Hills Price to Walt Whitman, 25 March 1967, and one from William D. O'Connor to Abby Price, 11 January 1866; I have quoted from both. I used passages of letters from Louisa Van Velsor Whitman to Helen Price courtesy of The Pierpont Morgan Library, New York, MA 918. I quoted from Louisa Van Velsor Whitman to Walt Whitman, M 30 evening, by permission of the Harry Ransom Humanities Research Center, The University of Texas at Austin.

Permission to print excerpts from the Susan B. Anthony Papers was graciously given by Mary Anthony Coughlin, whose great-great grandfather, D. R. Anthony of Leavenworth, Kansas, was Susan B. Anthony's brother. Portions of a letter from Elizabeth Cady Stanton to Susan B. Anthony, 1 March [1853], from the Elizabeth Cady Stanton Papers, is reprinted courtesy of Coleen Jenkins Sahlin, great great granddaughter of Elizabeth Cady Stanton. Portions of Elizabeth Cady Stanton to Paulina Wright Davis, 6 December [1852], Raritan Bay Union, Manuscript Group 285, New Jersey Historical Society, Newark New Jersey, were used by permission.

I appreciate the help that the Rare Books Room at the Ohio Wesleyan University Library offered. Photographs of Louisa Van Velsor Whitman in the 1850s and at age sixty are reproduced courtesy of the Bayley-Whitman Collection, Ohio Wesleyan University. An engraving and two photographs of Walt Whitman (Saunders 4, Folsom, 1850s, no. 2; Saunders 14, Folsom, 1860s, no. 24; and Saunders 28, Folsom, 1860s, no. 25) are also reproduced courtesy of the Bayley-Whitman Collection, Ohio Wesleyan University (for photographs labeled "Folsom," see "Whitman Photographs," *Walt Whitman Quarterly Review,* 4:2/3 [fall/winter 1986–1987]). The photographs of Paulina Wright Davis and of Ernestine L. Rose are reproduced courtesy of The Schlesinger Library, Radcliffe College. The exterior view of the Broadway Tabernacle appears in *View of Broadway* (from Anthony Street East Side looking up), a lithograph by G. Hayward for Valentines Manual 1858, and is reproduced courtesy of the Museum of the City of New York, The J. Clarence Davies Collection. The interior view of the Broadway Tabernacle appears in *Distribution of the American Art–Union Prizes,* Broadway Tabernacle, c. 1847, a lithograph by Sarony and Major, and is reproduced courtesy of the Museum of the City of New York, 29.100.1513, The Clarence J. Davies Collection.

Portions of this book have appeared in a modified form in essays in the following publications: *Walt Whitman Quarterly Review,* edited by Ed Folsom (fall 1989); *Approaches to Teaching Whitman's "Leaves of Grass,"* edited by Donald D. Kummings and published by the Modern Language Association; and *The Cambridge Companion to Walt Whitman,* edited by Ezra Greenspan and published by Cambridge University Press.

I also thank the following people for sharing their research with me: Gay Wilson Allen, Whitman scholar; Paul Curran, Milford, Massachusetts; John Holzhueter, State Historical Society of Wisconsin; Alice Lotvin Birney, American Literature Specialist, Manuscript Division, The Library of Congress; and Morris Schappes, New York City. Barton Lewis helped immeasurably, doing research for me in Manhattan on the many occasions when I could not make the long trip there. Shawn Lewis and Joan Smith Longorio encouraged and helped me, reading and commenting on some of the chapters of this book. Whitman scholars Ed Folsom, Ezra Greenspan, M. Jimmie Killingsworth, Donald Kummings, Jerome Loving, and Ken Price have steadily supported my work.

I am grateful, too, for the financial help I have received, which enabled me to travel long distances to do my research: a Gloria Lyerla Library Memorial Fund Research Travel Grant, from the Texas Tech Library; a South Central Modern Language Association Research and Travel Grant; funds from the Institute for University Research of the College of Arts and Sciences, Texas Tech University; the Feinberg Award of the *Walt Whitman Quarterly Review.* In addition, I received two University of Iowa Alumni Dissertation Travel Awards.

Nicole Mitchell, director of The University of Alabama Press, has steadily supported my work, and I am also grateful to Marcia Brubeck, who copyedited my book and whose careful eye helped the endnotes become more exact than they were originally. Suzette Griffith, Assistant Managing Editor at The University of Alabama Press, has carefully and graciously guided the text and me through the last stages.

Friends and colleagues in the English Department here at Texas Tech contributed to my work with their encouragement: Wendell Aycock, Thomas Barker, Bruce Clarke, Bryce Conrad, Leon Higdon, Carolyn Rude, John Samson, and Joseph Unger, as did librarians Bruce Cammack and Sandra River. Tech history professor Ron Rainger also read a chapter of my book and offered his assistance. Robert C. Wang, M.D., previously at Tech Medical School and now at the University of Nevada Medical School, performed wonders after I suffered a serious injury. Joel Reed, Syracuse University, offered steady encouragement, as did Katie Hauser, Skidmore.

My mainstay was and is Ed Folsom, University of Iowa, who not only directed my dissertation on Whitman but also continues to be there when I ask him for help. An exemplary reader, a fine writer, an astute scholar, an inspiring teacher—Ed is all of these. More than anything else, however, Ed is my friend.

My parents, Neva and Dewey Smith, gave me their love and support all of those years when I was growing up in Edinburg, Texas, as have Joan Smith Longorio, Sue Smith Waters, and Dewey Nelson Smith, my sisters and brother.

I feel especially lucky to have had Tommy Barker in my life for the past five years. He has been more than a colleague. He gently reminds me of the Whitmanian urge to celebrate, and we have, he and I, indeed celebrated.

Finally, as Whitman said that the body or the city or the Union were the real poems, so too do I say that my daughter, Shawn, and my son, Barton, are my real book. They have received my best, and they have given me theirs, in essence urging back my life when the medical profession felt it had no chance.

Walt Whitman
and
19th-Century
Women Reformers

Introduction

In 1889 Walt Whitman described Mary Whitall Smith Costelloe, a friend of his, as "quite a great woman in her way—a true woman of the new aggressive type."[1] Whitman lets us know here that his concept of "true woman" differs markedly from the stereotypically submissive, dutiful Victorian woman. Whitman admired Mary Whitall Smith from the start. She met him when she was a student at Smith College and soon brought him into her family circle, which included her father, Robert Pearsall Smith; her mother, Hannah Whitall; a brother, Logan Pearsall; and Alys, her sister.[2] In 1885, Mary Whitall Smith married Frank Costelloe, a lawyer and politician, and moved to London, where she led an active public life. She and Whitman exchanged letters until 1890.[3] Whitman, who also called Mary Smith Costelloe "the bright particular star,"[4] commented favorably on her newspaper articles, telling his friend Horace Traubel that they were about "all that pertains to progress, suffrage, such things." Whitman, said Traubel, "classed her as very radical indeed—almost along with the Anarchists." Mary Smith was, Whitman said, "much more advanced than her father."[5] Mary Whitall Smith is only one of many remarkable women to whom Whitman listened and from whom he learned.

Thirty years earlier, during the decade of the 1850s, using language like that which he used when speaking of Mary Smith Costelloe—"a true woman of the new aggressive type"—Whitman alluded to "woman under the new dispensation."⁶ The present book seeks to clarify Whitman's meaning when he used this phrase. I focus on the decade of the 1850s, the period of Whitman's most creative work and also the most radical period in woman's rights agitation in the United States until the recent movement that started in the late 1960s. My work on Whitman and antebellum women brings together dominant cultural voices not previously heard as part of the same cultural dialogue. I show how ten years of women's history, 1850–1860, become inscribed in the 1855, 1856, and 1860 editions of *Leaves of Grass*. In doing so, I add cultural contextualization to *Leaves of Grass* of the sort that Ed Folsom calls for in "Prospects for the Study of Walt Whitman": "Much remains to be done in gaining an understanding of just how the various editions responded to their historical moments, how the very forms of the books reflected ideological and philosophical struggles that Whitman was undergoing, not to mention publishing struggles. Each book reifies a moment of political and publishing history." My work addresses another need in Whitman criticism that the Folsom article cites—the need to enhance Whitman's biography: "to build a more fully detailed portrait [by writing] biographies of more of his friends, associates, and family."⁷

Unlike previous studies, this book places women's actual words, words readily available to Whitman in written and spoken formats, in juxtaposition with Whitman's language and analyzes the ways in which the lexicon of women's rights resonates in Whitman's work. The women I write about did not function as adjuncts to Whitman in a historical or literal sense, nor do they function in such a way here. Conspicuous by their absence in Whitman scholarship, they speak in this book as historical personages in their own right. Whitman, who himself was well aware of history's elisions, explained in the 1850s his own view of history's partiality: "Because women do not appear in history or philosophy with anything like the same prominence as men—that is no reason for treating them less than men:—The great names that we know are but the accidental scraps.—Mention to me the twenty most majestic characters that have existed upon the earth, and have their names recorded.—It is very well.—But for that twenty, there are millions upon millions just as great, whose names are unrecorded.—It was in them to do actions as grand—to say as beautiful thoughts—to set examples for their

Walt Whitman, July 1854. This steel engraving by Samuel Hol-
lyer of a daguerreotype by Gabriel Harrison appeared as a
frontispiece in the 1855 *Leaves of Grass*. Reproduced courtesy
of the Bayley-Whitman Collection, Ohio Wesleyan University.

race.—But in each one the book was not opened.—It lay in its place
ready."[8]

In the decade of the 1850s, Whitman published the 1855, 1856,
and 1860 editions of *Leaves of Grass*. Whitman scholars, by and large,
agree that these editions represent Whitman's best work. In that
same decade, the national woman's rights movement held yearly
conventions (but not in 1857), and there were countless state and
local conventions as well. I look at the links between the first three
editions of *Leaves of Grass* and the texts generated in this decade by
women Whitman knew, many of whom were radical activists in the

woman's rights movement. By providing a new and needed context for a revisionary reading of *Leaves of Grass,* then, I attempt to demonstrate that women's cultural history makes a vital contribution to a full reading of *Leaves of Grass.*

This study addresses a concern recently expressed by M. Jimmie Killingsworth: "Fitting Whitman into a category has meant neglecting the power of his poetic language to transform categories, indeed, to overwhelm them."[9] Though Whitman the person was frequently caught in the prejudices of his times, Whitman the poet was able, to an amazing extent, to write himself out of those prejudices. Whitman the theorist of American democracy believed that the world was moving toward the leveling of distinctions. This study tracks the moves Whitman made to inscribe sexual equality in his text and notes, as well, what contemporary consciousness *now* sees as his failures.

I have sought to discover Whitman the listener as well as Whitman the reader and writer, taking seriously the notes Whitman made of conversations, the records others made of him as a conversationalist, and letters to and from Whitman and the women I study. I take Whitman seriously as an attentive reader of newspapers and magazines, as a reader of his culture. After visiting Whitman in 1856, Bronson Alcott wrote in his *Journal:* "Listens well; asks you to repeat what he has failed to catch at once, yet hesitates in speaking often."[10] Helen Price, a friend, wrote in praise of Whitman's ability to listen: "As a listener (all who have met him will agree with me) I think that he was and is unsurpassed. He was ever more anxious to hear your thought than to express his own. . . . He seemed to call forth the best there was in those he met . . . seemed to feel, or at least made others feel, that their opinions were more valuable than his own."[11] She said that in 1883; in 1919 she reiterated the point: "I never knew any one more ready to listen to what others might have to say upon any subject under discussion. He seemed to be more anxious to see their point of view than to express his own. It was a pleasure somewhat rare to find a listener who, as Emerson puts it, entertains your thought.' "[12]

Gay Wilson Allen, in his definitive biography of Whitman, provides a view of Whitman based on long and careful study of countless sources. His repeated references to Whitman's reliance on the ear echo the comments made by those who knew Whitman. Whitman's notebooks, Allen says, "show that whenever he met someone who had traveled abroad, or possessed unusual knowledge, he made a practice of soliciting all the information he could."[13] No doubt Whitman developed many of his ideas of equality first by listening to his mother and then by establishing a close friendship with Abby Hills Price and by listening to her and others like her—women like Ernestine L. Rose, Paulina Wright Davis, Mary Chilton, and Eliza Farnham.

This book argues that *Leaves of Grass* became more of a woman's text in the 1856 edition than it was in 1855 and that the 1860 *Leaves* is the most radically "feminist" of all the editions. The editions therefore follow a trajectory parallel to the woman's rights movement: ten years of contentious reform debate culminated at the 1860 National Woman's Rights Convention. This study documents the movement through the lives of three of its leaders—Abby Hills Price, Paulina Wright Davis, and Ernestine L. Rose. It documents the effect on *Leaves of Grass* of these women's texts, and it argues that Whitman used many of the same arguments and rhetorical gestures that were used by these women, who took the radical line in the movement. In chapter 5, I also discuss women engaged in promoting woman's rights outside the national woman's rights organization. I preface my whole discussion of Whitman and woman's rights (chapters 2–5) with a chapter on Louisa Van Velsor Whitman, Whitman's mother, a woman who, while outside the women's rights movement, nonetheless strongly exerted her will. This book is organized not around a discussion of the different editions of *Leaves of Grass* or around Whitman himself but around the women. Like Jerome Loving's and Florence Bernstein Freedman's biographies of William D. O'Connor, my study enriches our understanding of Whitman by telling about people who influenced his life.

Ed Folsom emphasizes Whitman's cultural responsiveness in his essay " 'Scattering it freely forever' ": "Whitman picked up information here and there, depended heavily on the media of popular culture, read widely but never systematically, had incredibly broad interests, picked up a smattering of French but never really learned any foreign language, and appropriated as his classrooms museums, daguerreotype galleries, theaters, opera houses, beer halls, and phrenology parlors. He spent his formative years immersed in American culture. . . . He loved the chaotic mix of the culture and

Walt Whitman in the 1860s. The photographer is unknown. Reproduced
courtesy of the Bayley-Whitman Collection, Ohio Wesleyan University.

chose to make a poetry out of it."[14] The work that follows examines
an aspect of that culture—the vital world of women's rights—in
which Whitman immersed himself and out of which grew *Leaves of
Grass*. Whitman was aware of the cultural debate concerning women
as one of many cultural debates that influenced his consciousness
and expanded his sense of democracy's meanings and possibilities.
This connection between Whitman and the woman's movement of
the 1850s has been ignored until now.

My book can be visualized as a series of concentric circles. Each
chapter focuses on a discrete circle of friends with a specific individ-

Walt Whitman in the 1860s. The photographer is unknown.
Reproduced courtesy of the Bayley-Whitman Collection,
Ohio Wesleyan University.

ual at the center. My chapter on Louisa Van Velsor Whitman considers her relationship with Whitman as we learn of it from her letters to him. The letters mainly cover the years 1862–1873, the years that Whitman lived in Washington, D.C. But the letters give us a sense of Louisa Van Velsor, and we see why Whitman described her as the primary influence in his life. The letters reveal the unique quality of the relationship that developed over Whitman's lifetime. In this chapter, I provide a new interpretation of Louisa Van Velsor Whitman's life. I write about her not only to vindicate her and reclaim her as a healthy and strong-minded woman but also to show how her own character laid the groundwork for Whitman's appreciation of strong-minded women in general. Whitman's awareness of her strength of character enabled him more easily to perceive, accept, and celebrate strength in women like Frances Wright, Abby Price,

Paulina Wright Davis, Ernestine L. Rose, Juliette Beach, and Mary Chilton; it made him receptive to the woman's rights activists' claims and to their calls for change. It honed his view of an egalitarian society. I also discuss Louisa Van Velsor Whitman's influence in the creation of one of Whitman's favored images—the "Mother of All." Finally, I suggest how Louisa Van Velsor Whitman influenced Whitman's aesthetics, an approach radically different from that taken by most Whitman criticism, which holds that she stifled or at best ignored Whitman's creativity.

Chapter 2 relates the story of Whitman's friendship with Abby Hills Price and her involvement with the communal movement and with the woman's rights movement. Chapter 3 tells the story of the Whitman–Paulina Wright Davis friendship, of Davis's leadership in the woman's movement, and of her focus on women's health and anatomy; and chapter 4 explores connections between Whitman and Ernestine L. Rose, emphasizing her sound knowledge of the theory of democracy. Chapter 5 recounts the story of three women's defense of the 1860 *Leaves of Grass*. Whitman's poetry plays a major role in all five chapters. A brief retrospective conclusion considers what happened to the ideas that Whitman picked up from these women. "Democratic Vistas," which Whitman began writing in 1867 and published in its present form in 1871, is a culminating statement of Whitman's poetics and his politics. It contains his most mature statement of an ideal democracy, which would include active and independent women, as the historical "democracy" of his own time did not. I give the last words in the book to a group of women who wrote to Whitman toward the end of his life.

Finally, it is important to recall here Whitman's own view of *Leaves of Grass*. Significantly, in a culture that honored the male child, Whitman thought of *Leaves* as his female child. In day-to-day life, Whitman did not give priority to the male child, not when his siblings had children or when he, metaphorically, gave birth. In 1865, Whitman wrote to his friend William D. O'Connor: "Still *Leaves of Grass* is dear to me, always dearest to me, as my first born, as daughter of my life's first hopes, doubts, and the putting in form of those days' efforts and aspirations."[15]

In 1888, he told Horace Traubel: "Leaves of Grass is essentially a woman's book: the women do not know it, but every now and then a woman shows that she knows it: it speaks out the necessities, its cry is the cry of the right and wrong of the woman sex—of the woman first of all, of the facts of creation first of all—of the feminine: speaks out loud: warns, encourages, persuades, points the way."[16]

Whitman was not speaking idle words. This book explores what lies behind them: a wide range of relationships between Whitman and a group of radical women.

1

Louisa Van Velsor Whitman

In a letter to her son Walt dated 12 January 1872, Louisa Van Velsor Whitman wrote that she was getting a box together, one of a long train of boxes over the years, to send to her daughter Hannah: "i got 10 1/2 yds of muslin and two dresses one a gingam and one delain and a can of peaches and some other things and george will give me 2 dollar to put in." One week later, she wrote Walt again and described once more what had gone into the box: "we sent 2 dresses and lot of muslin and flannel skirts and can of peaches and new years cake and lot of french candy and 2 dollars in money and cotton and sewing silk and linings for the dresses." Louisa Whitman's boxes were compilations important to her. In some essential way, Whitman's poems were to him what Louisa Whitman's boxes were to her.[1]

Louisa Whitman's care packages serve as images for one side of the polarity that Whitman said exists in us all: "The soul has that measureless pride which consists in never acknowledging any lessons or deductions but its own. But it has sympathy as measureless as its pride, and the one balances the other, and neither can stretch too far while it stretches in company with the other."[2] Though the packages and letters to Hannah might seem to place Louisa Whitman on the sympathy side in her son's equation, she also had the "measureless pride" of which Walt spoke. Indeed, Whitman called his mother "the ideal woman, practical, spiritual, of all of earth, life, love, to me the best."[3] By discovering the details of Louisa Whitman's life and

Louisa Van Velsor Whitman (1795–1873) in the 1850s. Reproduced courtesy of the Bayley-Whitman Collection, Ohio Wesleyan University.

character, then, we may concretize Walt's notion of the ideal female citizen living in American democracy. Knowledge of the details of Louisa's life adds as well to our reading of Whitman's poetry, for Whitman's poetics and his sense of democracy are inextricably fused.

Louisa's "sympathy"—the threads of connection that Louisa established as she involved each one of her children in the lives of the others, as she interacted with her friends, boarders, and neighbors, and as she kept sending Hannah boxes and letters—finds resonance in Whitman. It is woven into a letter he wrote to his friend Abby Price from Washington in which he spoke of his work in the Civil War hospitals, listing in detail the oranges and stamps and gifts of small sums of money he made to the soldiers, a replication of Louisa's own boxes to Hannah. It is woven into his poetics and into his sense of community. Threads connecting Walt and Louisa—indeed Louisa's very ambience—wove themselves into Walt's very being: "How much I owe her! It could not be put in a scale—weighed: it could not be measured—be even put in the best words: it can only be apprehended through the intuitions. Leaves of Grass is the flower of her temperament active in me. My mother was illiterate in the formal sense but strangely knowing: she excelled in narrative—had great mimetic power: she could tell stories, impersonate: she was very eloquent in the utterance of noble moral axioms—was very original in her manner, her style. . . . I wonder what Leaves of Grass would have been if I had been born of some other mother."[4] Whitman speaks here of Louisa's style—her narrative skill, her mimetic power, her ability to take on personae, her eloquence "in the utterance of noble moral axioms," her originality: her style. He speaks of his debt to her style. He stresses here, then, not her gendered role of Mother/Nurturer (with its culturally created corollary, "sympathy") but her own creativity. In his poetry, Whitman often conflates the two: motherhood/creativity. It is criticism, not Whitman's poetry, which has focused on one to the exclusion of the other; it is critics, such as D. H. Lawrence, who see wombs as a negative. Not so Whitman.

Seeing Louisa in the light of her own creativity permits us to interpret her in a new way—new to scholarship, that is. Louisa is part of that long foreground of which Emerson spoke in his 1855 letter to Whitman. In addition to adding insight into this long foreground, seeing Louisa Van Velsor Whitman as an individual, an individual woman, will affect the way we read the images of women and of mothers in *Leaves of Grass*. Ultimately, it will also affect the way in which we read Whitman's concept of American democracy.

In 1949, Clarence Gohdes and Rollo G. Silver reprinted sixteen of Louisa's letters in their edition of Whitman and Whitman-related manuscripts, *Faint Clews and Indirections*. They did so because they wanted to add "to existing information on the poet's family and with the idea of illustrating the interest in politics and reading which Mrs.

Whitman also shared" and because they felt that a study of Whitman's family helped to account for Whitman's democratic ideas: "The poet was reared in the midst of the greatest democratic institution known to mankind—a large family. The center of it, until he himself took over, was his mother."[5] Though Gohdes and Silver regarded the family as a democratic institution—a view that hardly convinces many readers today—the fact that they saw Louisa's strength and her own intellectual interests distinguishes them as unusual readers of Louisa and sets them off from critics who followed. Twenty years later, for example, Edwin Haviland Miller, in his book *Walt Whitman's Poetry,* reads Whitman's mother as a negative, even malevolent, force in Whitman's life.[6]

Edwin Haviland Miller's dislike for Louisa is apparent in his comments about her in his notes in *The Correspondence* and in *Walt Whitman's Poetry: A Psychological Journey.* In the book, for example, Miller says of Louisa, "The sea-mother fails to 'gather' her castaway to her breast, just as the egocentric indifference of Louisa Van Velsor Whitman repelled her son but made him hunger for affection" (47). Miller links Walt senior's alcoholism and his failure in business to Louisa's "dominance": "Partly because of his failure but also because of her aggressive nature, Mrs. Whitman dominated the family. (That the father and two sons sought escape in the male society of taverns and that Walt ordinarily depicts passive males are consequences, I suspect, of the mother's emasculating rule of the family)" (48). The language equates Louisa's willingness to think and act for herself negatively; it becomes negative "dominance" and an "aggressive nature" that in its "dominance" runs the males in the family to drink and also renders them "passive," thus "emasculating" them. Miller counters an earlier scholar's conjecture that Whitman left home because he had difficulty dealing with his father: "It is more likely that, though he found the capricious behavior of an alcoholic father difficult, he found equally difficult the matriarchy which Mrs. Whitman had established in the household" (48). He charges Louisa with "nagging querulousness [which is] present in the hundreds of extant letters Mrs. Whitman wrote to her children, which are filled with self-pity and hostility toward anything that disrupted her way of life" (55).

David Cavitch's dislike for Louisa exceeds Miller's. Moreover, Cavitch's accounts contain factual inaccuracies. These accounts appear in his 1985 *My Soul and I: The Inner Life of Walt Whitman* and in shortened form in the 1985 *Walt Whitman: Here and Now,* edited by Joann P. Krieg.[7] Cavitch says, for example:

> The calm possessiveness of the earth in "This Compost" and the withering complacency of the woman in "Song of the Broad-Axe" reveal Whitman's horrified suspicion that he was betrayed in his deepest trust. He saw from a child's perspective the threatening self-centeredness of his mother to whom he again felt vulnerably exposed. She could allow her sick infant to die; she could exile her oldest child, who would not acquiesce to her denial of the squalor and misery of their life; she overrode her second child's feelings with her own, making him her favorite; she imposed on all her children a dependence and obligation as rankling as Eddie's helpless idiocy, which mirrored their plight; and now she could bury the worn-out and useless husband and father—all while acting as if nothing were seriously amiss. She appeared possibly treacherous, even while they continued to "stick by each other" as long as they lived. [96]

There is no basis for Cavitch's statement that Louisa allowed her infant child to die. As for Jesse, Louisa did not want to put him in an asylum. Louisa wrote to Walt:

> i got your letter walt about jesse Jeffey must have wrote very strong about him. . . . well walt jessy is a very great trouble to me to be sure and dont appreceate what i doo for him but he is no more deranged than he has been for the last 3 years i think it would be very bad for him to be put in the lunatic assiliym if he had some light employment but that seems hard to get i could not find it in my heart to put him there without i see something that would make it unsafe for me to have him he is very passionate almost to frenzy and always was but of course his brain is very weak but at the time of his last blow out we had every thing to confuse and irritate.[8]

Cavitch's statements simply are not true to the facts; they are not borne out by primary documents.[9]

Though by no means her only detractor, Miller is an especially influential one because of his prominence as editor of Whitman's *Correspondence,* with his explanatory notes and commentary a part of each of the six volumes of the twenty-two-volume *Collected Writings of Walt Whitman*. The notes and commentary on some level function as interpretation of Louisa and thereby guide readers' views of her. Also, Miller's Freudian study of Whitman's poetry has been influential. Contrary to the view that scholars such as Edwin Haviland Miller and David Cavitch hold about Louisa, I argue that she was a formative figure in Walt's life, offering him a role model that helped him redefine a restricted cultural conception of motherhood and instead valorize the potential strengths of mother[parent]hood. As the United States moved closer and closer to fragmentation in the 1850s—culminating in the Civil War—the need for images of cohesion became more immediate and apparent, and strengths such as those that Louisa possessed provided an obvious template for one of Whitman's most suggestive images for the Union—the cohesive "immortal mother" who would ensure national unity.[10]

Also, Louisa Van Velsor's own writing presented Whitman with a model for the syntactically loose, emotively *present* voice that he developed in his poetry. The lack of punctuation that readers today find off-putting Whitman perhaps found suggestive. Reading Louisa's letters forces us to pay attention to the rhythm of the syntax, forces us to supply the stops and pauses, since Louisa uses no standard syntactical signs. She was, finally, a more aware and creative person than Whitman scholarship has so far allowed us to see, and her influence on her son, far from being psychologically debilitating, was artistically and politically liberating.

A month before Louisa died, miserably unhappy living at the home of her son George and her daughter-in-law Lou, she wrote to Walt, "if i was younger i should show some of my dignity."[11] This is a telling line, for it shows her extreme self-awareness and her pride, the quality Whitman saw as necessary to keep a person from being subordinated to another's will. As such, it is an especially poignant remark, since at that time in her life, Louisa clearly knew she had been subjugated.

The theme of Louisa's financial dependence on her sons runs throughout the letters; the theme's persistence, and the change in her tone when she asks Walt for money, become painful. Walt was by far the most giving, the most dependable, and the most nurturing of her children, and Louisa acknowledged these qualities in her letters to him. Still, she was dependent, aware of the threat of the poorhouse.[12] She was not an exception in this respect; rather, the exception would have been for a nineteenth-century woman—regardless of class—to be economically independent. Christine Stansell, in *City of Women,* describes the kind of threat Louisa Whitman felt: "A woman's age, marital status, the number and age of her children and, above all, the presence or absence of male support determined her position in working-class life. Any woman, whether the wife of a prosperous artisan or a day laborer's daughter, was vulnerable to extreme poverty if, for some reason, she lost the support of a man."[13]

Louisa's awareness of her dependency is obvious: "i often think how loth many is to have children and what would become of me if i had none"; "people dont want to have children but i dont know what would become of me in my old days if i had none"; "we . . . have got one of the old fashion snow storms . . . but i think we have got enoughf to eat to stand through it if it dont last too long thank god and good sons."[14]

The many moves the Whitman family made only heightened Louisa's vulnerability. It had been customary to change houses when Walter senior was alive, and the custom remained after his death. Louisa herself formed the habit, at least by 1860, of renting a brownstone in Brooklyn, subletting the more desirable floors, and leaving the basement or ground floor for the family. Her son Jeff and daughter-in-law Mattie and their children frequently lived with her or at least in the same brownstone. She always made a home for Ed, her youngest son, who had suffered brain damage as a child; her son Jesse, who was eventually committed to a mental hospital, lived with her periodically; and her son Andrew and his children used her home frequently as a base, a necessity, since Andrew himself was financially completely irresponsible, as was his wife, Nancy. Louisa's daughter Mary visited occasionally. Walt himself moved in and out of this protean circle until he went to Washington. Only Hannah, Louisa's other daughter, did not frequent her home. Until Louisa moved to Camden, against her will, Walt always regarded the Brooklyn house as home, whatever its address.

Louisa well knew the power and powerlessness of money. She spoke to Walt of Jeff's and George's stinginess, though she never described it as such. She remarked once that it was odd that every time Jeff sent her money, fate somehow kept it from reaching her. She wryly noted that making a good salary did Jeff and Mattie no good, since they remained by their own account as short of money as ever: "matty sent me two 25 cent bills," she wrote Walt, "quite a lift wasent it walt."[15] Her frequent assertions that George would never fail to support her betray her fear. More than once she wrote to Walt comments such as "for all that[,] george would never see me want i have too high opinion of him to think he would ever shirk in any way if i was needy."[16] She grew tired of hearing constant talk of money after she moved to Camden: "the more we have the more we want," she said. She saw the difference between her enforced frugality and George and Lou's parsimony.

Her financial dependency created emotional dependency. Louisa felt threatened by George far more than by Jeff or Walt. After the Civil War ended and George returned to Brooklyn to live, he had trouble adjusting to civilian life, and the strain showed in their relationship. Louisa was aware of George's discontent, but perhaps because of her dependence on him, his moodiness exacerbated her own sense of unease over her own space—her fear of possible homelessness. She spoke to Walt of George's moodiness. Her letter speaks of her abasement:

> i was glad to have the letter and glad to have the 2 dollars at noon i hadent one cent and i asked georgee to give me 50 cents and after looking for a considerable time he laid me down 50 cents well Walt i felt so bad and child like i cried because he dident give me more if i had got the 2 dollars a little sooner i should not have asked i have got along very well up to about 2 weeks ago and since that time george has been moody and would hardly speak only when i spoke to him well of course you will say mother put the worst construction on it well walt i did not the first few days i thought perhaps something had gone wrong in his business affairs but up to to day he has been so different from what he was ever since i have been home but to day he is more like himself well Walt i thought of every thing sometimes i would think maybee he is tired of having me and edd and then i would think george is too noble a fellow for that to be the cause and i knew that i had not or he had not been to more expence than if he paid his board Jeffy told me to have a talk with george and ask him what made him so but i dident like to i would ask him if he wasent well and so on but i doo hope it will go over i acted just the same as if i did not notice any change but i felt awful bad and

what has made him act so god only knows but i beleive it runs in the
Whitman family to have such spells any how i hope they wont come
often.[17]

The shifts within this letter tell a lot about Louisa's disposition.
They move from Louisa's avowal of her abasement ("i felt so bad and
child like") to her sense of dependence ("maybe he is tired of have-
ing me and edd") to her desire to believe in George's sense of ethics
("george is too noble a fellow for that to be the cause") to her astute
awareness of the economics of the household structure ("i knew that
i had not or he had not been to more expence than if he paid his
board"). But she could not confront George with this awareness. Her
way to cope with her conflicting emotions was to see a genetic cause
("i beleive it runs in the Whitman family") and to hope George's
spells wouldn't come too often. The picture of George that emerges
from Louisa's letters is similar to the picture the poet-persona in
"There Was a Child Went Forth" gives of the father—a harsh man,
quick-acting, self-centered—though Louisa herself constantly affirms
George's goodness in her letters to Walt. Finally, the narrative struc-
turing in this vignette could be an example of what Whitman referred to when he told Traubel that his mother "excelled in narrative—had great mimetic skill." It's a well-told story.

While Louisa's boarders did not make her financially independent, they gave her the variety that she liked in her life. She
complained about them, but she missed them when they were gone.
Her home was an extended circle made up of boarders, grown children, spouses, and grandchildren, with countless friends coming
and going and sharing talk, tea, and food, her children's adult
friends, whom she would feed and bed down, and Whitman's Washington friends, who stopped to visit. For her, quiet times were a "lull
in the confusion." She liked the confusion, though at times she tired
of it. She talked about the tradespeople she dealt with—Ammerman
the grocer, the baker Mrs. Steers, the butcher, and the soap maker.
She spoke of the horse cars going by her door, of the dead horses
lying in the streets and the odor. She did not live in the isolated
home of the urban nineteenth-century white bourgeois lady, whose
space is described by Stansell as "an embellished inner space cut off
from the public world."[18] There was no sharp demarcation between
the borders of Louisa's home and the streets outside her home. Like

the urban working-class woman, Louisa identified closely with her neighborhood, just as her son Walt identified with the crowd.

A lot of the talk in the letters concerned home and the need either to rent a new place or to own a home. In the earliest letter we have from Walt to Louisa, written from New Orleans in 1848, Whitman introduces the theme: "I long for the day when we can have our quiet little farm, and be together again—."[19] Fifteen years later, after settling in Washington, Whitman lost no time in writing to his mother about a home; he kept telling her not to worry about a house; the "quiet little farm" became a "ranch," a "shanty," a "place on one or one half acres." Louisa responded in kind. "I often think," she said to him in 1867, "if i had a shanty i could be contented where i could be at peace and not have to move i will try to take things coolly as you advise."[20] In an April 1867 letter, Walt told her: "You must not be uneasy about a place—there will be some way provided—If not one way, it will be another, I hope—So mother, keep a good heart—I guess I must try to come on to Brooklyn & set you all right—."[21] Finally, in 1869, George built a home in Brooklyn and Louisa moved into it, renting out part of it. Louisa wrote Walt, "the house aint done but we shall have to move on saturday your next letter you must direct portland ave) i beleive the number is 71 opposite the Arsenal." She told Walt that she had "comfort . . . that i shant have to move again very soon," but she added, prudently, "but strange things happen in these days dont they Walt so its best not to make any calculation."[22] Three and a half years later, under protest, she made her last move—to live and to die at the Camden home of George and Lou.

The tension between Louisa's strong sense of self and her financial and resultant emotional dependency surfaces throughout her letters. In any one letter the tone will shift from her wry sense of humor as she comments on the pompousness of Charles Heyde, her son-in-law, to her lament over her dependency. Given the historical circumstances, she had no alternatives to this dependency. She admired resourcefulness in a woman; her daughter-in-law Mattie had that quality, and though she and Mattie at times were at odds with each other, they were extremely close. She admired women who resisted domination. She grieved because her daughter Hannah showed neither resourcefulness nor resistance. In an 1869 letter, she told Walt a chilling story of a young couple that lived on the floor

above her. The story reveals Louisa's acceptance of male abuse, but
it also shows the value she placed on any kind of resistance, which,
Louisa felt, Hannah lacked:

> i wish han was something like young chappells wife up stairs here
> he is awfull at times wishes to god he could find her dead when he
> come home she dont know i suppose i hear him swear at her the
> other night he made a great noise i thought he had knocked her
> down but i gess he dident the next day she was singing and lively as
> usual she says he has an awful temper but it goes in one ear and out
> the other her mother lives in brooklyn has her second husband she
> was in my room the other day she said Janey deserved a better lot
> that her father was a minester i think they are from the south but
> Janey gives as much back as she gets she goes to her mother and
> stays a week or two edd says he told him he liked to be alone).[23]

Louisa's attempts to get Hannah to exert a will of her own never
worked. Hannah seldom wrote; at times her husband Heyde wrote
in her place. In one letter, Louisa told Walt that she had received a
letter from Heyde telling her that Hannah "has very many dresses
to make but wears nothing but ragged dresses i wish han had more
exertion about her so i sent the money george gave me for her to
get her things made if she couldent make them herself."[24] Louisa,
however, *did* exert herself, and it is to Whitman's credit that it was
exactly this quality in his mother that he most admired, a quality
responsible for the charge that critics have made about her being
"dominant," "aggressive," and "emasculating." Her pride and her exertion prepared Whitman to listen to women like Frances Wright
and Abby Price and to recognize, to use his own phrase, "woman
under the new dispensation."[25]

After Walt moved to Washington, letters replaced the talks he
and Louisa were used to sharing. Correspondence soon came to be
an important part of Louisa's life: "here goes another of mothers
scientific letters when i get desperate i write commit it to paper as
you literary folk say."[26] Interestingly, Louisa's letters are filled with
references to her own compulsion to write (albeit letters and not
poems): "i feel as if i must write a few lines every time i get a letter
i cant feel satisfied until i write sometimes i think its real foolish to
write every week but if i dont it seems as if i had something to doo
that i had neglected."[27] Her lack of punctuation at first makes read-

ing her letters disconcerting. But soon her letters begin to take on a life of their own, demanding a new relationship between the reader and text. Her textual demands are not so very different from Whitman's with his innovative use of punctuation in the 1855 *Leaves of Grass* and Preface, where he uses ellipses as if they were standard punctuation and thus creates a flow of thought that is unbroken by standard grammatical signs. Louisa's omission of standard punctuation forces the reader to create line breaks and lexical units, to engage actively with the text as a reader. In addition, a certain distinctive rhythm emerges in Louisa's prose, a prose that has a leveling quality evident in her nonhierarchical use of "i" in place of "I." Also, her lack of punctuation forces each word to relate to the next on a more or less equal basis. It doesn't take long for her writing voice to assume a strong presence. Her use of written as well as spoken language may well have been part of what the poet-persona in "There Was a Child Went Forth" calls the "family usages"—in this case, the idiosyncratic use of language. To appreciate her letters, the reader must look for something other than formal literacy.

Louisa often used phrases that are familiar to readers of *Leaves of Grass;* she told Walt that George "was here to breakfast this morning but felt as if he would like *to loaf and live at his ease* there was no particular need as i told him of his going to work so soon but he seemed inclined to doo so" (emphasis added).[28] A phrase that she used in another letter, speaking about time on a simplistic level, articulates a principle that becomes a central theme in Whitman's "Song of Prudence." In this poem, Whitman develops his concept of constant regeneration:

> Who has been wise receives interest,
> Savage, felon, President, judge, farmer, sailor, mechanic, literat, young, old, it
>   is the same,
> The interest will come round—all will come round.[29]

The phrase Louisa uses is "time comes round."[30] Louisa uses this phrase as she reflects on an anecdote she has just written to Walt. In different permutations, Louisa reiterates the concept frequently, the concept of acceptance and of cyclic movement, which for Whitman becomes more complex as he factors into it a notion of history and science, of evolution. Louisa's anecdote and reflection on it bear out what Whitman meant when he speaks of his mother as "Illiterate in the formal sense but strangely knowing," having "great mimetic power" and skillful narrative techniques, and achieving a certain "eloquence in the utterance of noble moral axioms."

Her way of talking evidently suited her just fine. In a letter written to Walt from Hannah and Charlie's home in Vermont, Louisa dismisses Charlie Heyde's pompousness: "i will try to stand the gramatical phrases."[31] In another letter, she shows her awareness of a turn of phrase: "I have just received your favor as the business men say enclosing 3 dollars."[32] She told Walt that George thought it awfully funny when one of her boarders called her "Lady Whitman." She laconically commented "so your writing again leaves of grass well if it dont hurt you i am glad."[33]

Louisa and Walt discussed politics, on both the local and national level, and her letters allow us to track Whitman's own concerns during the traumatic Civil War period and its aftermath. In late 1863, she commented on the Union generals Burnside and Meade: "O i am so afraid the rebels will get the better of Burny i hope he will be ready for them sometimes i think i wish mead was removed but i know so little about it but the army of the potomac seems to me to always be a little too late."[34] She felt ambivalence about the movement to impeach Andrew Johnson: "well walt we have lived to see something that never was i suppose known before in america the impeachment) i think it rather sad but notwithstanding exactly as it should be."[35] She commented on Thaddeus Stephens's speech, read before the impeachment, which she felt was "very good indeed."

From February to May 1868, she closely followed the progress of President Johnson's trial. In March, she said, "doo you know walt i have always felt a kind of sadness when i read the articles of impeachment not but what i always thought he was bad but there is so many things to be considered)." In April, "i have read the impeachment articles every day i was in hopes it would be carried through without any postponement." And finally, in May: "i suppose the impeachment is dragging to a close george thinks Bingams speech is splendid . . . i havent read it yet their speeches is so long i hope this will not be so lengthy as the others poor old man i wonder how he feels) it will be rather sad if he is convicted for all i suppose he hasent done right i see in the papers if he leaves he will be escorted through the citys)."[36] She supported the nomination and election of Colfax and Grant. Six months after the election, however, she worried about Grant's ability: "i always said if Grant got to be president i hoped he wouldent disappoint his party but i dont know i hope he wont but i suppose time will tell."[37] She said in March of '69 that she felt some of the pardons given Confederate soldiers were perhaps good, but that too many had been given. As late as the spring of 1873, several months before she died, she still commented on politics.

Most important, however, was news from home, which Whitman said was more important to him than anything else. "Mat was going to send me a good long letter—hope it will be full of family matters—nothing is too trifling, nothing uninteresting," he wrote Louisa.[38] In the give and take of their letters, they created many ongoing narratives. One is the reading they made of Hannah's husband, Charlie. Heyde, pretentious and jealous of Whitman, was the one person Whitman said that he thoroughly disliked. Louisa consistently defused Heyde's pretensions and bombast through understatement: "O i must tell you i got a letter from charley heyde yesterday it certainly was the best i think he ever wrote he always when he writes to me begins with mrs whitman this was commenced with dear mother whitman . . . i thought to myself when i read his letter has charley heyde got religion it was so different from his former letters probably the next will be the old stile."[39] In another letter she told Walt she had received from Heyde "three sheets of foolscap paper and a fool wrote on them."[40] But Walt and Louisa also wrote about Jeff, Mattie, and their two children, about George, the Price family, and other family friends, and about their own health and activities.

Louisa was able to fulfill her desire to read as she grew older and had fewer children to care for. She received much of her reading material from Walt, who sent package after package of books, newspapers, and magazines to her.[41] He sent her *The Life of John Brown*, a book by George Sand, countless unnamed books, including copies of his own work. He sent her copies of the *Tribune*, the *Star*, the *Chicago News*, the *Sun*, *Harper's*, *Appleton's Journal*, the *Galaxy*, the *Graphic*, the *Atlantic*: "i got all the papers last week and have got three to day. . . . i dont know what i would have done yesterday without those papers i had harpers weekly."[42] On another occasion: "got your package yesterday with the envelopes and letter and 1 dollar and book to read."[43] In letter after letter Louisa acknowledges Whitman's packages: "i also got the books you spoke of and have read them both through."[44] And again: "i got the papers today with the letter walter i like the chicago news very much i never saw one before i wish whenever you have one you would send it to me."[45] She read almanacks:

"i wanted to see about the moon and the sun rising and all."[46] The following year, she wrote to acknowledge the 1868 almanack Whitman sent her: "i got the franklyn almanack but i have not got the papers you spoke of today. . . . the carrier . . . brought me a number of books and the almanac its a real good one much better than the tribune one."[47] Louisa preferred papers which carried politicians' speeches: "i like so to read the speaking in the house."[48] On another occasion she wrote: "got the big book i doo so like to have something to read."[49]

She read Whitman's poems: "i have the whisper of heavenly death it lays here on the table by my side i have read it over many times. . . . i liked it it was so solemn."[50] The view of Whitman as a poet not accepted within his own family circle—a common view within Whitman criticism and espoused by Whitman as well—is not entirely fair. Though Whitman's mother, sisters, and brothers did not read his poetry with anything like the level of understanding and appreciation that many of his contemporaries did, they *did* read it; Louisa frequently mentions his poetry in her letters: "where is all the Drum taps we have looked all over for one or two i thought you left some up stairs but cant find one i had one of the first ones on the table here and i cant find it i used to read some in it almost every night before i went to bed.[51] Helen Price, in her 1919 article describing her family's close relationship with Whitman and thereby illuminating facets of his personality, speaks of the family's reception of Whitman's poetry: "It was my impression in my frequent visits to his mother that those of Walt Whitman's family that I met there took little interest in his book, although they were devoted to him as he to them." Price goes on to say: "My mother once called upon Mrs. Whitman and read to her Walt's latest poem, 'The Mystic Trumpeter.' She told my mother that she had read it but did not understand it. She was not an educated woman, but she possessed what was far better than anything books could give her. One felt in her quiet, undemonstrative manner a tender, loving sympathy, a cheerful, uncomplaining spirit, although she had led far from an easy life, and a charm that made it a delight to be with her."[52] Gauging from her letters, Louisa did make an effort to read Whitman's poetry. That she did not always understand it and that she was not an astute reader are understandable. She frequently mentions critical reviews and comments on Whitman and his work, and she often sent these on to Whitman. She asked Walt in April 1867 if he had seen the

Times article "about your being the only american poet i cut it out
and was going to send it to Jeff if you havent seen it i will send it to
you."[53]

She made her own critical judgments: "i have got a union with
an article about your book [*Drum-Taps*] i told Jeff to take it and send
it to you would you like to have it or dont you care about it, it is not
so severe as the one in the nation of the 16th november tom Rome
left it here for me to read he is quite put out about it i should like
for mr Oconnor to see that in the nation it is a long piece with flourishes) the one in the union made me laughf."[54] For the most part,
Louisa disliked the writing style of William D. O'Connor, Whitman's
writer friend, because of what she called its "flourishes," though she
liked O'Connor's *Good Gray Poet* better than John Burroughs's book
on Whitman. She liked the presence of voice she heard in *The Good
Gray Poet:* "Oconnors shows the spirit its wrote in i should form an
idea of the man if i had never seen him by reading his writing i
suppose you see that piece in the sunday times as you dident say
anything about it i will send it."[55]

O'Connor's other pieces, however, irritated Louisa, who makes
the connection between conversational style and writing, a connection her son worked to achieve. She wrote to Walt in February 1868:
"I think we will get the galaxy and see the Oconor peice if its as
stupid as his others i dont think it will be worth 25 cents i dont see
into his writing such peices as he writes i should think him capable
of writing something more substancial a man that can converse as
he can."[56] She disliked O'Connor's *Galaxy* piece, "The Ballad of Sir
Ball," a mock-heroic poem attempting to clarify the authorship of
"Rock Me to Sleep," a poem published in 1860.[57] She wrote to Whitman: "It is signed w. i hope nobody will think you wrote it walt."
Louisa's critical sense expressed itself in her admiration of Anne Gilchrist, whose work Gay Wilson Allen says "rightfully won for herself a reputation in literature."[58] Gilchrist's article on Whitman, "A
Woman's Estimate of Walt Whitman," appeared in the May 1870 issue of the *Boston Radical.* Allen praises her assessment of *Leaves of
Grass,* and especially of the "Children of Adam" cluster, saying that
her insights were more "imaginatively expressed than [Whitman's]
own defense in the open letter to Emerson in the second edition."[59]
Louisa wrote of Gilchrist to Walt: "i got the 2 radicals one i got one
day and the other the next i set right down and read it that Lady
seems to understand your writing better than ever any one did be-

fore as if she could see right through you she must be a highly educated woman."[60]

The last nine months of Louisa Van Velsor Whitman's life are not
pleasant to read about. In 1881 Maurice Bucke wrote Helen Price,
Abby Price's daughter and Louisa's good friend, asking her to send
Louisa's letters, to help him as he prepared a biography of Whitman.
Helen Price refused his request because she felt Louisa's letters written to her after she moved to Camden misrepresented Louisa. Price
felt the move to Camden hastened Louisa's death. She said that, to
a stranger, the letters that Louisa had written her during this period
would give "no true idea of her, She was naturally so bright, sunny,
genial in her temperament."[61]

Louisa called George and Lou's Camden home, where she
moved in 1872, "scientific": "everything must be kept so scientific
here i dont know sometimes how it is i hope there will never be any
thing to annoy or disturb the manager i think sometimes a person
can be to particular Lou aint so nice about any thing but the appearance of the house that seems to be her hobby."[62] Louisa's dislike of
precision, in the ambience of her home and in her writing, was a
quality her son shared, both in the disarray of his own room in his
Mickle Street home and in his poetic aesthetic, which, he claimed,
was full of imprecision:

> Do I contradict myself?
> Very well then I contradict myself,
> (I am large, I contain multitudes.)[63]

Both were saying not that they wanted no structure but that they
preferred to structure their life, and in Whitman's case his poetry,
inductively. Both wanted to give the appearance, at least, of letting
form happen. For Louisa, the positive element of home lay in its
offering a space into which people came and from which they went;
there was an improvisatory quality to her life. Whitman wanted to
present the same quality in his poetry. Thus, Lou's conception of
home as an engineered space in no way fit Louisa Van Velsor's disposition: "i have two rooms on the second floor and george and lou
is kind," she wrote her young friend Helen Price—actually a surro-
gate daughter—"but o hellen dear i would rather have my own
shanty and my good friends come to see me this is a very lonesome
place every thing quiet and precise."[64] One month later she wrote

again to Helen Price, "camden is a very dull place every thing very precise and uneventful."[65]

The words "contented," "comfort," and "composed" become almost a leitmotif in her letters to Helen and Walt: "helen i try to be as contented as circumstances will admit"; "helen i knowed i should never be contented to live with any one but helen i try to be contented but them old brooklyn times comes to my mind very often i wish we had took more comfort and you had staid more with me"; "hellen i must try to compose myself and think its all for the best"; "i try to bee contented but the good old times to brooklyn will come to my mind"; "helen . . . i dont like it here i can never feel contented if walter gets well i shall have a hope that he will get some little place for his own comfort as well as mine . . . i cant write all my troubles . . . some is real and some immaginary."[66]

Her letters document her growing despair. Louisa felt useless, especially when Lou's aunt came and stayed.[67] Louisa spoke of feeling rebuffed by Lou and her aunt. They were both "English," Louisa said, and she felt that they looked down on her. She was lonely. She felt unwanted, even by George. She kept telling Walt that she missed Mattie and that she had only him and Helen Price to talk to—and she could only do that through letters.

At first she tried to adjust. It was right, she said, for Lou to be in charge, but still, she did not like living under another's rules. She did not want managed space. She was lonely. She disliked the sterility of George and Lou's life. She wanted the confusion of her own home, with boarders and friends and children and grandchildren and bills to the grocer Ammerman to worry about. She wanted her friends to come in for tea and for them to sit around and talk. She missed having someone to talk to. I think that loneliness and grief finally killed Louisa.

She died on 23 May 1873. Appropriately enough, she left one last letter, her voice persisting beyond her death (her version of Walt's "So Long"): "farewell my beloved sons farewell i have lived beyond all comfort in this world dont mourn for me my beloved sons and daughters farewell my dear beloved Walter."[68]

Edwin Haviland Miller's notes accompanying the letters in *The Correspondence* create a far different picture of Louisa from mine. Since Louisa's letters have not yet been published, Miller's interpretations of her dictate many readers' views of her. Miller footnotes a comment Walt made to Louisa ("I . . . hope this will find you comfortable"), for example, several months after she had moved to Camden: the footnote reproduces part of Louisa's 3 December 1872 letter, in which Louisa complained to Walt of George and Lou's frugality: "lou and george are very clever but i think they are a very saving couple. what they want to save so much for i cant see as they have no young ones but maybe its all right. george is so changed in regard to being saving but i cant get used to being so ecomical." Miller says: "This from Mrs. Whitman, who was the very model of thriftiness!"[69] Knowledge of the actualities of her situation calls into question Miller's reading of Louisa. At the time, Walt was paying George and Lou twenty dollars a month for Ed's room and board, though George made much more money than Walt. George and Lou were building a second home in Camden, and Louisa became impatient with all their talk about money. Louisa had no money except what Walt sent her. George and Lou bragged about the good deal they were getting from the man who was building their home—he was building it so cheaply for them, they said, that he would probably lose money on it (as did Walt senior on his house-building ventures). George and Lou's frugality and Louisa's were different in kind; throughout her life, Louisa had no choice but to be frugal.

In another footnote, Miller comments on a statement that Whitman made to Louisa three months before she died. Whitman wrote to say that if he and she had a house in Washington, they could invite George and Lou down to see the coming inauguration. Miller footnotes Whitman's remark:

Around this remark Mrs. Whitman was to construct a dream-house: annoyed by George's economizing and, more important, loath to accept a (rightful) secondary position in her daughter-in-law's household, WW's mother despite her years hoped for a home of her own. As early as October 9, 1872, hardly six weeks after she had moved to Camden, Mrs. Whitman complained to Helen Price: "i would rather have my own shanty and my good friends come to see me" (Morgan). Even more significant, she wrote to the same friend on April 18(?), 1873: "i wouldent mind living here if i had a place of my own but this living with and not being boss of your own shanty aint the cheese" (Morgan). WW himself referred to the possibility of purchasing a house in Washington; see [letters] 485, 491, and 494.[70]

Since we know from the record that Walt wrote Louisa as early as 1848 about her having a home of her own, we know that she didn't just "construct a dream-house" all of a sudden. As for the remark about her desire to own a home "despite her years," Walt was sixty-five years old when he bought his first and only home on Mickle Street. Finally, Walt soon criticized George and Lou's home on precisely the same grounds that Louisa did.

Miller quotes from Louisa's letters in which Louisa tells Walt that if they had their own home, it need not be large nor fancy. She also says that "we couldent have many visitors to stay all night." Miller remarks about this: "The last sentence is especially interesting."[71] Evidently, Miller sees this sentence as evidence of Louisa's possessiveness or "unnatural" attachment to Walt, or perhaps he sees it as a veiled hint of Whitman's habit of bringing men home to sleep with him, if indeed he did so. A reading grounded in the actual circumstances, however, suggests a quite different interpretation. Louisa was tired and dying. She had taken care of grown children, sick children, dying children, and grandchildren for years. She was old. She needed her own place in which to die. Nurturing others—providing for visitors—was not on her mind in the last few months before her death.

In January 1873, a stroke paralyzed Whitman. He was still more or less immobile when he reached Camden three days before his mother died. He made a brief trip back to Washington after her funeral but then returned to live with George and Lou—to live in the same rooms where Louisa had lived and to use the same furniture. He said to Peter Doyle a month after Louisa died that he thought the move would be a good one for him. He could recuperate at the Camden house. Miller comments in a footnote: "WW's description of life in George's home is in sharp contrast with the querulous letters of his mother in the six months preceding her death."[72] Within three months, however, Whitman was saying the same kinds of things about this home that Louisa had said. He wrote to Ellen O'Connor: "It is socially here an utter blank to me—my cynical dread of being bored by any one is now completely gratified with a vengeance—." He told her that he looked "long & long at my mother's miniature, & at my sister Mat's—& O the wish if I could only be with them—."[73] Three weeks after that, he wrote to Peter Doyle: "I don't know a soul here—am entirely alone—have not

formed a single acquaintance here, any ways intimate—My sister-in-
law is very kind in all housekeeping things, cooks what I want, has
first-rate coffee for me & something nice in the morning, & keeps
me a good bed & room—All of which is very acceptable—(then, for
a fellow of my size, the *friendly presence & magnetism needed,* somehow,
is not here—."[74]

In another letter to Doyle, his words resonate even more with
Louisa's, as he speaks of his situation: "My *heart* is blank & lonesome
utterly."[75] In a letter he wrote three years later to his niece Hattie, in
words remarkably reminiscent of his mother's, he indicts Lou and
George's home for its sterility, which makes it a place far different
from Louisa's and different too from the kind of extended family of
friends that he had cultivated in his Washington years: "Dear Hattie,
it is real lonesome here since you went away—it is more a 'receiving
vault' to me than ever. Thank God though I am certainly better this
winter, & more like a prospect for me physically, than for now nearly
four years. . . . This makes me more cheerful & buoyant under the
chilling atmosphere, (both moral & meteorological) of this house.
Dear girls, I sometimes lately feel as if I was going out in the world,
to take some hand again in some work that suits me, even if ever so
little. Wouldn't it be a blessed thing? You see, dear girls, I just talk
freely & confidentially to you both—I want some one to talk to—&
it does me good—."[76]

In 1884 Walt finally bought a home, thirty-six years after writing
the note to Louisa in which he told her someday the family would
own its own place, "a farm" he called it then. He lived in his modest
Mickle Street home until he died. After one of his particularly bad
spells, Dr. Maurice Bucke, his personal friend as well as his doctor,
tried to talk him into going to Johns Hopkins hospital to live. Whitman refused, saying that he preferred his own home to Johns Hopkins, with its promise of "apartments hygenically arranged" and the
"best eating." Like Louisa, Whitman did not want managed space.
He told his friend Horace Traubel: "No man will willingly abdicate
his own dung hill. Allowing for all else, what can return to him the
price of freedom but freedom?"[77] Louisa had said much the same
thing eleven years earlier to Helen Price: "every one seems so different and formal and unlike our new york and brooklyn friends such
kind of half city places as camden is generally just as this place is but
i wouldent mind living here if i had a place of my own but this living
with and not being boss of your own shanty aint the cheese."[78]

Louisa did not willingly abdicate her own home; finally, she had no voice in the matter. Her sons George and Jeff demanded that she move. In the end, she was that child she referred to in her letters—if by child, she meant a dependent—when she realized her total lack of control over her space and movements. In her culture, there was no way for an old woman who was no longer "useful" and who had no economic independence to show some of her dignity. The sense of her powerlessness comes out in a letter she wrote to Helen Price, in October:

> i little thought the last time you came over to help make my dress and we were all so cheerfull and you were so kind hellen dear to get it completed that it would be the last time you would come) i looked for you hellen every day after your return home but you dident come to see me and i came away feeling as if i should never see any off you again)
>
>   your good mother or emma or you i thought to see you all before i left but fate decided otherwise i dident think to leave until some time in september but george and lou came and the canal boat that was to bring my things george thought would not come in a long time again) but O hellen the breaking up was almost too much for me i had been very miserable for some time the thought of breaking up my old home made me very nervious and i was very lame, but hellen dear i have survived it all."[79]

While Louisa Van Velsor was alive, Whitman sought to make the circumstances of her life mirror the sense of dignity she carried inside her. He greatly helped make her life what she wanted it to be except that, finally, he did not (or could not) see to it that she had her own home. He consistently sent Louisa self-addressed and stamped envelopes to use when she wrote to him, Jeff, Mattie, Hannah, Mary, and her friends. And he took responsibility for many other details as well; by this gesture he ensured that she could continue to write, and writing letters became increasingly important as one of the few meaningful activities remaining to her. The letters allowed her to envelop a larger world—a larger space—than she otherwise could have. Whitman's other gestures included urging Louisa to spend some of the money he sent her on herself: he begged her to buy herself shoes, underwear, a good steak for dinner. The envelopes, however, were especially important because they gave her a lifeline to circles outside her immediate one, and they enabled her to maintain the connection with her children. The sad thing is that she depended on Walt for them. She managed to circumvent many of the disadvantages that her lack of education and the restrictive attitude toward women's place created for her, but she did not circumvent them all. The envelopes represent one of the many bonds between Whitman and his mother. In a way, like Louisa's and Walt's boxes, they represent an ethic of care. In a way, they are *her* poems; they express her yearning.

Louisa wanted more than letters, however, to bequeath to her children. In a letter to Walt dated 12 July 1870(?), she wrote about having her photograph taken: "well Walt i have been to day and had my picture taken i have been saving money for it for this 2 months and to day i have been to pendletons on the corner of fulton and Johnson st and had six large ones taken i went alone i told the man i wanted very extraordinary ones for they were to go to a distance and he said he would take the best that could be taken i set three times the last one did look very good the others was good only the eyes wasent so good they will cost nearly 20 dollars yours and georges i will have framed and one for myself i shall send han one in the package so you see walt i bequeath something to my children so they will not forget me." Two photographs of Louisa are reprinted in Randall Waldron's *The Letters of Martha Mitchell Whitman*.[80] Unlike Walt, whose early aging is vividly dramatized in his photographs taken in the 1860s, Louisa seems hardly to age. Her hair has not grayed; the lines around her mouth are only slightly etched.

After an 1868 visit with Louisa, John Burroughs described Louisa as "a spry, vivacious handsome old lady worthy of her illustrious son." At another time, he said that Louisa was a "large handsome woman, a strong character."[81] Ellen O'Connor's comments add to our picture of Louisa. In her draft of the 1907 *Atlantic Monthly* article on Walt, in a paragraph that was deleted from the published version, O'Connor writes: "I went to Brooklyn and saw Mrs. Whitman, Walt's mother. . . . She received me very kindly, hearing of me, of course, through Walt, and we spoke a good deal of him. She spoke of him as Walter. . . . She was the type of the good mother. Good, large-hearted, great-natured character, the type of the mother. A benignant face, too. Her eyes I think were a darker blue than Walt's, but she had a rosey complexion, very fresh for a woman of her years. Mrs. Price once said that she believed if half a dozen people were to

Louisa Van Velsor Whitman at age sixty (daguerreotype). Reproduced courtesy of the Bayley-Whitman Collection, Ohio Wesleyan University.

make bread, she could detect Mrs. Whitman's from the others; she could feel by that quality of magnetism which she possessed in common with Walt."[82] Whitman favored his maternal bequeathment. He told Horace Traubel that it was lucky for him if he "took after the women of my ancestry, as I hope I do: they were so superior, so truly the more pregnant forces in our family history."[83] When Mattie and Jeff's second daughter was born, Walt wrote Louisa: "as to its being a girl it is all the better. (I am not sure but the Whitman breed gives better women than men.) "[84] He wrote to his friend Ellen O'Connor, 15 November 1863: "Mother is very well & active & cheerful—she still does her own light housework, & keeps up handsomely under her surroundings of domestic pressure—one case of sickness & its accompanying irritability—two of grown helplessness—& the two little children, very much with her, & one of them unsurpassed in volatility & restlessness—Nelly, I have thought before that the real & best bravery is to be discovered somewhere else than in the bravery of war, & beyond the heroisms of men."[85] Two days later, he wrote to his friend Charles Eldridge: "Charley, I think sometimes to be a woman is greater than to be a man—is more eligible to greatness, not the ostensible article, but the real one."[86] Three days after that, in a letter to another friend, he spoke of Louisa: "But the greatest patriot in the family is my old mother."[87] "The best part of every man is his mother," he once said to Traubel.[88] He spoke of Louisa's role as peacemaker in the family.[89] "My Mother was a Van Velsor," he said to Traubel. "I favor her: 'favor' they call it up on Long Island—a curious word so used, yet a word of great suggestiveness. Often people would say—men, women, children, would say—'You are a Whitman: I know you.' When I asked how they knew they would up with a finger at me: 'By your features, your gait, your voice: they are your mother's.' I think all that was, is, true: I could see it in myself."[90] The letters and photographs give us Louisa's tangible legacy; the effects of her presence come to us in the poem Whitman wrote in her honor, "As at Thy Portals Also Death" and more generally in the many images of Motherhood that appear in Whitman's poetry.

The horrors of the Civil War demanded that Whitman put peacemaking into the public perspective. Even before the war, in an 1860 notebook entry, Whitman showed his concern for cohesion and inclusivity, as political dissension moved toward disunion:

To Picture-Makers

Make a picture of America as an IMMORTAL MOTHER, surrounded by all her children young and old—no one rejected—all fully accepted—no one preferred to another. For as to many sons and daughters the perfect mother is the one where all meet, and binds them all together, as long as she lives, so The Mother of These States binds them all together as long as she lives.[91]

Our views of Whitman's image of the mother have been short-sighted. Much of the criticism of these images has centered on essentialism, arguing that Whitman saw women only as agents of reproduction, as wombs. My view, however, is that Whitman wanted to expand the meaning of the term "motherhood," to go beyond biology. In a 1990s context, Leora Tanenbaum—reviewing Ellen Willis's *No More Nice Girls: Countercultural Essays*—succinctly states the essence of Whitman's view of parenthood: "A mother does not have to be a woman."[92] Motherhood (parenthood) became an analogue for the inclusivity and cohesion Whitman felt his country lacked and without which the democratic experiment would eventually fail. The most compelling image of the heterosexual-based family comes in "There Was a Child Went Forth," a poem which images for readers a far from inviting view of the "family." There are no images in the poetry of two men parenting, or two women, but in "Drum-Taps," there are images of male/male nurturing.

Whitman's friend John Burroughs even called Whitman a "mother-man": "Whitman was the lover, the healer, the reconciler, and the only thing in character for him to do in the War was what he did do—nurse the wounded and sick soldiers—Union men and Rebels alike, showing no preference. He was not an athlete, or a rough, but a great tender mother-man, to whom the martial spirit was utterly foreign."[93] In terms of contemporary criticism, Burroughs's statement reveals a Whitman who resisted socially constructed gender roles. Whitman wanted to blur all sorts of boundary lines, and thus it is difficult to imagine that he wanted human possibilities to be prescribed and predetermined by a person's biological sex. He wanted the body to be a freeing force in a person's life, not constricting. In the following notebook entry, his language indicates an awareness of the role society plays in the construction of gender roles: "Could we imagine such a thing—let us suggest that before a manchild or womanchild was born it should be suggested that a human being could be born—."[94] This entry places the emphasis on similarity—on humans' common membership in the species—rather than on difference, on distinctions made through biological structure, so that Whitman, in this entry at least, seems to be in contemporary critical terms closer to social constructionists than to essentialists. Thinking as he does here could also allow him to contemplate his own sexual orientation and the ways in which society treats a person who does not accept standard definitions of "man-child" and "womanchild."

Whitman, the "great tender mother-man," did not learn nurturing from his father; it was Louisa Van Velsor Whitman's model of care that he practiced in his public role as "wound-dresser" during the Civil War. When Whitman said "Motherhood," however, on some level he meant that motherhood was not gender specific. The push is to make family mean something more than the nuclear family, but there is no strong pattern of imagery of alternative family patterns in a contemporary sense in Whitman's poetry. But like his communitarian friends, Whitman saw the problem in defining family as only one's biological children. He defined comradeship more inclusively than as male lovers only, the alignment that the "Calamus" cluster inscribes. *Leaves of Grass* in its entirety inscribes "comradeship" in the broadest sense to mean the world, to move from the experiences of the "I" in "Song of Myself" to the search for a world community, a "Passage to India." "I think," Whitman said, "there is nothing beyond the comrade—the man, the woman: nothing beyond: even our lovers must be comrades: even our wives, husbands: even our fathers, mothers: we can't stay together, feel satisfied, grow bigger, on any other basis."[95] Contrary to what Helen Michael said in her 1897 article, "Woman and Freedom in Whitman," about Whitman's not recognizing an "impersonal mother," Whitman's definition here of comradeship is doing just that, that is if we accept Michael's definition of "impersonal mother": "she who, whether for her own offspring or another's, holds out to the tender being her care and love because she is actuated by the highest motives of kindliness based upon universal brotherhood."[96] For Whitman, the concept of impersonal mother need not be gender-marked. Comradeship is the Santa Spirita in "Chanting the Square Deific"—the most inclusive of the deities, the most inclusive of terms.

In a 1985 article, Betsy Erkkila emphasizes the role of the Patriot Mother in Whitman's thinking and imagery: "It was out of his radical commitment to the ideals of the American revolution, projected as a potent female genius, that Whitman began to forge his sense of identity and calling as a poet."[97] "Whitman," she says, "moves from his earlier emphasis on the poet as a creator of strong individuals to an emphasis on the poet as a creator of national unity; and in so doing, he shifts in his poems from a primary identification with the male to a primary identification with the female dimensions of the universe" (435). Erkkila also emphasizes this point in the closing chapter of *Whitman the Political Poet:* "The future that Whitman imagined—and the only future possible for America—was in the image of a divinely charged matriarch, self-poised, swinging through time."[98]

In December 1862 the Whitman family read that "G. W. Whitmore" was among the wounded at the second battle of Bull Run. Whitman, fearing that it was his brother George, immediately left Brooklyn to find him. George, not seriously wounded, was an exception to the norm. The Civil War was a war of amputation, the fracturing of human connection, of community: the southern states were removed from the Union; families cut off from one another geographically and politically; arms and legs and hands severed from bodies. Whitman had already labored over the theoretical question of amputation—of what secession meant to America. When he got to the front, he encountered literal amputation. He wrote to his mother: "One of the first things that met my eyes in camp, was a heap of feet, arms, legs, &c. under a tree in front of a hospital."[99] Those feet and arms and legs to Whitman represented not only the human body dismembered but the Union as well.

Whitman responded to the fragmentation that he saw everywhere by staying in Washington and tending the wounded.

> With hinged knees returning I enter the doors. . . .
> Bearing the bandages, water and sponge,
> Straight and swift to my wounded I go.[100]

Actually, it wasn't bandages, water, and a sponge that Whitman carried to his wounded but rather psychological bindings. He visited the soldiers daily, talked to them, read to them, wrote letters to and for them, and touched them. "Mother, I feel so sick when I see what kind of people there are among them, with charge over them, so cold & ceremonious, afraid to touch them."[101] He became their arms and legs, joining his life to theirs to heal the fracture, volunteering his presence for their near absences. He said that simple touching seemed to mean as much at times to a wounded and sick soldier as anything. He said he almost feared the world: "Mother, when I see the common soldiers, what they go through, & how every body seems to try to pick upon them, & what humbug there is over them every how, even the dying soldier's money stolen from his body by some scoundrel attendant, or from some sick ones, even from under his head, which is a common thing—& then the agony I see every day, I get almost frightened at the world—."[102]

He cared for the wounded in much the same way his mother had cared for her family. He brought them food, stamps, clothes, and crutches. He told his mother that it was "awful to see so much, & not be able to relieve it."[103] Whitman was blessed or cursed by his empathy. He became in his imagination the wounded: "These . . . tens and twenties of thousands of American young men, badly wounded, all sorts of wounds, operated on, pallid with diarrhea, languishing, dying with fever, pneumonia, &c. open a new world somehow to me, giving closer insights, new things, exploring deeper mines than any yet, showing our humanity, (I sometimes put myself in fancy in the cot, with typhoid, or under the knife,)."[104] He gathered up the duties, responsibilities, and cares delegated culturally to the mother into a voice of cohesion, inclusivity, and peace, and he spoke to his culture with that voice.

Even the most radical of the women activists in the 1850s—those least bound to the domestic role for women—occasionally used the concept of motherhood in the same way, as a resonant voice of cohesion and inclusivity. They used the Republican motherhood argument—that an educated and strong mother made strong and responsible citizens.[105] We need to keep in mind as we read Whitman's images that Whitman heard woman's rights activists use the same maternal images in their speeches that he used in his poetry. As activists fought for suffrage, married women's property rights, and divorce reform, many also celebrated motherhood.

In the 1855 poem "Great Are the Myths," Whitman uses the phrase "the mother of the brood":

> It is the mother of the brood that must rule the earth with the new rule,
> The new rule shall rule as the Soul rules, and as the love, justice, equality in
>   the Soul rule.[106]

In the 1855 poem "Faces," he uses the phrase "the mother of many children." These phrases become slightly transformed after the war.

The "immortal mother" he mentions in his 1860 notebook entry becomes in his poems "the Mother of All" in "Over the Carnage Rose Prophetic a Voice" (1865), "Pensive on Her Dead Gazing" (1865), "The Return of the Heroes" (1867), "Virginia—The West" (1872),

"Thou Mother of Equal Brood" (1872), and "Old Chants" (1891). The phrase "Mother of All" appeared first in 1865 in two "Drum-Taps" poems—"Over the Carnage Rose Prophetic a Voice" and "Pensive on Her Dead Gazing" (moved later to "Songs of Parting"). Material from the 1860 poem "Calamus #5" ("States") makes up a large portion of "Over the Carnage." One of the lines Whitman added to this poem was the line "Sons of the Mother of All, you shall yet be victorious." Victory, the poet-persona says, would not come from war; it would come from affection: "Affection shall solve the problems of freedom yet." Affection shall "tie you and band you stronger than hoops of iron . . . ":

> (Were you looking to be held together by lawyers?
> Or by an agreement on a paper? or by arms?
> Nay, nor the world, nor any living thing, will so cohere.[107]

The ethic of care ("sympathy") clearly takes precedence over law in this poem.

In "Pensive on Her Dead Gazing," the persona hears the "Mother of All" calling to her earth while she stalks the battlefields:

> Pensive on her dead gazing I heard the Mother of All,
>
> . . . .
>
> As she call'd to her earth with mournful voice while she stalk'd,
> Absorb them well O my earth, she cried, I charge you lose not my sons,
>   lose not an atom,
>
> . . . .
>
> My dead absorb or South or North—my young men's bodies absorb, and
>   their precious precious blood,
> Which holding in trust for me faithfully back again give me many a year
>   hence,
> Exhale me them centuries hence, breathe me their breath, let not an atom
>   be lost, [108]

The image of this 1865 Mother stalking the battlefields and charging the earth to do its work has parallels to the 1856 poem "This Compost," in which the persona wonders at the earth's power to grow "sweet things" out of corruption, to distill "exquisite winds" out of "fetor," to renew, to give "divine materials" to humans, to accept. The point of view used in the two poems, though, is markedly different.

In the 1856 "This Compost," we hear the poet-persona speaking in a voice that wonders, questions, and hopes. In the 1865 "Pensive," we hear the poem through the Mother of All's voice, mediated by the poet-persona's ears. She is an empowered mother, or a desperate mother. Hers is a commanding voice, calling to the earth to absorb, hold in trust, and then to exhale the dead soldiers "centuries hence": "Let not an atom be lost / Exhale them perennial sweet death, years, centuries hence." The Mother of All speaks the poet's concern that these dead have not died in vain, that their deaths will not be forgotten. The Mother of All commands: "absorb," "give me back again," "exhale." The persona in "This Compost" asks questions, wonders. The contrast in mood between the two poems is marked; Whitman's choice of the word "pensive" does not modify the mother in the later poem. The Mother of All is not pensive; she is desperate, as the second line of the poem states: "Desperate on the torn bodies, on the forms covering the battlefields gazing." The poet-persona listening to her is pensive, but the Mother of All becomes charged, in 1865, to act. She is very much a public mother.

The absorbing and exhaling motions she commands are invoked, though in a different manner, in still another poem, "Reconciliation": "That the hands of the sisters Death and Night incessantly softly wash again, and ever again, this soil'd world."[109] Here, sisters witness and put into motion the regenerative powers of the earth—recreating life from death (power from defeat?) and implicitly memory from poems, memory, and conscience—that the war, the dead, *actually* happened and that if we forget that, it is to our peril. The mother and the sister put into motion regenerative acts, which bind rather than fracture.

In "The Return of the Heroes" (1867), the Mother of All watches her heroes in fields for planting, not battle. Arms hold rakes and hoes rather than firearms. Arms are attached to the body rather than amputated. The "Mother of All" gazes down on the fields. This is the familiar point of view that the Whitman-persona takes in "Song of Myself" and "Song of the Open Road," which enables the persona to imagine a unity. More and more in the later poems the poet-persona employs the Mother of All to speak from this vantage point rather than assuming it himself.

Though in 1860 Whitman feared that the only way to overcome the divisiveness in America was to go to war, his attitude toward the war became less clear to him, became more difficult for him to understand, as the war continued. In July 1863 he wrote to his mother: "Mother, one's heart grows sick of war, after all, when you see what it really is—every once in a while I feel so horrified & disgusted—it seems to me like a great slaughter-house & the men mutually butchering each other—then I feel how impossible it appears, again, to retire from this contest, until we have carried our points—(it is cruel to be so tossed from pillar to post in one's judgment)."[110] He mentioned frequently the need for touching, for a way of binding: "Well, dear mother, I will not write any more on the sick—& yet I know you wish to hear about them—every one is so unfeeling. . . . Mother, I feel so sick when I see what kind of people there are among them, with charge over them, so cold & ceremonious, afraid to touch them."[111] A week later, on 22 March 1864, he wrote: "What an awful thing war is—Mother, it seems not men but a lot of devils & butchers butchering each other—."[112]

He continued to believe that there was a way to put together the fragmenting Union. Or he tried to believe. His 1872 poem "Virginia—the West," one of four poems written and added to "Drum-Taps" after 1865, allegorizes the war. In this poem the Sire, Virginia—the South—uses his hand not to give a loving touch to his mate, the Mother of All—the Union—but to attempt to kill her. Her voice saves her (her "calm voice speaking") and her children ("the Prairie States"). That same year Whitman wrote "Thou Mother with Thy Equal Brood," called at that time "As a Strong Bird on Pinions Free." In that poem, the Mother of All democratically nurses her children:

> Thee in thy larger, saner brood of female, male—thee in thy athletes, moral,
> spiritual, South, North, West, East,
> (To thy immortal breasts, Mother of All, thy every daughter, son, endear'd
> alike, forever equal,)[113]

Democracy, Whitman said in "Democratic Vistas," "alone can bind, and ever seeks to bind, all nations, all men, of however various and distant lands, into a brotherhood, a family."[114] To represent the binding nature of democracy, he looked to his own fractured family and remembered Louisa, who held her own contentious brood in a fractious harmony. She was the source for Whitman's resonant image of the Mother of All, and she enacted the ethic of care.

Whitman's obsession with the public possibilities for the qualities he associated with motherhood are clearly evident in his poem "With All Thy Gifts" (1873), published two months before his mother died. In this poem, America stands secure, overlooking the world. She is powerful and wealthy—one might say smug. But, the poet-persona asks her:

> What if one gift thou lackest? (the ultimate human problem never solving,)
> The gift of perfect women fit for thee—what if that gift of gifts thou lackest?
> The towering feminine of thee? the beauty, health, completion, fit for thee?
> The mothers fit for thee?[115]

In 1873 when Whitman wrote this poem insisting that there is an "ultimate human problem" not negated by a nation's wealth or military power, he could find no solace in his country's governmental policies to respond to the human problems created by his society. In this poem, Whitman posits virtue in women and reaches out—in desperation?—to the female image as a cure-all for his country's ills. Though the emphasis in this poem is on the failure of the United States to achieve the spiritual democracy talked about in "Democratic Vistas," the solution—"the gift of perfect women"—both essentializes women and ignores the power economics play in creating a society that deals with the kind of problems the poem suggests. Whitman fails to take into account that though his own mother possessed qualities he associated with a strong democracy—a strong sense of her own self, a commitment toward caring for her family and friends, a drive for self-education, etc.—she also was, finally, dependent. Economics made Louisa part of the "ultimate human problem." Louisa felt this identity. I don't think that Whitman ever did.

In 1881, eight years after Louisa Van Velsor Whitman died, Whitman wrote a poem in her honor. He called it "As at Thy Portals Also Death" and placed it in "Songs of Parting." In it, Whitman speaks of the binding quality of the Mother, his mother—of "the divine blending, maternity"—and he speaks of sitting by her coffin: "I kiss and kiss convulsively again the sweet old lips, the cheeks, the closed eyes in the coffin."[116] It is a short poem, a modest elegy in comparison with his elegy to Lincoln, but it is only one of the many public acknowledgments of his grief over his mother's death; frequently he spoke of his loss to his friends, in letters and in conversations. We see his grief from eyes other than his own in an account written by Helen Price, his friend and also that of Louisa Whitman:

> At her funeral a gathering of thirty or more persons were sitting in the front room of the little cottage in Camden waiting for the services to begin. On taking my seat among them, I noticed a curious thumping at intervals that made the floor vibrate beneath my feet. I was so absorbed in my own grief that at first I was hardly conscious of it. I finally left my chair, and going to the back of the room where we were sitting, I noticed a half-opened door leading to another room. Glancing in, I saw the poet all alone by the side of his mother's coffin. He was bent over his cane, both hands clasped upon it and from time to time he would lift it and bring it down with a heavy thud on the floor. His sister-in-law told me that he had sat there all through the previous night.[117]

In the many letters that he wrote to his mother during the Civil War, Whitman told her of the vigils he kept at dying soldiers' bedsides. And in "Drum-Taps," the poet-persona wrote about a vigil he kept one night in a field watching over a dead comrade, the kisses he gave that comrade. Death infuses "Drum-Taps," death and the pounding beat of the funeral-march drum:

> I hear the great drums pounding,
> And the small drums steady whirring,
> And every blow of the great convulsive drums,
> Strikes me through and through.[118]

"The strong dead-march," the poet says in "Dirge for Two Veterans," "enwraps me." The moon shining down on the funeral march is "some mother's large transparent face."

> The moon gives you light,
> And the bugles and the drums give you music,
> And my heart, O my soldiers, my veterans, My heart gives
> you love.[119]

The gesture of bending down to kiss his enemy's lips that the poet-persona makes in "Reconciliation" is the gesture of a Peacemaker:

> For my enemy is dead, a man divine as myself is dead,
> I look where he lies white-faced and still in the
>   coffin—I draw near,
> Bend down and touch lightly with my lips the white face in
>   the coffin.[120]

In yet another "Drum-Taps" poem, "Spirit Whose Work Is Done," the drum sounds hollowly and harshly, "Now as the sound of the drum, hollow and harsh to the last, reverberates round me."[121] Those sounds resonated in Whitman's ear as he sat by his mother's coffin, his cane thudding the death march. He said that there were some things for which there are no words. His grief for Louisa was one of those things. The drum he beat as he pounded his cane throughout his all-night vigil beat in her honor. *That* was his elegy.

2

Abby Hills Price

For its time, the 1855 edition of *Leaves of Grass* is revolutionary in explicitly addressing women as readers; the next two editions, however, reflect woman's rights consciousness more and more. The 1856 and 1860 editions contain passages and even entire poems that resonate with the image-making work of women writers and activists leading the first woman's rights movement in the United States, from 1848 to 1861. Just as the woman's rights convention on 10–11 May 1860 in New York City marks the most contentious of the conventions taking place in this first wave of the movement, the 1860 edition of *Leaves of Grass* outsteps the 1856 edition in its woman's rights awareness and inscription. The book's length is responsible for much of the effect of the 1860 *Leaves of Grass* as a text aware of and responding to the woman's movement. In 1860, Whitman had not yet begun to weed out his radical representations of women; the process began in the 1867 edition. The 1860 edition contains the radical poems of the 1856 edition, with more added. In terms of woman's rights consciousness, the distinguishing factor between the 1855 edition and the 1856 and 1860 editions lies in the move toward specificity. A poem that effectively exemplifies this move is the 1856 poem "Song of the Broad-Axe." Section 11 of this poem, "Her shape arises," depicts the scenario that woman's rights advocates called for, that of the American woman moving freely in public space and, even more specifically, voting. The increase in references to the woman's

Abby Hills Price (1814–1878). From a photograph by H.
S. Wyer, Yonkers, N.Y., in "Letters of Walt Whitman to His
Mother and an Old Friend," *Putnam's Monthly and the
Reader* 5:2 (November 1908):168.

rights movement culminating in the 1860 *Leaves of Grass* occurred
thanks in part to Abby Hills Price, who was Whitman's close friend
from 1856, the year of their meeting, to 1878, when Abby died. Whitman's friendship with Price personalized his awareness of and involvement in women's fight for equality.

From the very beginning of the movement, however, Whitman, an avid newspaper reader, had every opportunity to read what
women were saying about their essential lack of citizenship in American society. Though brutalized by the press, the woman's rights
movement received wide coverage, beginning with Seneca Falls
in 1848. James Gordon Bennett, editor of the *New York Herald,* attempted to discredit the movement by printing the entire 1848 Declaration of Sentiments, but by doing so, he spread woman's rights
ideas throughout the nation. Horace Greeley commented: "Nothing

is so good for a weak and popular movement as this sort of opposition. . . . The mass of people throughout the country who might otherwise not know of its existence, will have their attention called and their sympathies enlisted in its behalf."[1] Once the National Woman's Rights Conventions began convening in 1850, the major New York newspapers carried detailed reports of the speeches and descriptions of the activities. Horace Greeley's *Tribune,* for example, printed the convention proceedings in full-page spreads on its oversized sheets. In 1850 when Price delivered one of the key speeches at the first National Woman's Rights Convention, her words began appearing in New York newspapers, and so, though Whitman would not meet Price in person for several years, he encountered her words five years prior to the first edition of *Leaves of Grass.*

Another forum for Whitman's cultural immersion in the woman's rights movement was the publishing firm of Fowler and Wells. In 1842, Orson S. and Lorenzo N. Fowler took over the editorship of the *American Phrenological Journal* and, in 1848, the *Water-Cure Journal.* Whitman read both journals, and both supported woman's rights reform. Whitman maintained a close connection with these two popularizers of phrenology. In addition to reading their publications, in 1849 Lorenzo Fowler performed the phrenological reading of Whitman's head that remained important to Whitman throughout his life. Fowler and Wells distributed the 1855 and 1856 *Leaves of Grass;* and between 1 November 1855 and 30 August 1856, Whitman contributed articles to yet another Fowler and Wells publication, *Life Illustrated.* Lydia Fowler, medical doctor, author, and wife of Lorenzo Niles Fowler, participated in the woman's rights conventions alongside Abby Price. Whitman had every opportunity to hear about the conventions and about Abby Price from conversations with Lydia Fowler. In fact, Lydia Fowler served as secretary for the September 1853 convention held in New York, called the Mob Convention because of the harassment the speakers received. (The World's Fair had opened two months earlier, and Whitman attended it daily.) Abby Price spoke at the Mob Convention; Paulina Wright Davis and Ernestine L. Rose spoke and served as officers. In addition, a general reciprocity existed between the Fowler and Wells firm and the Hopedale community, where Price lived from 1842 to July 1853. The community's official newspaper, the *Practical Christian,* regularly carried the firm's advertisements and supported its phrenological tenets. Fowler and Wells frequently published in tract form the

Broadway Tabernacle, New York City, exterior view. The Tabernacle, the building with the columns, was the site of woman's rights conventions held in 1853 and 1856. Lithograph by G. Hayward for Valentines Manual 1858, reproduced courtesy of the Museum of the City of New York.

woman's rights convention proceedings, which contained Price's speeches. In addition to the published accounts of the conventions in newspapers like the *New York Tribune,* then, Whitman's knowledge of woman's rights reform became particularized through his connection with Fowler and Wells.

Finally, one other forum links Whitman with the woman's rights movement and may have introduced Whitman to Abby Price. That forum represented the conflation of two circles: the circle of reform-minded activists and writers whose paths intersected Whitman's and the Bohemian circle that gathered regularly at Charley Pfaff's café. The latter group of people has been well studied by Whitman biographers.[2] The former has not been treated at length.

Gay Wilson Allen does, however, document the 1856 fall meetings that took place between Whitman, Thoreau, Bronson Alcott, and Sarah Tyndale, all reform-minded thinkers, with Tyndale qualifying as an activist. These meetings took place at a time when Alcott and Thoreau were also spending time at the Raritan Bay Union, a commune that began in 1853 but had already dissolved as a reform-oriented community by the fall of 1856, though its school, "one of the most innovative and progressive schools in ante-bellum Amer-

Broadway Tabernacle, interior view, c. 1847. Lithograph by Sarony and Major reproduced from the J. Clarence Davies Collection courtesy of the Museum of the City of New York.

ica," continued until July 1861.[3] Whitman had connections with this commune. In addition to Thoreau and Alcott, such culturally important figures as William Cullen Bryant, Horace Greeley, Octavius Brooks Frothingham, James Freeman Clarke, Joshua Giddings, Moncure D. Conway, Gerrit Smith, and Henry Bellows spoke and conducted discussions at the Raritan Bay Union.[4] (Conway sought out Whitman in 1855 after Emerson recommended *Leaves of Grass*.) Theodore Weld directed the school. Angelina Grimké Weld and Sarah Grimké taught there, as did Elizabeth Peabody Palmer, William Henry Channing, Steele MacKaye, and Edward Livingston Youmans. Youmans, who met Whitman in the 1840s, became a force in American science education.[5] During the time when Youmans was teaching at the Raritan Bay Union, Fowler and Wells published his book, *Alcohol and the Constitution of Man; being a popular scientific account of the chemical history and properties of alcohol and its leading effects upon the healthy human constitution* (1853). Three entries for Youmans appear in Whitman's notebooks, two of which are in the 1850s note-

books. In the "Left 5 at Jones" notebook, Youman's name and address are followed with some of Whitman's notes on his dealings
with Fowlers and Wells. In the "Dick Hunt" notebook, Youman's
name appears with that of Ernestine L. Rose, Abby Price, and Mary
Chilton, all of whom were activists for women's rights and were also
involved with reform communes. In this group too is Frank Bellew,
an illustrator who spent time at Pfaff's.

Abby Price and her family lived at the Raritan Bay Union from
July of 1853 until 1855 or 1856, when they moved to Brooklyn. Since
Youmans taught at the Union and knew Abby, he may have introduced her to Walt, or perhaps the young writer George Arnold, who
frequented Pfaff's café and knew Whitman, did so. George Arnold's
father was George B. Arnold, onetime president of the Raritan Bay
Union. George B. Arnold, whose wife Lydia died in the summer of
1854, is mentioned in connection with Abby while both still lived at
the Union in a letter a young student at the school wrote to her
friend: "Mr. Arnold and Mrs. Price go to New York together most
every day!!?!! I should think Mr. Price would get jealous. Mrs. Price
wears her hear [*sic*] up. Only think how sweet she must look!"[6] Price
and Arnold may have made these trips to New York to find a brownstone to rent, since George B. Arnold and members of his family
shared a brownstone with Abby and Edmund Price and their family
after leaving the Union.[7] Possibly, too, Price and Arnold went to
Pfaff's, where Henry Clapp, Abby's friend from the 1840s, could
regularly be found. Regardless, Arnold and Abby Price fused the
Raritan Bay reformist circle with the Pfaff Bohemian circle, Arnold
through his son and Abby through Henry Clapp, editor of the *Saturday Press,* which in 1860 vigorously promoted the 1860 *Leaves of
Grass.* Though now the leading Bohemian, Clapp had experienced
life as a reformer back in the 1840s when he first met Price. They
had served together in the New England Anti-Slavery Society and
the Non-Resistance Society. Both the Pfaff circle and the reform circle were "ultra," to use the word of the day. Whitman moved in and
out of each one. Both circles provided Whitman with the kind of
intellectual stimulation he would receive in the decade of the 1860s
in the O'Connor/Burroughs circle in Washington, D.C. And both
groups vigorously supported woman's rights.

Finally, pertinent to the discussion of Whitman's knowledge of
and sympathy with the woman's rights cause, there is the matter of
two newspaper articles. One article, titled "A Chapter on Females,"

appeared unsigned in the 26 March 1849, issue of the *Practical Christian*. Its subject matter is women's health. The second article under discussion appeared in the editorial column of the 17 December 1858 issue of the *Brooklyn Daily Times,* entitled "Health Among Females." The 1858 *Times* article is an almost verbatim copy of the one appearing in the 1849 *Practical Christian.* Emory Holloway and Vernolian Schwarz, editors of *I Sit and Look Out: Editorials from the Brooklyn Daily Times,* include "Health Among Females" in their section on women, "Women—Sex—Marriage."[8] While Whitman might possibly have written the article, say, in 1848 when he was editor of the *Brooklyn Daily Eagle,* and the *Practical Christian* might have copied it from the *Eagle,* attribution is risky, given the journalistic conventions of the times. And attribution is the real point, for by and large the *Times* articles that have been attributed to Whitman reflect views that are anachronistically (for Whitman) negative toward women. Thus, these two articles dramatize the dilemma facing Whitman scholars. The whole problem of validating the authorship of Whitman's journalism has been so formidable that there is no collection of it in the twenty-two volumes of *The Collected Writings of Walt Whitman.*

At issue here is the extent of Whitman's involvement with the *Brooklyn Daily Times.* Gay Wilson Allen says Whitman edited the paper from the spring 1857 to June 1859, though Whitman says 1856. Overall, the point of view and tone of the articles in Schwarz and Holloway's chapter "Women—Sex—Marriage" differ dramatically from those of Whitman's earlier journalism. Ezra Greenspan, in *Walt Whitman and the American Reader,* remarks about Whitman's *Times* experience: "There was less of Whitman in the paper than there had been of him in his previous papers—less of his personality; fewer of his personal convictions, activities, and stylistic idiosyncrasies; and, most interestingly, none of his creative writings. As far as readers of the paper were concerned, the editor of the *Times* and the author of the volume of poems which had been reviewed in its pages just several months before his accession to the editorship could have been two entirely separate personalities."[9] My own feeling is that they were more than separate personalities; I feel that Whitman did very little of the *Brooklyn Daily Times* writing that has been attributed to him by scholars.

Gay Wilson Allen bases his theory largely on conjecture in connection with an 1885 letter that Whitman wrote to Charles M. Skinner, editor of the *Times,* in which Whitman said, "In hasty answer to your request asking me to specify over my own signature what years I worked as an editorial writer in the *Brooklyn Times* office I would say that if I remember right it was along in 1856, or just before."[10] Whitman does not mention the *Times* in *Specimen Days* when he lists the various papers he had worked on, though he adds: "I have had to do, one time or another, during my life, with a long list of papers, at divers places, sometimes under queer circumstances."[11] The articles about women in the *Brooklyn Times* that have been attributed to Whitman give a perspective on Whitman's views of women's role in American society that differs from that which Whitman expressed in his 1856 notebooks, his poetry, his "Primer of Words," later published by Horace Traubel and titled *An American Primer,* and earlier newspaper articles. Until further work is done on Whitman's journalism, I cannot agree that *Times* editorials were written by Whitman and represent authoritative statements of his views toward women and woman's rights.

Whitman said in his 1876 Preface that his general objective in writing *Leaves of Grass* was "to make a type-portrait for living, active, healthy Personality, objective as well as subjective, joyful and potent, and modern and free, distinctively for the use of the United States, male and female, through the long future."[12] I suggest that Abby Price was one of several women who furnished Whitman with models for his female type portrait, his representation of the democratic woman. The more we understand antebellum women's lives and the more we develop a sense of their history, the more readily we will begin to understand just what Whitman meant when he spoke of *Leaves of Grass* as a woman's book. Once present-day readers see that Abby Price was an extraordinary person who lived an extraordinary life, they have a context for reading the images, the language, and the scenarios that Whitman creates in his poems when he speaks of women. It is a context that has been lacking until now in Whitman criticism and biography. In Abby Price we find a concrete referent for Whitman's gendered female pronoun. In her we see the degrees to which Whitman met and did not meet her own lived, radical, "feminist" experience. The story of her life is one of those books that Whitman has in mind when he speaks of history, one of the leaves that lies unturned, waiting.

Walt's letters to Abby tell us relatively little about her life, but they do let us see his regard for her, his affection, and the care he took to include the Price family and George B. Arnold in his queries. His letters also show that he spoke to this close friend in language that was affectionate and familiar, with overtones of Victorian sentiment. But still, it is somewhat surprising to the late twentieth-century sensibility to realize that Walt Whitman used such language in addressing a female friend. The letters also reveal that the bond between Abby and Walt was reciprocal. Likewise, they show us that Walt valued his talks with Abby. Except for one business letter, Abby's letters to Walt have not survived. In a February 1874 letter to Ellen O'Connor, Whitman tells O'Connor that he has recently destroyed letters: "Besides moving into this house from the former one—I have twice hurriedly destroyed a large mass of letters and MSS.—to be ready for what might happen."[13] Some of the letters were from Abby Price. There is good reason to believe that Abby's letters were prime candidates for the fire especially because she and Walt both engaged in confidential communications. In November 1874 Walt wrote again to Ellen O'Connor: "Nelly, I just send you, (although one or two items confidential, sort o') Mrs. Price's last letter to me, two days since—read it, & destroy it— I also send Mrs. Davis's, she (Mrs. P) sent me, as you are interested in her—."[14]

The twenty-three extant letters from Whitman to Price need to be read consecutively and in their entirety so that their tone can reveal itself and tell us about the friendship. As with many friendships, the tone is more intimate in letters written after meetings. A good example of this intimate tone is the letter Walt wrote Abby from Boston, where he had gone to help see through the Thayer and Eldridge publication of his 1860 *Leaves of Grass*. Walt begins the letter: "As I know you would like to hear from me, my dear friend, I will not yet go to bed—but sit down to write to you, that I have been here in Boston, to-day is a fortnight, and that my book is well under way." He then gives Abby details about the book itself; he comments on "this Eastern race of yours"; he speaks of Emerson; he speaks of missing his and Abby's talks; and he closes with a modestly self-mocking paragraph: "Let me see—have I anything else to say to you? Indeed, what does it all amount to—this saying business? Of course I had better tear up this note—only I want to let you see how I cannot have forgotten you—sitting up here after half past 12, to write this precious document. I send my love to Helen and Emmy." He signed the letter "Walt." In an 1863 letter responding to Abby's news that her daughter Emily was thinking of coming to Washington to nurse the wounded, Walt wrote to Abby: "But, my darling, [the war] is a dreadful thing—you don't know these wounds, sicknesses &c—the sad condition in which many of the men are brought here, & remain for days, sometimes the wounds full of crawling corruption &c—."[15] The language Whitman uses in his letters as he addresses his friends and those whom we suppose are his lovers provides an unexplored context in which to interpret comparable language in *Leaves of Grass*.

Like his letters to his mother, Whitman's letters to Price have a tone of forthrightness, with no condescension; for her part, Abby is not at all in awe of Walt. In the only extant letter we have of Abby to Walt, written in 1867, she asks him to do what he can, in Washington, to see that her firm is not taxed twice for the ruffles it makes. She explains that her firm has just received notice of the law concerning the tax, which stated that "articles of clothing made by sewing from materials already having payed tax" had been exempted. Abby and the firm thought that their goods came under this head, but, she said, the assessor said they did not. Abby ends her letter: "You see Harland right away and tell him about it and find out who the Committee are, and I guess if you have time enough you can get it done and I shall have the fun of sending you the check!"[16] She talks to Whitman like a friend, confident in the relationship and confident of herself.

Whitman assisted Abby Price in another case as well, helping to free from jail a postmaster who she felt had been unfairly charged.[17] Abby assisted Walt in various ways: she provided a place for him to stay while on leave, in 1866 and 1868. In 1870, when Whitman's thumb was so badly infected that he couldn't write, she wrote letters for him. He also asked her to send him magazines that he couldn't get in Washington. She provided a circle of people with whom he could discuss his poetry and topics of interest. She promoted his books. And she and her daughters befriended his mother. Her primary assistance, however, lay in her own intellect, her spirit, and her talk. Her experience and her beliefs gave Whitman access to a world he would not have experienced without her. He brought her his friendship and *Leaves of Grass*.

William O'Connor spoke of the importance of Price's circle to his own project, that is, O'Connor's championing of Whitman and his poetry. He wrote to Price in January 1866 thanking her for a letter she had written to him, a letter of appreciation for his book on Whitman, *The Good Gray Poet*. O'Connor told Price: "I read gladly that you personally intend to spread it as much as you can for this is the most efficient service that can be rendered."[18] People like those in Price's circle—"that vast mass of thoughtful and elevated people," O'Connor called them—were the audience O'Connor said he wanted to reach but could not through journals or reviews, from which, he said, he expected only abuse and ridicule.

In addition to the comfort that Whitman felt with the Prices, evidenced by his staying with them in 1866 and 1868 and apparent in the tone of his letters, he found in Price and George B. Arnold the blend of intellectual, dissenting, artisan consciousness associated with Frances Wright and Thomas Paine, two of Whitman's heroes. Whitman recorded in a notebook a March 1857 conversation that he had with George B. Arnold in which Arnold spoke to Whitman about Joseph Priestley, the radical Unitarian, scientist, and political theorist. Whitman heads his note "Dr. Priestly (or Priestley)" and "Conversation with Mr. Arnold, March 1 '57."

> Dr. Priestly was quite a thorough man of science, (physical science) as well as of morals and mentals.—Mr. Arnold says the Dr. first made the definite discovery of oxygen—Can this be so?—He was a Unitarian. . . . Mr. Arnold went to Pittsburgh to preach in a little Unitarian church owned by Mr. Bakewell, a rich person; a follower, admirer, and personal friend of Dr. Priestley. . . . [Dr. P.] must have been a *real man*.—He was not followed by the American Unitarians.—
>
> (How these Unitarians and Universalists want to be respectable and orthodox, just as much as any of the old line people!)[19]

George B. Arnold was at various times in his life a Unitarian minister, an orchardist, an inventor, a scientist, and a believer in spiritualism.[20] As a young Unitarian minister, Arnold worked among the poor in New York City; he then moved west to Pennsylvania and Illinois and back east to New Jersey, where he was at one time president of the North American Phalanx and the Raritan Bay Union, before settling once again in New York. He married Lydia Spring, the sister of Marcus Spring, who was a New York businessman, philanthropist, and major stockholder in the North American Phalanx and the Raritan Bay Union. In 1848, Arnold was a barnburner delegate in Illinois, the same year that Whitman was fired from the *Brooklyn Eagle* because of his barnburner politics. The *New York Times* obituary states that after the failure of the North American Phalanx and the Raritan

Bay Union, Arnold "exercised his talents as an inventor, and secured patents upon valuable attachments to the sewing machine."[21] Helen Price and Whitman both refer to talks that he and Arnold had in the Price home.

Justin Kaplan distinguishes between the people in Pfaff's café and Abby Price's parlor, but Price's circle of friends was inclusive. Kaplan says, "Despite some qualifications, Whitman had found in that gloomy vault beneath the sidewalk a more *gemütlich* and inspiriting social base than Abby Price's Brooklyn parlor."[22] Kaplan's view misrepresents the Price home. Abby Price's Brooklyn parlor housed some of the most radical thinkers of the day, and her circle overlapped Pfaff's circle. Since George B. Arnold was the father of George Arnold, a regular at Pfaff's and a writer, one would suppose the son also visited the Price/Arnold home. Henry Clapp, the spirit behind the Pfaff circle, publisher and editor of the *Saturday Press* and an important supporter of Whitman's poetry, published a poem of Price's in his 5 March 1859 *Press,* nine months before he first published a poem of Whitman's. It is possible that Whitman first met Clapp at Price's home. Her home offered Whitman a space for his artistic and intellectual development just as surely as did Pfaff's. Louisa Van Velsor Whitman mentions Clapp to Whitman in a letter: "the clapp i wrote about is the one hellen price spoke to you about being to the falanks Jersey."[23] In another letter, written in fall 1870, Louisa goes into more detail about Clapp. The letter further illustrates the connection between the Prices, Clapp, and Whitman: "Hellen had a letter from Clapp wishing to know if you was in washington as there was nobody out of his own family that he thought as much of as you that he had written to you but had got no answer he has been to new york and put up at lessey farlands i believe thats the name and she gave him cloths to make him desent and there has been a collection to get him paper and materials to write hellen said he was tipsey nearly all the time he was in new york he wrote to hellen she had the letter here he was never so glad to get back out of new york that all was changed."[24] Albert Parry says that "it was the death of George Arnold (the son), whom Clapp dearly loved, [that] started Henry on his course of suicidal drinking."[25]

Price's home also gave Whitman an outlet for his poetry. Before "Out of the Cradle Endlessly Rocking" appeared in Henry Clapp's *Saturday Press* (titled "A Child's Reminiscence"), Whitman brought it to the Price home and asked one of the circle to read it. George

B. Arnold first read it; then Price; and then Whitman. After the reading, Whitman asked for comments on the poem.[26] Abby Price also furnished Louisa Van Velsor with her own readings of Whitman's poetry. Helen Price in her letters says that Abby visited Louisa Van Velsor, read Walt's poems to Louisa, and discussed them with her. Helen Price speaks of Whitman as "a member of my own family when on his vacations from Washington."[27] In an 1868 letter to Abby, Walt refers to the Prices as "those that are almost the same as *my own folks.*"[28]

There, at Abby Price's home, Whitman met the numerous reformers who made up her circle. He saw in her and her activist friends people with *hopes* for a different kind of society. But the strongest draw was Abby. Helen Price describes the friendship: "It was in talking with my mother on the spiritual nature of man, and on the reforms of the age and kindred themes, that [Whitman] took special delight. These appeared to be his favorite topics, and she, having similar sympathies and tastes, would take an equal pleasure with himself in discussing them. It was the society of my mother that was certainly Walt Whitman's greatest attraction to our house."[29] Whitman offers a view of them, sitting around the kitchen table talking: "I was down late to breakfast this morning," he wrote Ellen O'Connor; "had a good breakfast though—nobody home but Mrs. Price & Mr. Arnold . . . after breakfast we sat leisurely & had a good chat—subject, the Roman Catholic religion—."[30] Abby Price was one of those leaders of reform Whitman spoke of in a notebook entry: "*My final aim* To concentrate around me the leaders of all reforms— transcendentalist, spiritualists, free soilers."[31] Helen Price emphasizes the conversations that took place on a regular basis in her home, and she repeats the value Whitman placed on listening and on her mother: "It was in her friendship," Helen says, "and in this *women's circle*—a mother and two daughters—that Mr. Whitman passed not a few of his leisure hours during all those years."[32]

In the twenty-three extant letters that Whitman wrote to Price, he frequently mentions their talks: "I wish you lived here—" he wrote her from Boston in 1860. "I should visit you regularly every day—probably twice a day." In his letters from Washington, he speaks of their long talks: "Abby, I think often about you, & the pleasant days, the visits I used to pay you & how good it was always to be made so welcome," he wrote in 1860. In 1863: "O I wish I could come in this afternoon, & have a good tea with you, & have three or four hours of mutual comfort & talk, & be all of us together again." In an 1869 letter he speaks to Abby of the monotony of his life in Washington: "Abby, I have little to write about, only I wanted to write you something. . . . I shall leave Washington soon after the middle of August—then I will see you all, & we will have some good talks."[33] In 1871, Walt writes to Abby of her new grandchild: "What with the baby & all you women—what jolly times you must have—I wish I could just drop in and take part in them—."[34] The last time Abby and her daughters saw Walt was in March 1873. The occasion was Louisa's funeral.

The good talks that Whitman keeps mentioning as he writes to Price had to do with the spiritual nature of man, the reforms of the day, and kindred themes—these are the topics that Helen Price says Whitman and Abby discussed. By the time Whitman met Abby Price, she had lived a full and challenging life; indeed, her own pathway had been, at best, rugged. Abby was forty-two years old at the time of their meeting; Walt, thirty-seven. Prior to their meeting, Abby had been one of the reformers that Whitman said he wanted around him. She was also a mother. The story of Abby Price's life factored into the story of Whitman's life creates a new context for *Leaves of Grass,* one that obliges us to rethink aspects of Whitman's biography and his representations of women in his poetry and prose. Though Price early focused her attention on pacifism—which for her was closely aligned with spirituality—on community building, and on abolitionism, woman's rights absorbed the better part of her energy. An explication of her radicalism in this area serves three purposes: it brings to light the interrelationship between Whitman's first three editions of *Leaves* and the 1850s woman's rights movement, it affords a new and necessary context for our reading of *Leaves of Grass* and the role it inscribes for women in American democracy, and it writes Abby Hills Price's story into our cultural history.

Abby Hills was born in Franklin, Connecticut, on 18 July 1814. She married Edmund Price in 1837. Their first two children were born in Willimantic, Connecticut. In 1842 the Prices moved to the Hopedale community, near Milford, Massachusetts, the year the community began its experiment in Christian Socialism. Edward K. Spann describes the history of this community as a story "that recapitulates the history of idealism, of an inspired society successful enough to assure its own failure . . . the story of how the religious devotion of some helped lay the foundations for the industrial wealth of others."[35] Hopedale, in its inception, was one of those "admirable communes" of which Whitman spoke in "Song of Myself" until he excised the line in 1881: "It is for the admirable communes of literary men and composers and singers and lecturers and engineers and savans."[36] The move from "spiritual socialism" to capitalism that Spann traces in his book picks up on the moves M. Wynn Thomas sees in Whitman's poetry: the conflict between Whitman's desire for equality and the reality of mid-nineteenth century capitalism.[37] That is, on a deep level, Whitman's affinity lay in the kind of spiritual socialism to which Hopedale dedicated itself in its inception.

Idealistically, Whitman and Price shared the dream of a society different from their own. A few days after Price's death, in 1878, the *Woman's Journal* honored her with a laudatory obituary. The *Woman's Journal,* edited by Lucy Stone and her husband Henry Blackwell, called Abby a co-worker in woman's rights and mentioned her involvement in early American socialism. The obituary alluded to her failed hopes: "The *high hope and imagination* of her earlier years were not always appreciated; and in her latter life, she seemed to retire from public spheres of effort" (emphasis added).[38] This high hope and imagination was something that she and Whitman held in common. Price also tenaciously resisted adhering to doctrinal thinking and exhibited a rare courage in her willingness to act on her principles. She lived the life she preached. She was that ideal model for which Whitman called in his 1856 poem "By Blue Ontario's Shore": "He or she is greatest who contributes the greatest original practical example."[39] Whitman as a poet used language to bring about his vision of democracy; Price lived her vision, and though she did not have Whitman's power of the written word, she also wrote her vision. In a strange rounding of the circle, she chose to die back within the folds of her early dreams; in 1876, Abby moved to Red Bank, New Jersey, to end her life at a boardinghouse that in the 1840s and 1850s had been a phalanstery—the communal home of the North American Phalanx, a Fourierist commune, which differed ideologically from the Christian Socialist commune of Abby's once-beloved Hopedale.

Little is known about Edmund Price, who is as vague a presence in the Price story as Walter senior is in the Whitman story. Adin

Ballou, who served as the area's genealogist and also made time to found the Hopedale community, is the only person who left behind a description of Edmund Price: "Mr. Price was by trade a hatter. He was a very honest, industrious, hard-working man, in whatever business engaged, often consuming 15 to 18 hours of the 24. Had he been as successful in preserving the fruits of his toil as in earning them, he must have become wealthy. But, with no vicious or spendthrift habits, through misjudgment or ill-luck in the investment of his funds, he frequently lost in large sums what he had acquired by laborious diligence."[40]

Because Abby Price also made time to write, her presence, unlike her husband's, is not vague. Her story is told—eleven years of it, that is—in the issues of Hopedale's newspaper, the *Practical Christian,* a newspaper fascinating for its account of the Hopedale community. Reversing Whitman's pattern, Price went from being a poet to being an orator/journalist. In the early years of Hopedale, she figures in the *Practical Christian* mainly as the town bard; she wrote poems in honor of deaths, births, national holidays, and any event of communal interest. In this capacity she recorded the town's history, and she wrote political or protest poetry. A letter from Edmund Quincy, in 17 September 1844, provides us with an early view of Price:

> Sister Price I saw who is the Sappho of the community—brother Price is a hatter so he clothes the outside of the head while she adorns the inside—which I take to be a fair division of labor. She is a very modest well-behaved young woman and looks as if she had considerable talent. She has certainly improved amazingly in putting her verses together since the article I remember sending to you from the Practical Christian, two or three years ago.[41]

Though Price appeared "well-behaved" to Quincy, in actuality she was nothing of the kind if "well-behaved" means accepting group opinions. One month before Edmund Quincy's letter, Price wrote to her friend Abby Kelley Foster, an early leader in the antislavery movement and controversial because she insisted on speaking publicly despite being a woman. The letter reveals Price's independent spirit as she questioned the value and spirit behind antislavery fairs. These popular fairs ostensibly sought to raise money for the cause, but Price did not always regard altruism as their reason for being:

I believe in going at things deliberately and counting the cost—before setting the time to feed the multitude for we shall have no miraculous power given us at that time and I have my doubts about the Christianity and [illegible] of Fairs. I think it will cost more than it will come to. I do not have so great faith in loud talk and scolding as many have—And it will take more than Joanna & Stacy to make me believe that my duties interfere with each other and if I am bound to take care of my children at home I am not to take care of the Fair at Milford. I have written in great haste—excuse incoherence. I hope you will be very prudent and not get into any bad scrape—.[42]

George Stacy, who withdrew from the community in 1845 but who continued to be involved in its activities,[43] remained an irritant to Abby Price. Stacy claimed the communal structure of Hopedale infringed upon an individual's rights. Price, however, placed her faith in a community organized on the idea of social equality and shared communal responsibilities, a vision that she believed incompatible with capitalism.

Price expressed her belief in Hopedale as an ethical alternative to society at large in a public letter she wrote. For a brief period in 1846 the Price family had to move away from the commune into the nearby town of Milford, apparently for financial reasons. Abby wrote a letter at that time to the Hopedale association, addressing the community as "dearly beloved" and pledging her loyalty to it. "Never, never shall I cease to love the friends associated at Hopedale as my dearest friends; and the object they are struggling for I must esteem as the highest and first among the reforms of the day."[44] Soon the family returned to Hopedale, and Abby became even more involved in the community's life.

In Price's years at Hopedale, her writing appeared in two book publications. Her poem warning of the inevitable consequences of war if slavery was not abolished ("The Nation's Destiny") appeared in *Liberty Chimes,* published in 1845 by the Providence Ladies' Anti-Slavery Society. "And, left alone, thy suicidal race / Will slay each other in a fell embrace." The collection included the following writers, many of whose names are familiar to nineteenth-century historians and literary scholars: Nathaniel P. Rogers, Wendell Phillips, Adin Ballou, Abby H. Price, Richard Hildreth, George W. Stacy, C. K. Whipple, Eliza Storr, S. E. Coues, E. Burritt, James Russell Lowell, Henry Clapp, Jr., Frances H. Green, S.L.L., John Brown, and Sarah

H. Whitman. In 1850, Price's poems/hymns appeared in a collection compiled by Adin Ballou: *The Hopedale Collection of Hymns and Songs, for the Use of Practical Christians.*

For the eleven years that she lived at Hopedale, Price consistently served as officer and committee member for the New England Non-Resistance Society and the Anti-Slavery Society. At the same time she held some of the most important positions in her own community. Because she lived at Hopedale, she had opportunities most other women of her time never even dreamed of. She became, as Edward Spann notes, "the leading spokeswoman for equal rights at Hopedale," which came, Spann says, "with the exception of the Shakers . . . as close to equality between the sexes as any place in America."[45] She voted in Hopedale elections; she held high offices in her community; she preached; she gave speeches at neighboring villages; she urged Hopedale women to work the farms and gardens as the men did; she wrote repeatedly in the Hopedale newspaper of the need for a Hopedale communal kitchen in order to give women time for self-development and for work outside the home; she defied conventional coding and wore the bloomer. She gave speeches at the first three national woman's rights conventions. Again and again she stressed the need for women to have healthy, strong bodies. Whitman found in his friendship with Price one of the richest resources possible for understanding the issues underlying the early woman's rights movement in America during its formative and radical years, 1850–1860. She was a "woman under the new dispensation"[46]—in no way a Victorian lady.

By 1850, Price was a seasoned activist, and she had also become a friend of Paulina Wright Davis. Davis, who had come to Hopedale the year before to lecture on women's health and anatomy, organized the first National Woman's Rights Convention, held in Worcester, 23 and 24 October 1850. Price, along with Davis, gave one of the key speeches at the convention. The following two years she also presented speeches at the national conventions and served as well on major committees. Her name appears on committee lists along with that of Lucretia Mott and other luminaries. Though she demanded a sweeping and varied range of reforms, Price articulated these demands under the broadest of rubrics: she renounced the ideology of separate spheres. This ideology, so pervasive in nineteenth-century white American middle-class culture, required assumptions to be made about gender and gendered roles that Price simply did not accept. She saw the control and power underlying the ideology, and she did her best to subvert it.

Simply put, Abby Price demanded that women have access to public space and that they share in the privileges and responsibilities such access affords. In her own life she was not representative of antebellum middle-class white women. The *Practical Christian* is filled with announcements of the speeches that she delivered at Hopedale and at surrounding communities. Her participation in the nonresistance and antislavery movements took her away from Hopedale. Her drive to tear down the artificial boundary lines circumscribing a person's physical space and her own success in doing so gave her an analog for the erasure of all sorts of other artificially constructed boundaries, which, in turn, made her, from Whitman's point of view, the ideal reader of his own similar desires. From 1850 to the summer of 1853, her public voice boldly demanded change and focused on woman's rights.

Price saw economic independence as a prerequisite for personal, legal, and physical freedom. At a minimum, she believed, women had to have such independence as an option. She demanded equal pay for equal work, and she demanded what we now call comparable worth.[47] She asked that women have the chance to compete fairly with men for jobs, an aspect of women's rights with regard to which Whitman, in his poetry, lagged far behind Price and other radical activists. She indicted the male power structure, but she also spoke of women's responsibility in transforming the way women thought about the private space of home and their complicity in their own subjugation. Women, she felt, would have to create a new image of themselves. Price's words give us the viewpoints that Whitman heard in all of his talks with her.

"Cramped, dwarfed, and cowed down" was one way Price phrased her conception of women's lives: "In the name of eternity, we ask our brothers no longer to proscribe our sphere. I say, then, that we are cramped, dwarfed, and cowed down, for the want of pecuniary independence."[48] She did not feel that the home rewarded women with the high sense of morality and spirituality that her society kept telling her it did. She saw such claims as bogus, as ways to flatter women in order to keep them "in their place." Over and over in her speeches she urged women to move out of the home into the life of the public world. She wanted opportunities for women. In her speech at the 1850 National Woman's Rights Convention she declared: "Employments and occupations being opened . . . woman, at every step, becomes greater in all respects; more free and dignified." She told men and women to look around them. Women's space, they would see, "is circumscribed not by [women's] ability, but by [their] sex."[49]

Woman's rights needed much explanation "because woman suffers the inferiority of caste without knowing it and man as he prevents her development and growth thinks he is doing God's service."[50] Here, Price addressed the ubiquity of sexism: sexism was invisible precisely because it permeated society. She addressed in part the problem of gender formation: the distinction (or balance) between genetics and culture in forming one's subjectivity, one's notion of individualism. Though at times Price spoke of inborn character and personality traits, she was not an essentialist. She believed women held the position they did, not because of biology, but because men had dictated the circumstances and had assigned women roles that stunted their development. A "false public sentiment," a "scornful public sentiment," she called it.[51] Women contributed to this false public sentiment, however, through their own lack of consciousness as to their position in society, their own failure—refusal—to *see* that their servile position was a result of their exclusion from the body politic, both politically and economically, and not of biology. Part of Price's goal was to reveal the ideological assumptions that supported an essentialist view, a view claiming that one's biological sex dictated one's destiny.

In her 1851 convention speech, Price gave a graphic picture of what she considered typical of the American woman and her allotted space. The home becomes an "inferior circle of industry." The images she uses speak of reduction, of a woman being whittled down until she becomes nothing more than a "femme covert":

Woman is expected to be frail, delicate and dependent in order to be loved. She must be thus lovely to expect marriage, and she must be married to have a home and a subsistence. Hence she is limited to an inferior circle of industry, in which she can act only in helpless dependence upon Man's wiser guidance, and preserve her feminine character, the beauty of which consists in graceful weakness, timidity, and submission to the conventionalisms of life. In this condition she must patiently continue until some favorable circumstance affords her an opportunity of yielding up her personal identity and becoming a "Femme Covert" for the sake of a sure living! Thus marriage for a home becomes frequent, necessarily so, from the proscriptions under which Woman suffers. Should she attempt to make herself independent and selfsupporting, she would be pronounced "out of her sphere," "masculine" and "unlovely."[52]

Price kept repeating the need for women to be "pecuniarily independent."[53] In her 1850 speech to the National Woman's Rights Convention, she lists three changes needed in order for women to "enjoy" the right to happiness: "Women ought to have equal opportunities with men for suitable and *well compensated* employment"; "women ought to have equal opportunities, privileges, and securities with men for rendering themselves *pecuniarily independent*"; "women ought to have equal legal and political rights, franchises and advantages with men." The term "pecuniary independence" runs like a motif throughout her work. Women had to get out of the house. They had to work or at least move in the world of the human (not just the biological) family. "Doom the wife and mother to the cares of home life, sacred and beautiful as it is," Price said, "and her nature is never satisfied, because it is never fully aroused and applied." Her reiterated theme was that the roles of women were far more inclusive than those of nurturers *only* and as decorations to men: "A nobler destiny is hers, than to be the doll of a parlor."[54]

In a move rare for her times, Price turned the glorification-of-home argument in on itself. If, as her culture kept declaring, home was so important and rendered such an important service to society, why didn't men take over domestic duties or at least share the role? She is sarcastic as she inverts gender roles: "If then the domestic duties are so important, to be attended to with the undivided thought that is claimed of woman, why should not the man, who has them resting upon him equally with his wife, be relieved from public affairs by those well qualified—mature and unengaged women: and so the young father have leisure to train his family, whose sons, learning soon of society contempt for the opinions of disfranchised woman, need other authority than that considered by society on a par with the idiot, the insane and the criminal."[55] Her other point in the above speech was one she made frequently: many women preferred not to marry; motherhood was not the *only* profession for women. She argued for the rights of single women.

Price's speech at the first National Woman's Rights Convention is filled with language trying to push away barriers, wanting to extend the human potential, desiring opportunities for women: "Say not to [women] you have done all you may do, keep your minds and attention within that narrow circle, though your nature and ripened intellects would fain be interested in whatever concerns the larger family of man, and your affections, strong in a healthful growth, yearn towards the suffering and the afflicted of every country." She kept using the word "narrow": "By thus narrowing their sphere, and curtailing their rights and resources, women are doomed to an endless routine of domestic drudgery, to an indoor sedentary life, with little or no stimulus to great or noble endeavors."[56] She wanted space, "a larger circle of wants": "[Woman] needs to have her whole nature developed and strengthened by exercise; her attention directed to a larger circle of wants than those of her own household. She needs fully to apprehend the condition of the world; in fact, to realize the actual of the life she wishes her children to fill. This she cannot do, without some experience in its struggles and its triumphs."[57]

Price knew that behind the "false public sentiment" keeping women out of public life and space were very tangible material realities at work that created and maintained the constricting boundaries. These boundaries kept women out of public office and public space and, for the most part, out of work: because of them women remained dependents—in essence, children. The strongest material force working against women was patriarchy's success in making women deny the strength of their bodies. This denial was accomplished through various forces. One was the physical debilitation that women experienced through excessive childbearing, which was presented as a civic or eugenic duty, one might say, a duty to fill up America with the "native-born";[58] another was the kind of medical care available to women during pregnancy and childbirth (having a woman's body often insured a premature death);[59] and another was women's dress. Price knew the power patriarchy exerted by controlling each woman's body. She understood the politics of dress, the mixing of the personal and the public. She made it clear that she connected a woman's dress with her health, her sexuality, and her work.

The kind of clothing women (or men) wore determined quite primary things—for example, a person's physical mobility. If a woman was threatened physically, could she run away? Could she, Price asked, work in the garden, on the farm, ride horseback, sail a boat, go upstairs and down without having to hold up her skirts; could she operate heavy machinery without having to worry that her skirts would get caught and cause injury or death? And what about the body itself? Corseted and weighed down by the heavy material of antebellum costumes, women's very bodies were physically over-taxed and weakened and distorted. At the second National Woman's Rights Convention in 1851, Price linked dress and dependence:

Woman is at present to a great extent unfitted by her *dress* for self-support and independence; she is almost necessarily restricted to sedentary pursuits by this attire, and although not the cause of this restriction, yet it is a style that she long ago would have discarded, had she had equal rights to employment according to choice, and as many and as noble objects placed before her for personal achieve-ment.[60]

Price no doubt had mixed feelings when four years later she saw the frontispiece of the 1855 *Leaves of Grass,* with Whitman dressed in the loose-fitting, simple clothes that were not fashionable for mid-dle-class men and were unthinkable for middle-class women. Whit-man's clothes, which Bronson Alcott called his "man-Bloomer" ("he wears his man-Bloomer in defiance of everybody"),[61] were even less cumbersome and ornamented than the bloomer that Price wore in 1851–1852. She had led the way in her part of Massachusetts in the hope that women would adopt this new kind of clothing; she wore it, and she gave speeches promoting it. After a year of public censure, however, she finally gave up wearing the bloomer in public because she felt that instead of bringing benefits, it actually harmed her cause. She was then publicly criticized for giving it up. She replied to one of her critics: "I honor the dress and still enjoy its convenience and neatness wherever I deem it wise to wear it; and only regret that I have not done more to advance its interests. As I feel at present I cannot, without being false to my highest convictions of what is wis-est and best for me to do, wear the dress away from home alone. While I still award the new style the superiority, on all points that I ever did, I must be allowed to act freely, as my own conscience and experience dictate. Had I been more heroically organized, I might have held out better. But let me not be utterly condemned for admit-ting that I have not the courage *I thought I had.*"[62]

When she looked at the frontispiece of the 1855 *Leaves of Grass,* then, she recognized the opportunity that Whitman had for reform. Controversial though Whitman's acts and words were, as a male he had a wider range of possibilities for resistance than she. All she had to do was to look at Frances Wright's life to see the price women in America paid for stepping out of their space. She had only to think of Wright's last years, isolated, impoverished, deprived of her income by her husband, and separated from her daughter, with her work largely at an end because she had defied Victorian conventions.

Unless the stress on women's physical strength is placed in the context of the times, the contemporary reader is likely to miss its significance. Price insisted that physical strength and physical mobility provided an analog for intellectual and imaginative possibility. Whitman works with the same idea in his 1855 Preface: "The largeness of nature or the nation were monstrous without a corresponding largeness and generosity of the spirit of the citizen" (*Leaves of Grass,* Comprehensive Reader's Edition, 710). Abby Price told women that in order to secure their rights, they may, as she wryly put it, "be called on to omit homage to some household god for the acquirement of health and strength by out-door exercise."[63] She could be caustic in her impatience with women's resistance to change. In the transcript of her speech at the 1852 convention that appeared in the *Liberator,* we hear her impatience, even disdain: "Women are so enervated by habit as to despise their own sex. Talk to them of women-preachers, women-lecturers, they reply with contempt. . . . The men are more favorable than the women themselves." The transcript continues: "At a lyceum at Milford, she had requested that Mrs. E. Oakes Smith be invited to lecture. The men consented, but on going home, decided not to have the lecture. They were willing to hear her, but the ladies at home did not think it proper for woman to lecture and away they went, and got an Orthodox minister to come and lecture on woman's sphere!"[64]

In January 1853, Price wrote an article attacking the lie in her society: "We boldly declare that 'all men are born free and equal,' equal, if at all, in political rights and privileges. This is asserted in the same general sense that the term man is used in our account of the Creation, where it is said 'God made man in his own image, male and female created he them.' " Price creates, in the article, a male voice speaking to women: " 'You [the male voice says] are disfranchised. We shall not allow you the right of suffrage; the right of acting with us as rational human beings, and of guarding your own peculiar interests in common with ours.' 'Give to us your homage and we will govern you at home,' by the work of our own mouths daily. Man says to woman 'We want you *there,* and we will take care of you—we'll keep you in business; mind you *that business.*' " Near the end of the article, Price, as before, states, "[Woman] has a right to choose her own sphere." She wryly points out circumstances that have proven the need for her to do so. If women's need for independence does not rest on philosophical or moral grounds, then, it is necessary for survival in the broadest sense. Men abandon women, she says. In this article, she alludes to the Gold Rush and the practical consequences it had on women and children: "[In case] another gold excitement shall break out, enticing thousands of husbands and fathers—perhaps to Central Africa and the residue be summoned to the South, to protect the property of slaveholders—women shall have political power enough to manage the business that is left and properly take care of the children."[65] Six months later, speaking of the laws that denied women the right to govern their own lives, she asks, "Is this the genius of our Government for one class to represent another?"[66]

We know that Whitman and Price spent time together for a period of seventeen years, up to the time Louisa died, and that they wrote each other for another three years after Louisa's death. We know they had long periods of time together, talking. We also know that they talked about reform. We know Abby Price's views. It comes as no surprise, then, that in 1856, the year Price and Whitman met, Whitman's notebook entries became more focused on the issue of women's rights. Two entries furnish an excellent example of this awareness. These entries occur in the "Dick Hunt" notebook and appear to have been written early in 1857. One entry sounds like the start of a lecture, one of the many that Whitman planned but never delivered, as if, like Abby Price and other women's rights activists and orators, Whitman too were going to speak at a woman's rights convention. The notebook lecture has a tone much like Price's when she challenges women to change their thinking, when she attempts to jolt them out of their acquiescence (you "might be called on to omit homage to some household god for the acquirement of health and strength by out-door exercise"). Whitman's entry is brief: "(to women—sternly) Do you suppose you have nothing waiting for yourselves to do, but to embroider, to clean, to be respectable and modest, and not swear or drink?" The other note reads: "Women rely on men / the spiritual influence of women, & sex—Mrs. Tyndale's theory/."[67]

The "(to women—sternly)" entry makes the same kind of admonitions that Price made in her articles or speeches. Price alternated between blaming the male power structure for women's wrongs and taking women themselves to task for being, as she saw it, all too ready to relegate responsibility for themselves to others—to their husbands, brothers, and fathers. The "(to women—sternly)" entry, however, also indirectly says that women *can* move in the outside world. Women can be decision makers rather than passively accepting the decisions made by others. The "(to women—sternly)" entry thus represents the radical side of the woman's rights movement. It represents the side that called for the development of the individual to the fullest potential. The use of the word "sternly" in the opening line indicates Whitman's awareness of the resistance to change that the reformer faced in women as well as in men. The writer/orator names the confining boundaries: domestic work (sewing and cleaning), personal characteristics (such as passivity, modesty, and the like), and the personal sphere (where supposedly such things as swearing and drinking did not happen). Whitman, the lecturer, wants his audience to see that in accepting these socially formed boundaries as if they were intrinsic ("natural"), women deny themselves self-development. Abby Price's words ring through Whitman's.

The "women rely on men" entry represents another position in the woman's rights movement. Here the woman's body supposedly dictates the woman's role in life, dictates her characteristics. She is passive, submissive, moral, spiritual, and giving. Her body, smaller than the male's and less muscular, means she needs protection. This body, which furnishes the physical environment for the fetus, means that she exists for the other, not for herself. The "women rely on men" woman is a Cult-of-True-Womanhood woman. Though female activists like Antoinette Brown (Blackwell), from whom we have many more texts than from Sarah Tyndale, did not subscribe wholeheartedly to the view of women represented here, Brown did argue, as Tyndale appears to argue here, for women's intrinsic morality and for a separatist stance—women and men had intrinsic differences. In contemporary terms, Tyndale's and Brown's views represent the more conservative stance in women's rights, nudging close to essentialism. Whitman is astute in juxtaposing these two views; they were juxtaposed and fought over in the woman's rights conventions throughout the decade of the 1850s and also at Price's home when she and her friends talked about reform issues. They are still part of the feminist dialogue.

Sarah Tyndale's endorsement of this second theory—"women rely on men"—illustrates the tensions within individual women as well as the movement at large. Sarah Tyndale, an organizing force in the early woman's rights conventions, a friend of Price's, and, importantly, an astute businesswoman, took over and successfully ran the family business in Philadelphia for a number of years after her husband died before she turned it over to her son Hector. In 1857, Sarah Tyndale gave Whitman fifty dollars to buy back his plates from Fowler and Wells; she was one of the early stockholders in the Raritan Bay Union, a confirmed associationist. Through all of these developments, she clung to the theory that, to bring about change, women needed to work seemingly passively through men. It is instructive to note that though Price and Tyndale held opposing views on the "nature" of "woman," they worked together and were friends. From these women, then, Whitman heard opposing points of view as they all met at Price's home to talk. These opposing views of the "nature of woman" permeated women's discussions; they also appear in Whitman's poetry. Though many contemporary feminist readers of *Leaves of Grass* want to hear only Price's voice, Whitman did not always subscribe to views as radical as Price's, nor did many women of the time.

One woman active in the national woman's rights movement who found Whitman's poetry too "gross" was Martha Coffin Wright, Lucretia Mott's sister. In a letter written to her husband, David Wright, Martha Coffin Wright speaks of *Leaves of Grass*. The letter was written 26 October 1856, right after the second edition went on the market. It is not clear, however, which edition was read. The scene Wright paints in her letter of a group of people coming together in the evening to read aloud from *Leaves of Grass* recalls the scene Helen Price describes when she tells about similar evenings at the Price home. Martha Coffin Wright said:

> We had a pleasant evening at Morris' [Morris Davis]. Mrs. Yale, a superior woman, who talks profoundly & oracularly, was enthusiastically recommending "Leaves of Grass" wh. Emerson had pronounced the work of the age, & wh. Morris thought so full of new & beautiful thought. I told Mrs. Yale I had only looked into it and read

enough to see that the writer was a profound & original thinker, but there were blemishes, in the little that I read, that I thought ought to exclude it from my table. She was surprised that I shd. say so—the same objection wd. apply to the Bible & Shakpeare. Yet one could admire their beauties without dwelling on their defects. I told her those were written in an age when grossness was tolerated but there seemed to me no excuse for writing, in this day, what was unfit to be read. Morris selected some of the passages that pleased him, and read aloud—.[68]

Another notebook entry, in what also looks to be notes for a lecture, was an entry Whitman called "a simpler system of the Table." Perhaps since this entry deals with domesticity (rather than such things as sex or war), it has not been noticed by critics. It deals with the seemingly mundane, which women such as Price knew was not mundane at all. Kitchen time and hence gender-inscribed roles controlled a woman's life. Excessive kitchen time, for Price, meant stripping women of power. For its time, Whitman's notebook entry makes a radical proposal by even suggesting a shift in gendered roles. Whitman's poetry, however, does not make this kind of radical move—that is, not in his representations of women's and men's domestic roles. Almost without exception, Whitman follows traditional gender roles in his poetry when he depicts specific trades or domestic roles but not when he depicts female sexuality. This notebook entry, however, which calls for equal distribution of domestic roles must be considered when one comments on Whitman's belief in gender equality. This passage shows Abby Price's influence on Whitman:

No house, no woman, can be disenthralled until the society arrives at a simpler system of the table.—One dish, cheap, nutritious, plentiful, is enough for a meal.—The complex array of dinner, and the labor-costing and money-costing dishes, shall sink away.—A live man must eat;—A great appetite is grand;—Beef, rice, fruit potatoes, bread—these in plenty, become a man, twice a day—perhaps even thrice a day;—They are to be plain and rude.

It is observed in civilized life in the matter of the table, as in other matters, the trouble and expense are mostly for what is needless, and mars rather than mends—while that really needed is cheap and is soon done.—As to who shall do the work it is just as becoming, when both understand it as, that the man cook for the woman as that the woman cook for the man.[69]

The first and last sentences, of course, go against convention. Price wrote often of the need for a communal kitchen at Hopedale and in general society. In a particularly well-argued article that appeared in the 20 November 1852 *Practical Christian* and was entitled "The Combined Household," Price argues for a communal kitchen to achieve economies of time, resources, and expense. She frequently made this argument. She does not, however, in this article push for a reversal of gender roles. It is clear in her article that the communal kitchen will benefit women, not that men will take part in the work done there. Here she tries to work within the existing structure as she expresses herself expediently. "There being therefore no doubt about the economy and convenience of an organization of domestic labor, what is there at present in the way of establishing a common table for such as may choose? Capital would be well invested thus. I can conceive of no other way for woman to be free and at liberty ever to attend to the cultivation of her mind, or indeed properly to attend to her children—women's highest, noblest mission."

She does not use the sarcastic tone here that she uses in the *Una* when she argues that if the role of wife and mother was sacred, then so was the role of husband and father; therefore, why not prohibit the male, as the female was prohibited, from acting in any role other than husband or father? Here she moderates her argument. My point is that Price varied the persona and rhetorical strategy that she used to argue her case. She did, however, publicly argue it. On the other hand, Whitman's suggestion for a "simpler system of table" shows his readiness, like Price, to abandon the gendered roles firmly inscribed in his and Price's culture. Though the evidence is confined to his notes, the fact that Whitman could see the need for reciprocity in the everyday acts of private life shows bolder thinking than some of his heretical statements having to do with the church.

One month after Price's article "The Combined Household" appeared in the *Practical Christian*, the "Provisional Prospectus of the Raritan Bay Union" was printed in New York papers and in the *Practical Christian*. Among the stockholders listed were George B. and Lydia Arnold, Sarah Tyndale, and Paulina and Thomas Davis. In a letter written to Paulina Wright Davis that same month—December 1852—Elizabeth Cady Stanton voices a belief similar to Whitman's

statement "No house, no woman, can be disenthralled until the society arrives at a simpler system of the table." By this time Stanton
had five children. She wrote:

> My eyes turn longingly to "the Association" as a truer mode of life.
> Woman must ever be sacrificed in the isolated household. It did re-
> joice me to see your names appended to the Prospectus of the Rari-
> tan Bay Union, for I am resolved to go there. But how I am to reach
> the goal is the question. I have nothing yet that I can call my own
> except the house I live in of which I have a deed. This is worth 2000$.
> Could I go there with my five children by taking so small a share?
> would my firm health, strength my capacity for & love of work be
> considered as capital? I should be a *jewel* in an Association for *they
> say*, I am good natured, generous, & always well & happy. Oh what
> bliss is yet in store for us. *All our talk about woman's rights is mere moon-
> shine so long as we are bound by the present social system.* Henry has a
> horror of all associations of the kind proposed—what shall I do with
> him?—as he seemed greatly pleased with you when you last met, as
> well as on the previous occasion when he kept you blushing in the
> stage coach. I think I shall hand him over to your eloquence.[70] [Em-
> phasis added]

Stanton's observation that "all our talk about woman's rights is mere
moonshine so long as we are bound by the present social system"
complements Whitman's belief that universal suffrage would not
solve the ills of society. The change must come in the private realm
as well as the public. In Whitman's eyes, literature's image-making
work would play a key role in this regard.

In May of 1852, two-year-old Henry Edmund Price died. As a way
of dealing with her grief, Abby Price went to Brooklyn to visit former
Hopedale residents Clement O. and Lydia B. Read, who had left
Hopedale in 1849 and had moved to Brooklyn where Clement Read
"played a leading role in founding an 'extensive Bathing and Washing Establishment' designed especially for the poor."[71] She visited the
site of a new commune while there—the Raritan Bay Union near
Perth Amboy, New Jersey—and also the nearby North American Phalanx, a well-established Fourier association. While she was in Brooklyn, Price wrote two articles about her experiences for the *Practical
Christian*. The articles show how this visit sharpened her view on as-
sociationism, another term for communitarianism, or, loosely, early

American socialism. The visit caused her to begin questioning the use of the "test" as a basis of membership in the Hopedale community, where prospective residents had to affirm that they shared the community's beliefs in such matters as pacifism, temperance, and antislavery. Price, like Whitman, was engaged in a quest for the "Great City," a theme Whitman explored explicitly in poems like the 1856 "Song of the Broad-Axe." Like Whitman, she was committed to the principle of a spiritualized government and citizenry. But unlike him, in 1852 she was still committed to the idea of a select society. Her journey to the site of the Raritan Bay Union and her visit at the North American Phalanx plus her own experience living at Hopedale gave her a lived experience in alternative concepts of democracy that made her a valuable source of information for Whitman in his own search for the Great City.

Price begins the first article written after her return from Brooklyn—17 July 1852—with a positive appraisal of Hopedale. In the first half of the article, "Things at Home," she takes the reader with her through the village as if on a guided tour. As the tour guide, she sees familiar sights in a fresh manner. She comments that the "new arrangements" that Hopedale had adopted the previous winter "of forming independent branches of industry, under the general organization . . . have given a new impetus to enterprise, reducing the number of hours needed for discussion, and giving greater freedom of individuality, with all the advantages of combination."[72] At this time in her life Price was wrestling with the delicate balance between the "greater freedom of individuality" and the "advantages of combination," an issue with which Whitman continually dealt. Edward Spann's reading of the "new arrangements" (the forming of independent branches) disproves Price's. Spann, with his advantage of historical hindsight, believes that the fragmenting of industry set a tone that made it relatively easy for George Draper, the brother of longtime Hopedale resident Ebenezer Draper, to convert the town from communal living into a company town run by the Drapers.

Underlying this article were Price's specific concerns that agriculture not be given short shrift (a point she develops in her next article) and thus that women's opportunities not be curtailed: "A Garden Branch has been formed whose efficiency has been proved. . . . This branch also affords healthful and remunerative employment for woman. . . . Not what she can do very well encased in whalebones and long skirts; but dressed loosely in a convenient Bloomer—

she finds it *womanly* employment. . . . Why should not these be as well paid; for who made us to differ?"[73]

Price then states that there is no competition between the different branches—"The Machine, the Box, the Carpentry, the Agricultural, the Fruit-growing and the Printing Branches." Into all of these "woman is welcomed, to do what she may find herself able, as equal co-laborer." Price ends with an argument for women's economic independence. In this particular article, she does not indict the "false public sentiment" for women's oppression, as she often did in her speeches to the national women's rights conventions. Rather she takes it as a given that at Hopedale women have the opportunity to work outside the home, and she charges Hopedale women to do so:

> [That women are equal co-laborers] is right and just, and takes away from the well woman, who is free from the care of children, the fear of dependence, that broods like a fearful nightmare over her shadowed future. Woman must learn to be self-helpful, in order to be independent and happy. She must learn to contribute as much as she receives, in order to realize the glory of her own destiny. She has been too long the weak angel, asking help to breathe fragrance and love. She should become the strong one, graceful in healthful vigor, imparting aid and courage and hope to man, who has too long wrestled alone with fate. Her *help is meet* for him in all life's toils. Then will he look to her as an equal—a companion, a friend, and not to be regarded as a ward, a pet, a plaything, an inferior, to bear along on his arm up the steep of adversity, for at best, a rugged pathway is human life.[74]

Price's use of the intensives "must learn" and "should become" indicate that Price felt Hopedale women were not taking full advantage of their opportunities.

She follows this article with one titled "Things at Home-Continued," 31 July 1852. In it she makes serious accusations against unnamed persons who were threatening the stability of Hopedale. Price opens this piece stressing the need for agriculture: "Agriculture should be the basis of a prosperous Association." Agriculture was indeed the basis for associations organized under Fourier's principles. Hopedale shared the Fourier plan in that it was a joint-stock community, but Hopedale also relied a great deal on its industry. In this article on Hopedale and its needs, Abby Price criticized the un-named source or sources who had the power to withhold capital from the commune. In "Things at Home—Continued," Price said there was not enough capital being invested in the community: Hopedale needed more waterpower, and having more would benefit both industry and agriculture: "We have proved both by our deeds and by our words . . . that Association is the true policy, both to the capitalist and the laborer; and now what is the reason the means are not forthcoming to realize our highest ideal? There are friends of Association possessing wealth that might be profitably invested, as well to themselves as to others, in improving our water power for mechanical purposes, and in bringing out the full power of our land. Why is so much wealth consecrated to bloated, oppressive corpora-tions . . . ?" She took a scolding tone: "He who has power that he withholds from the cause of Human Progress, has a fearful account to render for his stewardship." By 1852, the balance of share-holding in Hopedale had tipped; one man held most of the stocks—Ebenezer Draper. In 1852, Ebenezer Draper replaced Ballou as the community president. As the community structure weakened, the opportunity for a takeover intensified, and when George Draper, Ebenezer's en-terprising brother, moved to Hopedale, the move to end the com-mune accelerated. In March of 1856, to use Spann's words, the "paradise of Christian socialism" had turned to dust.[75] It became a company town controlled by George Draper, with the help of his brother Ebenezer. By 1856, Abby lived in Brooklyn. Her bravery in taking on the moneyed powers assuredly helped to bring about her departure from this experimental community that she had loved and had helped to build.

Thus in July 1853 Price wrote a farewell letter to the community. Because she had served as confidant for three of her townspeople who were involved in what turned out to be an adulterous triangle, she had been publicly stripped of her authority as a spokesperson for the community, or at least that is how she took the proceedings of the Council of Religion, Conciliation, and Justice, which tried the case. The investigating council issued a report saying that Price was seriously implicated in the incident, since, they said, she had known too much to keep still. She called on the council members to prove that their report was accurate. Perhaps if she had not called their hand (as she had a year earlier in her article on Hopedale's need for more communal investment by the principal shareholders) and if she had accepted their report in silence (as a woman was expected to do), her part in the affair would soon have been forgotten. But she did question them. As a result of her demand, "a searching investigation," she said, "was entered into by them, and I was charged, 1, with knowing too much to keep dark, and 2, with double dealing." Price responded to the charges, saying that had she known the end in the beginning, she would have acted differently and that her errors had been errors of judgment, not of intention:

> In the panic and dismay of the excitement I found I could not make myself fully understood by the Council and that injustice has been done me, I am sure time will prove. I therefore quietly withdrew from the Community membership. Should we go to the Raritan Bay Union, I shall be received with a cordial welcome by friends who know me better than do the persons who so bitterly condemn me. I have no views in regard to "free love" different from the others here.
>
> In relation to the whole matter, my opinion is that in their zeal for principle and purity, our people have been less merciful than their better judgment will incline them to be after mature deliberation.[76]

Four weeks after Price's letter detailing her expulsion, a brief announcement appeared in the *Practical Christian*, "To Whom It May Concern":

> As the communication of Abby H. Price . . . has left a doubt on the minds of some persons as to the degree of guilt that should be attached to her in the matter of which that communication treats: The undersigned, members of the "Council of Religion, Conciliation and Justice," hereby attest that she was not charged before them with *designedly* abetting criminal intercourse between the condemned parties named in her communication.
>
> *D. B. Chapman   Anna T. Draper   Ann F. Fish   William G. Comstock*[77]

Anna Draper was married to Ebenezer Draper. The *Practical Christian* for 29 January 1853 lists the officers for the Council as follows: Dudley B. Chapman, William G. Comstock, Ann Fish, Henry Lillie, and Abby J. Spalding. Ebenezer Draper was listed as president; Abby Price was part of the Relief Committee, along with Edmund Soward, Joseph B. Bancroft, and Almira Humphrey. I have read no explanation as to why Anna Draper officiated at Abby's trial or why Lillie and Spalding did not.

Price's letter in the *Practical Christian* appeared on 2 July. On 5 or 6 July, she wrote a personal letter to Samuel May, a prominent Unitarian minister and activist in the temperance, pacifist, abolitionist, and woman's rights reform movements. She first told him about an antislavery meeting she had led at South Milford. Part of the day, she told May, had been "given to the presentation of woman's rights," by request. She then spoke of a meeting scheduled to be held at Hopkinton:

> About Hopkinton I feel sadly for I hear the most unfavorable rumors have been carried by Mr. Stacy perhaps, or some unfriendly person. Mr. Ballou advises me however, to go there and not fear. You will please write to any one you please for their opinion about my blame. I mean any one here. No person that I know of accuses me of intentional wrong—only that my confidence was too easily imposed upon, I have suffered, I cannot tell you how much, both on my own account and for Henry's sake, and for the sake of all. If you think the odour of the affair, will bring a shadow upon Anti Slavery tell me frankly— and what I do, I will do as I have done, upon my own responsibility.[78]

May responded:

> Since I wrote to you last, I have had a conversation with Abby K. Foster. I had every reason to believe her to be your friend. It was she who first proposed & advised that our County A. S. Society should invite you to become a Lecturing Agent for them; first privately to me; and afterwards at a meeting of the Exec. Committee. I felt therefore that, in talking with her, I had at once the judgment of a friend to yourself and a friend to the Antislavery cause. She had then heard nothing about the unpleasant business at Hopedale; it was entirely new to her.—I showed her your letter in the *Practical Christian*, and told her what I had heard, from Hopedale people, about the matter. Her judgment was, that, until matters were more fully cleared up, it was not best that you should continue lecturing for our County Society. This, as you know, was my own opinion.—I have felt great regret that the affair, as regards your own connection with it, has not been more clearly explained, I hoped that the last P.C., would have

contained something explicit. It is, at least, unfortunate for you, as I see the matter, that nothing more definite has appeared in the P.C.

May added a postscript: "I have felt no inclination, but rather a repugnance, on every account, to talking with any other of the Committee about it—and have not done so." As my own postscript to May's 1853 letter to Abby, I record a comment that May made in 1858, about Walt, in a letter he wrote to the British antislavery activist Richard D. Webb: "In all Boston I can find but one copy of Walt Whitman's Leaves of Grass; it is a second hand copy, much the worse for wear, and they ask for it a dollar & a half, double its value. I therefore do not send it, and I do not think you will be much the loser if you never see a copy. Still, judgments differ, and should I see a copy at a reasonable price, I will send it to you."[79]

As far as I know, Price did not speak at any more antislavery events. She did attend the woman's rights convention held in New York 6 and 7 September 1853, at the Broadway Tabernacle, called the Mob Convention, the last woman's rights convention I have found a record of her attending until 1870, at which time she delivered a poem written for the celebration of the twentieth anniversary of the national woman's rights movement. The 1853 Mob Convention provided an excellent opportunity for Whitman to attend. At this time he routinely attended the World's Fair, also held in New York, embracing the opportunity to mingle with the crowd. The Woman's Rights Convention provided one more opportunity for him to mingle with the crowd. If he did attend the convention, he had the opportunity to hear Price's terse comments on equality:

> An equality of rights among those on whom the laws press with an equality of weight, seems a demand founded on first principles so obvious, that the only matter of surprise is, how it can be denied for a moment; or rather, that would be a matter of surprise, did we not know how little, hitherto, the world has been guided by rationality, and how completely spell-bound have the customs of society become under the frost of prejudice and old habit. I can fancy this frost dissolved; indeed, I already see the sun of progress play on its cold surface. I hail the light of progression. Indeed, history teaches us that we have progressed a little way.[80]

Somehow, less than three weeks after the July 1853 farewell letter appeared in the *Practical Christian,* the Price family moved from Hopedale to the Raritan Bay Union. "Co-Operative Industry," an open letter addressed to Paulina Wright Davis, the editor of the *Una,* appeared in its August issue. In this 20 July open letter, full of Abby Price's praise for the Raritan Bay Union and hope for and belief in its success, Price never names the Hopedale community, but it forms the subtext for the letter. Her idea of the basis for the "Great City" had changed.

The Raritan Bay Union did not, like Hopedale, require a pledge (or "test") in order for people to live there, nor did it, like the nearby Fourierist community, the North American Phalanx, dismiss Christianity as an element of communal life. Completely changed now in her view toward written agreements, which she had at one time considered a necessity, Price now saw the lack of a pledge as positive. Like Whitman, she thought that laws would not create the Great City; rather, affection among citizens would engender community and, on the national level, for Whitman especially after the War, preserve the Union. Price wrote in the 1853 "Co-Operative Industry":

> They [Raritan Bay Union communitarians] depend more upon the inspiration of the Divine Spirit, for their moral progress than upon any prescribed rules and arguments entered into to-day, for their guide on the morrow. The principles of Christianity as revealed by the Great Teacher, they hold to be eternal truth; while therefore individual obedience to these principles is required of all, an individual enforcement of their obedience rests equally upon all. Without the living vitality of these principles . . . all constitutional laws, all judiciary tribunals, all solemn meetings, to enforce obedience, may prove but instruments of prejudice and hate, cruel and unjust in degree as the engine of the inquisition. God save the fraternity, that depends upon its written laws for life! Such is already dead! May this *new* Union strive to cultivate the largest liberty, the highest harmony, the truest, the divinest love, and the most perfect development.[81]

Unlike Price, Carl Guarneri, in his 1991 *The Utopian Alternative,* sees the Raritan Bay Union in a less than sanguine light. But it did not take Price long to lose her optimism. The Prices moved to Brooklyn in 1855 or 1856. By that time, the Raritan Bay Union was in effect defunct. Speaking of the directors of the Raritan Bay Union—Marcus Spring, George B. Arnold, and Clement Read—Guarneri says that the Raritan Bay Union was "far less democratic than the NAP [North American Phalanx]" and was "controlled by a kinship network of successful business families."[82] In 1856, Spring, acting much like George Draper at Hopedale, "bought back most shares of the community's stock."[83] Price's hopes for an egalitarian city were once more dashed.

This tumultuous period in Price's life—1853–1856—was likewise a tumultuous time in Whitman's life, though largely in a positive sense, since it saw the most important poem in American poetry— "Song of Myself"—first come to public view in the 1855 *Leaves of Grass.* Though not so specifically reflecting woman's rights consciousness as the 1856 and 1860 editions of *Leaves of Grass,* the 1855 edition was indeed revolutionary in its insistence on equality and in its persistent and specific inclusion of women as its readers. In this sense, in 1855, *Leaves of Grass* was already the woman's book that Whitman called it. In the forty-sixth line of the poem the persona (who will identify himself as "Walt Whitman, a kosmos") declares equality as a given: "Out of the dimness opposite equals advance. . . . Always a knit of identity . . . , always distinction" (*Variorum,* 1:3). Line 70 tells readers that the persona makes no distinctions between the sex of potential loved ones: "The real or fancied indifference of some man or woman I love." Line 132 contains the first use of paired gendered pronouns, "him or her," used throughout *Leaves of Grass,* so compelling when one realizes that Whitman's insistence on this usage has taken almost 150 years to achieve, with yet a less than complete compliance. The poet declares his intended audience: "I am the poet of the woman the same as the man." He adds what might now seem trivializing because of its self-evidence: "And I say it is as great to be a woman as to be a man" (*Variorum,* 1:26–27). This point, however, was one that the woman's rights activists made again and again. It was *not* part of the public consciousness. They and Whitman had to inscribe it into consciousness. Just as Whitman declared androgyny when he specified the indifference of "some man or woman I love," so also did he cross boundary lines when he took on the voice of the wife: "My voice is the wife's voice" (*Variorum,* 1:50).

Much of the liberating force of Whitman's *Leaves of Grass* for female readers came from its insistence that women were just as much the intended audience as were men: "Accepting the rough deific sketches to fill out better in myself, bestowing them freely on each man and woman I see" (*Variorum,* 1:64). *Leaves of Grass* insisted, repeatedly, that the liberating vistas it projected were for both:

> But each man and each woman of you I lead upon a knoll,
> My left hand hooking you round the waist,
> My right hand pointing to landscapes of continents and the public road.
> [*Variorum,* 1:75–77]

Such lines as these opened up *Leaves of Grass* for women in a way that specific images did not, images that all too often identify women only with domestic crafts, only with domestic work, and only as mothers. They deflected such lines as "And there is no trade or employment but the young man following it may become a hero" (*Variorum,* 1:79). It helped a great deal to follow that line closely with "And *I say to any man or woman,* Let your soul stand cool and composed before a million universes" (emphasis added).

Though the 1855 *Leaves of Grass* fails to make the specific political connections with the woman's movement that the 1856 and 1860 editions of *Leaves of Grass* make, it does indirectly open up space for women. One line in particular in "Song of Myself" suggests what Whitman was seeing in the culture and his subsequent modification of this cultural fact. The line reads: "On the piazza walk five matrons stately and friendly with twined arms" (*Variorum,* 1:19). The image, with modification, replicates the image found in the "Symbolical Head," the phrenologically illustrated human head with the thirty-odd different compartments of the brain illustrated to depict the specific trait each compartment controlled. The Symbolical Head, so named in Lorenzo Fowler's 1847 *Marriage: Its History and Ceremonies; with a Phrenological and Physiological Exposition of the Functions and Qualifications for Happy Marriages,* used the image of two women standing with their heads and bodies touching, their outer arms crossed in front so that they can hold hands, to illustrate adhesiveness. The *American Phrenological Journal,* published by Fowler and Wells, at times used the Symbolical Head on its cover and accompanied its illustrations of the Symbolical Head with a "Definition of the Faculties, According to Their Numbers." That is, each separate illustration had its number. The text then defined each illustration.

The illustration of the two women, numbered "3," represented Adhesiveness, which the *Journal* defined:

> 3. Adhesiveness.—Friendship; love of company; disposition to associate, adapted to man's requisition for society and concert of action. Abuse: Excessive fondness for company. Deficiency: Neglect of friends and society; the hermit disposition.

(Floyd Stovall, in *The Foreground of* Leaves of Grass, says that Whitman was almost certainly a regular reader of the *American Phrenological Journal* during the years 1850–1856.")[84] Thanks to Fowler and Wells, the head was ubiquitous and frequently appeared in almanacs, magazines, and newspapers. In the 1855 *Leaves of Grass,* then, the women strolling in public space represent the definition of adhesiveness that the Fowler and Wells firm had inscribed into the cultural consciousness. The 1855 *Leaves of Grass* offers the image of women as representative of Adhesiveness ("On the piazza walk five matrons stately and friendly with twined arms"), if read within the context of its times. In 1856, Whitman begins his inscription of what he desired and saw missing in his culture: male adhesiveness. Female adhesiveness was already there in fact and image, though equal rights were not.

Though sympathy was culturally marked as feminine and was therefore culturally a weak and powerless quality, Whitman did not see it in this way. The threads of connection that Louisa Van Velsor Whitman established as she involved each one of her children in the lives of the others, as she interacted with her friends, boarders, and neighbors, and as she kept sending Hannah boxes and unanswered letters find resonance in Whitman. The threads of connection between Louisa and Walt and Abby Price and her children—daughters Helen and Emily and son Edmund—find resonance as well.

On some level, the urge to establish community lies behind Louisa Whitman's care boxes to her daughter Hannah and her general overall maintenance of her family, as it lies behind Whitman's own boxes of books and the papers that he regularly sent out to friends and family, up to his death. This push to nourish with clothes, food, and words, then, is a movement outward that finds its most honed expression in Whitman's poetry. Whitman himself made the connection between his words and sustenance, referring to his words as chyle, nutriment for the reader's body and soul. In no other prose passage is Whitman's connection between physical need or desire for connection with the other and his poems so sensuously expressed as in his 1876 Preface: "I also sent out 'Leaves of Grass' to arouse and set flowing in men's and women's hearts, young and old, endless streams of living, pulsating love and friendship, directly from them to myself, now and ever. To this terrible, irrepressible yearning, (surely more or less down underneath in most human souls)—this never-satisfied appetite for sympathy, and this boundless offering of sympathy—this universal democratic comradeship—this old, eternal, yet ever-new interchange of adhesiveness, so fitly emblematic of America—I have given in that book, undisguisedly, declaredly, the openest expression."[85] "Democratic comradeship" and "eternal yet ever-new interchange of adhesiveness" fuse the private and the public. These terms "adhesiveness" and "comradeship" appear often in Whitman's poetry and prose and have received considerable critical attention. Critics have focused on precisely who receives the love that adhesiveness entails—on who the comrade is and on the definition of "community." Is Whitman meaning that the community is a restricted one? Is he writing to and for gay men? Is he writing to and for women? If for women, does he tacitly acknowledge their sexual orientation? Is he writing for specific ethnic groups? For specific classes? Who is the reader? How inclusive is Whitman's community?

If one accepts the idea of a nonaligned ideal reader, a number of female readers have not, as attested by the number of responses in which women profess to feeling that they have been singled out, or at least that their lives were being addressed, a claim for alignment made as well by a number of gay scholars. Whitman would have said, in keeping with his embrace of contradictions, that both conceptions of the reader were what he had in mind, and he would not have created an either/or choice, as we theorists so often do.

When Whitman said in 1888 that *Leaves of Grass* was essentially a woman's book, possibly he had in mind the Utopian underpinning of his poetics and politics, that is, his project of inscribing an egalitarian mode of government, a government that recognized all people as equals under the law, in distinction to what actually existed. In that respect, the groups that the culture marginalized could feel addressed by *Leaves of Grass*. Just as Whitman consciously worked into *Leaves* an address that incorporated marginalized peoples, so did these people feel the singled-out quality of his address. In addition to using both of the gendered pronouns and the words "woman" and "women," part of the reason women felt singled out might lie in Whitman's incorporating such culturally loaded words as "adhesiveness," a word that had strong cultural overtones. Women, especially, would recognize the concept for which it stood, a phrenological concept well inscribed into the culture by 1855 through the agency of the Fowler brothers, the same Fowler and Wells responsible for the distribution of the 1855 and 1856 *Leaves of Grass* and of numerous journals and books dealing with the subject of phrenology, as well as for the *American Phrenological Journal*. The phrenological sign for the concept of adhesiveness, or friendship, on the symbolical head was, as stated earlier, the image of two women, as Michael Lynch points out in his " 'Here Is Adhesiveness': From Friendship to Homosexuality": "For Fowler, self-knowledge was primarily useful for self-improvement. Fowler and his associates devised and spread widely over midcentury America the familiar drawing of a head in profile with small iconographic drawings on it, as if from a tattooist gone mad on a noggin. The adhesive 'bump' . . . was indicated by two young women holding hands, their heads tilted together so that, presumably, their adhesive organs were as close as possible. I have found only one such sketch, from the Fowler establishment late in the century, showing two men to represent Adhesiveness; their arms are linked in a distinct male friendship pose."[86]

If one of Whitman's goals in *Leaves of Grass* was to etch into his culture what he saw lacking, then it seems consistent that he would take a term like "adhesiveness" and attempt to supply referents for it that he did not see in actuality. Thus possibly Whitman took the phrenological term "adhesiveness," culturally signified by the sign of two women embracing, and expanded it to mean male/male friendship and as well male/male lovers. If Carroll Smith-Rosenberg is correct, the culture already accepted a wide range of expressions of friendship/sensuality between women:

> In contrast [to the twentieth century], nineteenth-century American society did not taboo close female relationships but, rather, recognized them as a socially viable form of human contact—and, as such, acceptable throughout a woman's life. Indeed, it was not these homosocial ties that were inhibited but, rather, heterosexual leanings. While closeness, freedom of emotional expression, and uninhibited physical contact characterized women's relationships with one another, the opposite was frequently true of male-female relationships.

One could thus argue that within such a world of female support, intimacy, and ritual it was only to be expected that adult women would turn trustingly and lovingly to one another. It was a behavior they had observed and learned since childhood. A different type of emotional landscape existed in the nineteenth century.[87]

Whitman wanted the same kind of acceptance for men.

Smith-Rosenberg emphasizes the physicality of the relationships: "These bonds were often physical as well as emotional. An undeniably romantic and even sensual note frequently marked female relationships" (71). ("Bonds" was the word Sarah Grimké used to sign her fifteen *Letters on the Equality of the Sexes*, published in 1838, "Thine in the bonds of womanhood.")[88] A survey of women's diaries and journals has led Smith-Rosenberg to believe that some of the women surveyed experienced "an emotional intensity and a sensual and physical explicitness that are difficult to dismiss," and these relationships were perfectly acceptable to all concerned (58–59).

Possibly, then, one reason that many women in the nineteenth century responded to *Leaves* so enthusiastically was for the very reason that some present-day scholars have by and large reasoned that *Leaves of Grass* would reach primarily male readers: its valorization of adhesiveness, that is, adhesiveness defined ahistorically as meaning only male/male relationships. Nineteenth-century women, however, could readily see Whitman's references to adhesiveness as addressing them. What Whitman did, then, was to take the nineteenth-century popularized sense of the term, a term culturally understood to mean female/female relationships (via Fowler and Wells), and, rather than restrict it, to expand its range of referents to include male/male love.

In its broadest sense, "adhesiveness" meant friendship, the "other," community; for Whitman, it meant acceptance of diversity. In terms of Whitman's personal (sexual) yearning, the fact that the culture "permitted" physical intimacy between women (adhesiveness) gave credence to his own desire for physical intimacy between men. In terms of Louisa Van Velsor, Whitman could see the gendered roles at play—that "sympathy" was designated feminine and therefore weak and therefore an acceptable trait for his mother to have, whereas her "pride" (her will, her "strong-mindedness") was not. In terms of the woman's movement, thanks to Louisa Van Velsor's sense of self (her "pride") and to friends such as Abby Price, Whitman could hear the woman's rights activists' call to be a part of the community, to be considered as equal citizens under the law. Just as the national woman's rights movement served the function of inscribing into public consciousness women's demand for equal rights, so too did Whitman's poetry serve the complementary function of inscribing the fact of male/male love into the body politic, though through the indirectness of poetic language.

To go back to the discussion of the line in the 1855 "Song of Myself," the line reading "On the piazza walk five matrons stately and friendly," I see stemming from this line Whitman's desire to inscribe into the culture for males what he often saw in the culture in actuality in the lives of Abby Price and her reform-minded friends. For instance, "Salut au Monde!" initiates Whitman's desire to inscribe a new concept of adhesiveness—inscribing its representation of male/male relationships—with the 1856 line: "Who are the three old men going slowly with their arms about each others' necks?" (*Variorum,* 1:162). In 1881, Whitman demoted the number of friendly matrons from five to three. In 1871, he promoted the number of old men from three old men to "groups of old men." ("Who are the groups of old men going slowly with their arms about each other's necks?")

By his pattern of promotion and demotion, Whitman lessens the chance that his readers will recognize the similarity of the "Salut au Monde!" line ("Who are the three old men going slowly with their arms about each others' necks?") to the 1855 "Myself" line ("On the piazza walk five matrons stately and friendly with twined arms") by changing the number "five" to "group." This pattern accomplishes three things. First, it dissociates adhesiveness from the 1855 more or less culturally obvious connection of women and adhesiveness as illustrated by the Phrenological Head. Second, by 1881 the piazza line has three matrons, not five; thus Whitman demotes the pervasiveness of the matron's "friendliness" (adhesiveness) and thereby lessens women's power in terms of female/female bonding. The pattern works to inscribe male bonding into public consciousness—at the expense of female bonding, some would say. "Groups" inscribes Whitman's desire for a democracy founded on *affectional* bonding, not on the unbridled competition that Gilded Age capitalism exacerbated. "Groups" indicates a culturally accepted behavior or action because of the number. Males expressing physical/erotic love for males would be accepted, just as females expressing physical affection for females was accepted. By saying it, Whitman hoped to create the material reality. Though I am generalizing, the cultural lack lay in the male world, which did not fit Carroll Smith-Rosenberg's reading of the female world, that of "love and ritual."[89] The male-bonding image continues to evolve throughout subsequent editions of *Leaves of Grass*. The radical female image of the single woman realizing and expressing her singularity, furthered by women such as Abby Price, becomes, after the Civil War, increasingly the Mother of All. "Adhesiveness," like Whitman's use of the term "comrade," has no single referent. "Adhesiveness" and "comrades" can be narrowly focused, referring to males loving males; "adhesiveness" can suggest females loving females (as in the 1855 line); the terms can be more broadly focused, referring to people in general, as when Whitman talks about comrades in his conversations with Traubel that deal with the abstractions germane to his concept of democracy.

"Song of the Broad-Axe," a poem about the making of great cities, first appeared in the 1856 *Leaves of Grass*. Whitman's consciousness of women's entrance into public and political life heightened in 1856. This heightening is foregrounded in "Song of the Broad-Axe."

"Song of the Broad-Axe" can be given many different readings, but one inescapable reading is Whitman's view of history: the progress of civilization from feudalism with its despotism to democracy with its (supposed) egalitarianism. M. Wynn Thomas, in *The Lunar Light of Whitman's Poetry*, effectively deconstructs the positive image that Whitman wished to project of an America moving toward the realization of liberty for all. With the image of the ax, Thomas says, Whitman "has developed an ingenious image of the ideal, which he can conveniently confuse, or at least credibly connect, with the existing state of affairs."[90] Thomas stresses what Whitman doesn't say, noting Whitman's use of images to naturalize and elide the acquisitive nature of American capitalism (and democracy) and Whitman's idealization of the pioneer and the miner, with no apparent awareness of the price the land and humanity were paying in American's race for acquisitions. Thomas writes: "The ax is ingeniously used . . . as an organizing symbol which allows him to restructure society drastically, so as to make it into a nonprofit association of purely heroic adventurers and spirited workingmen, in anticipation of the brave New Jerusalem . . . to be built eventually on American soil."[91]

Thomas's reading of Whitman focuses on Whitman's nationalistic fervor. One can certainly see in "Song of the Broad-Axe" Whit-

man's partial view and what to many now is an embarrassing reading
of American history. But there is another reading as well, not mentioned by Thomas. What do we make of stanza 5?

> Where women walk in public processions in the streets the same as the
>   men,
> Where they enter the public assembly and take places the same as the men,
>   and are appealed to by the orators the same as the men, . . .

And stanza 11?

> Her shape arises,
> She less guarded than ever, yet more guarded than ever,
> The gross and soil'd she moves among do not make her
>   gross and soil'd,
> She knows the thoughts as she passes, nothing is conceal'd from her,
> She is none the less considerate or friendly therefor,
> She is the best belov'd, it is without exception, she has no reason to fear
>   and she does not fear,
> Oaths, quarrels, hiccupp'd songs, smutty expressions, are idle to her as she
>   passes,
> She is silent, she is possess'd of herself, they do not offend her,
> She receives them as the laws of Nature receive them, she is strong,
> She too is a law of Nature—there is no law stronger than she is.[92]

Stanza 11 in essence daguerreotypes Abby Price, or at least an
Abby Price. In 1864, four years after the Civil War halted the national woman's rights conferences, Eliza Farnham's *Woman and Her
Era* was published.[93] Farnham uses the above passage as an epigraph
for both volumes of her two-volume work. The passage faces the first
page of text, is centered, and has a border drawn around it, as if
to frame a portrait. Farnham met Whitman at Abby Price's home.[94]
Farnham and Paulina Wright Davis were also friends, having known
each other since the 1840s. Farnham, who used phrenological principles in her reform work in prisons, is especially notable for her
stint as woman's matron at Sing Sing. She also served as a nurse
during the Civil War. Though friends of Price and Davis and active
in reform, Farnham did not participate in the woman's movement
until 1858, when she agreed to attend her first National Woman's
Rights Convention, where she delivered an address on the supe-

riority of the female sex. The address became in essence the focus of her 1864 two-volume work. Farnham believed that the superiority of the female—she regarded women as superior to the men in the evolutionary chain because of their reproductive organs—made it retrogressive to demand equal rights, since by assuming males' place females would *lower* their own status in evolutionary history. Farnham "glorified woman's reproductive role as a creative power second only to that of god, and revealed a strong belief in the prenatal influence of the mother upon the emotional and physical development of the child."[95] Both of these views are found in Whitman's *Leaves of Grass*. No doubt her reading of stanza 11 stressed the biological superiority suggested in its last line: "She too is a law of nature—there is no law stronger than she is."

Stanza 11 as a whole, however, gives us an image that is very much grounded in the discrete historical circumstances of the woman's movement. One of patriarchy's main arguments against "giving" women the "right" to vote was the degrading milieu of election places. Cartoons showed women going to the voting place with men heckling them and, by implication, sullying them. The argument was that the voting box was men's space (public space) and that women's virtue would be compromised by "penetrating" it. This stanza answers those arguments. It clearly represents the views of the woman's rights activists of the times; it shows women moving out into public space. By implication, it develops Price's views: the argument holding that women's virtue would be compromised by moving out of the domestic sphere, and furthermore by voting, was absurd.

Woman's strength and assurance as Whitman depicts them in stanza 11 mirror the strength of women like Price, Paulina Wright Davis, Ernestine L. Rose, Elizabeth Cady Stanton, Susan B. Anthony, and Frances Wright. Why is it, then, that Stephen Black in his 1975 *Whitman's Journeys into Chaos* considers this woman strong not because of her own force of character but through pregnancy? "Perhaps sheer pregnancy guards this woman's movements through an offensive world."[96] What Whitman depicts as composure, David Cavitch depicts as withering complacency: "The calm possessiveness of the earth in 'This Compost' and the withering complacency of the woman in 'Song of the Broad-Axe' reveal Whitman's horrified suspicion that he was betrayed in his deepest trust."[97] Alvin H. Rosenfeld, in the winter 1968 issue of *American Imago,* protests against what he sees as Whitman's blurring of gender lines and roles:

"The reader will observe a movement in the poem from an un-defined sexuality, to a strong assertion of the masculine, to a collapse of the masculine, and its final replacement by an emerging feminine personality of *dubious* nature" (emphasis added).[98] Rosenfeld sees bisexuality as Whitman's new "strong being" and does not like it: "With his or her appearance [the "strong being's" appearance], there is a *regression* to a vague bisexuality" (emphasis added).[99] The portrait in stanza 11 is, for Rosenfeld, "that of a homosexual walking through 'the whole earth' confident that he belongs."[100] Rosenfeld's apparent homophobia needs no comment.

M. Wynn Thomas does not discuss stanza 11, but his implication that things female lack power lies in his diction in his discussion of other parts of the poem. He says of the ax, for example, that it is "curiously invested with attributes that not only emasculate it, but also incline to feminize it by rendering it in passive rather than active terms."[101] Dorothy Gregory, in a 1984 article in the *Walt Whitman Quarterly Review*, says that the "solitary woman" of stanza 11 "bears no resemblance to ordinary humanity."[102] It is true that the woman's rights activists of the 1850s were *not* representative of the status quo, and in this regard, they were not representative of "ordinary human-ity," but they were part of humanity and they did want to inscribe into public consciousness a new image of female "ordinary human-ity." The "solitary woman "of stanza 11 did bear close resemblance to many of Whitman's female friends and to their own desire to change the image of women. Betsy Erkkila reads the poem in just this context, as Whitman's inscription of the democratic dream: as a "city where people are sovereign, slavery is abolished, and women participate equally in the government of the nation—a city, in short, that reverses the political order of his time."[103] Only Erkkila reads this stanza in the way that Price, Rose, Davis, Stanton, and Wright would read it.

In a December 1852 article, Price had this to say about election days at Hopedale:

> Hopedale Election days are calm days. . . . We have no disputing, no ruffianism, no brawling, no low tricks thought of, but all is fair and open and courteous. I should like to have an internal and an exter-nal picture of our Annual Meetings taken with Daguerreotype ac-curacy (wishing to be sure it would be larger) and hold it up before the tyrannical, onesided, unjust, elections of the world, as evidence

of the better *policy* of the righteous recognition of all human rights.[104]

Though Hopedale ultimately failed to realize Abby Price's dreams for the "great city," it did provide her models—which she shared with Whitman—of a world different from mainstream American society, a world in which women had voice.

The two lines from stanza 5 (lines 128 and 129) and stanza 11 are closely related in theme to a passage in Whitman's 1856 *American Primer,* written at about the same time as "Broad-Axe," which also reflects the sentiments of Price and the woman's rights movements: "I expect to see the time in politics, Business, Public Gatherings, Processions, Excitements, when women shall not be divided from men, but shall take their part on the same terms of men. Sometimes I have fancied that only from superior, hardy women can rise the future superiorities of These States."[105]

The effects of the women's rights movement show in the 1856 edition of *Leaves of Grass* in the passages where Whitman sharpens his images of women who appropriate public space as their right; he also increases the number of these images. In the 1855 *Leaves of Grass,* the poet-persona indicates possibilities for women; in the 1856 edition, women *act.* For these reasons, the 1856 edition of *Leaves of Grass* provides a dramatic echo of the public voices of women Whitman either heard at the convention halls or read about as he picked up the New York papers. It also echoes the words he heard Abby Price speak. The 1856 edition, then, reflects not only the public agitation and the heightened visibility of women's issues that grew out of the conventions; it also responds to Whitman's remarkable friendship with Abby Price.

The intertwining of the Price and Louisa Van Velsor circles continued until Louisa moved to Camden in 1872. Louisa repeatedly mentions Helen and Emily Price's visits to her. Abby visited also but not as often. The Prices brought Louisa gifts and sewed for her. She reciprocated their gestures of friendship—fixing them tea and cake or cooking them meals. In one letter, Louisa told Walt that Abby "helped me get dinner and made some nice tea and bread and butter and peaches and cake and mince pie and it did mrs price so much good she seemed to really enjoy it i had to insist upon her staying she said she had quite a family home but i insisted on her taking of her hat and so did helen."[106] Frequently, Louisa mentions Abby's hard work and bad health.

Helen's letters to Louisa speak of the people who went in and out of the Prices's lives, for example Olive Logan (novelist), Eliza Farnham, O. B. Frothingham (minister and writer), and Miss Larned (probably Augusta Larned, writer and editor).[107] Helen frequently mentions the Urners (Abby Spring Arnold Urner, her children, and printer husband) in her letters to Louisa. (In 1857, Sarah Tyndale suggested that Walt get Benjamin Urner, who was a printer, and George B. Arnold to print his book.) Helen had a close friendship with Lizzie Harland (married to Thomas Harland, chief clerk in the Patent Office). Abby was exceedingly close to Paulina Wright and Thomas Davis, and their niece Katy Hinds. Helen speaks of the trips to the theater to see Charlotte Cushman she and her mother used to make. These letters present a broad and interesting circle of friends, active in social, political and artistic movements.[108]

In 1870, Abby Price made her first appearance at a woman's rights convention since the 1853 convention in New York. Possibly work had kept her from active participation; possibly the woman's rights activists, like Samuel May, preferred that she not publicly promote their cause as a result of the 1853 Hopedale publicity—scandal, as it came to be known—which ended with the accused couple claiming their actions were sanctioned on free love grounds and moving to the radical commune Modern Times. The 1870 occasion was the second decade celebration of the national woman's rights movement, held October 20, at Apollo Hall, in Manhattan. Price's good friend Paulina Wright Davis took charge of this meeting. Abby Price read a poem that she had written for the occasion, "Decade Meeting."[109] The October 20 issue of *Revolution* listed the names of the "pioneers and speakers to be present": Paulina Wright Davis, Lucretia Mott, Elizabeth Cady Stanton, Amy Post, Samuel J. May, Martha C. Wright, Matilda Joslyn Gage, Olympia Brown, Sarah Pugh, Josephine S. Griffing, Robert Purvis, Adelle Hazlett, Abby H. Gibbons, Phebe A. Hannaford, Charlotte B. Wilbour, Susan B. Anthony, Lillie Devereaux Blake, Theodore Tilton, Reverend Henry Ward Beecher, Mr. and Mrs. S. E. Sewell, Abby H. Price, Mary Anna Johnson, Adeline Thompson, and Sarah H. Hallock. Whitman was putting the finishing touches on "Democratic Vistas" as Davis was in New York organizing the meeting. Davis had stayed at Price's home before; possibly she stayed there at this time as well. In addition to the contexts already discussed, if we keep in mind Whitman's frequent visits at Price's home and his visit to the Davis home in the fall of 1868 and also realize that at the time of the decade meeting, Whitman had just left New York for Washington, we realize that Whitman's statements about women in "Democratic Vistas" are grounded in the history of the woman's rights movement.

The friendship between Whitman and the Prices was not without strain. In 1872, Walt became angry with Helen Price when she left the Whitman home wearing one of his rings as part of a joke planned by one of Helen's friends. Abby wrote Louisa: "I feel very sorry such a thing has happened. It has hurt Helen very much indeed, but I hope they both will learn a good Lesson from it—Helen not to touch other peoples rings—and Walter will learn to throw his broad mantle of charity over small things as well as larger ones. However it has all passed by—and let us forgive as we are hoping to be forgiven."[110]

And they did forgive. Abby offered space in her home to Louisa after Louisa moved to Camden to live in George and Lou's home. Louisa wrote Walt: "i got a letter from Helen. she and her ma wants me to come to their house and stay a while but i shall never go of course but its very kind of them."[111] Abby invited Walt to come stay at the Price/Arnold home after he suffered his paralytic stroke and Louisa died. He wrote to Abby and Helen in January 1874: "We are in the new house my brother has built—very nice. I find myself *very* [underscored twice] *lonesome* here, for all social & emotional consolation—(Man cannot live on *bread alone*—can he?)—I want to come & see you—*must* do so before long—want to pay a moderate board, (same as I do here,) if convenient for you to have me—*Shall not come on any other condition*—Well, Abby, I have just *skurried* rapidly over the sheet, & will send it to you just as it is, with love."[112] He wrote again in March: "I should prefer the upper room. . . . I shall come on— cannot now [pla]n the time, but will write before—& take up my quarters a while with you, as it seems to be agreeable, & the moderate sum you mention I should pay thankfully—."[113] In the last extant letter between Abby and Walt, written in October 1876, Walt wrote: "got your letter—write again—believe me, Helen and Abby dear, I appreciate the letters, & most of all your persistent & faithful friendship."[114]

3

Paulina Wright Davis

The following announcement appeared in the June 1849 issue of the *Water-Cure Journal:*

> BROOKLYN DAILY FREEMAN. Walter Whitman, Editor. Price six cents a week. This is a new, spirited, interesting reformatory daily newspaper, which has recently been laid before the public. Although small in stature, it is clothed with material of the finest fabric, well-manufactured, and made up after the most modern fashion in every particular. It belongs to the progressive school, and will not be found away back, behind the lighthouse, on any occasion, on any subject. May its success and patronage be equal to its merits![1]

Since only one copy of the *Freeman* has survived, that of 9 September 1848, we do not know the extent of Whitman's "reformatory" interests, but we do know the politics of the *Water-Cure Journal,* which provided a mouthpiece for many of the reforms so pervasive in the 1840s and early 1850s. It worked against numerous conventions of middle-class Victorian culture: women wrote for it as well as men; it called for dress reform for women and men as early as the 1840s on the grounds of health, safety, and mobility; it argued for water cure, a less invasive form of medical treatment than the prevailing modes of leeching and bleeding; it spoke for sexual equality. It also published illustrations of the body. One illustration, used to emphasize the role that exercise and dress played in creating and maintaining a developed and well-aligned body, was entitled "The Human Form Divine" and showed nude male and female figures. The male has a fig leaf over his genitalia; the female form, with breasts, has a simple line drawing for her genitalia. The *Journal,* which functioned as a self-help medical resource, is striking in its use of illustrations. There are diagrams of the human skeleton in which each bone of the body is named, and there are illustrations of the various organs of the body. There are discussions of the need for well-ventilated rooms and detailed illustrations that attempt to teach readers how to swim. There is also a series of illustrations that teach basic first aid and many that teach water cure. The journal is one of many that Whitman read, and as I have indicated, in its turn it promoted Whitman's paper, which had its own reformist intent, the short-lived *Brooklyn Daily Freeman.*

Paulina Wright's name began appearing in the *Water-Cure Journal* soon after Francis Wright, her first husband, died in 1845. At this time, she chose to make her living by giving lectures on female anatomy and health. These lectures were announced regularly in the *Water-Cure Journal* in the 1840s. In 1853, four years after Lorenzo Fowler read Whitman's skull, the *American Phrenological Journal,* also published by the Fowler and Wells firm, printed a biographical/phrenological sketch of Paulina Kellogg Wright Davis, part of a series of such sketches run that year. The biographical part of the sketch comprised the bulk of the article. Not surprisingly, the biographical sketch confirms the skull analysis, noting that Davis differed "from most females in possessing more energy and executive power, self-possession, independence, perseverance, will and varied business capacity, with less veneration, respect, and regard for public opinion, and less fear of consequences."[2] Davis, forty years old when the sketch was written, had been born in 1813 in Bloomfield, New York, and was, as Mary Ryan says in *Cradle of the Middle Class,* a radical feminist.[3]

Whitman and Davis had the opportunity to read about each other, to peruse each other's words, to hear about each other through mutual acquaintances (such as Lydia Fowler) and to meet each other long before 1856, when Abby Price moved to Brooklyn and Whitman became part of her circle of reform-minded friends, with Paulina Wright Davis one of that circle's most constant members. Whitman's friendship with Paulina Wright Davis, however, was never as intense as was his friendship with Abby Price, though he saw

Davis during her frequent and regular visits to Price's home and also stayed in her home in Providence, Rhode Island, for a week in October 1868.

The friendship between Price and Davis began in the 1840s when their reformist interests brought them together. In 1849 Davis (then Paulina Wright) lectured in Hopedale on health for women. Shortly thereafter she married Thomas Davis, and in September 1850, she organized and presided over the first National Woman's Rights Convention and gave the keynote address. Price also spoke at this convention. The friendship grew as the two women continued to work together. They both spoke at the next two woman's rights conventions. When Price's participation in the woman's rights movement ended late in 1853, Davis kept up her activities, and she and Price also maintained their friendship until Davis died in 1876.

For thirty years (from the middle 1840s to her death in 1876), Davis wrote and gave speeches, many of which, in turn, were reproduced in the major New York newspapers. For three years, she wrote for and edited a major woman's rights journal, the *Una*, 1853–1855. Because of the reciprocity between the journals, more than likely the Fowler and Wells firm carried the *Una* in their store. Davis, a public figure, was one of the reformers whom Whitman said he wanted around him. She speaks for an important period in women's history, and her varied interests provide rich contextualization for the complexities of the period from 1840 to 1876, the year she died. Though Whitman was fortunate to hear her insights and her strongly held beliefs in person, the access he had to them by reading newspapers and journals also gave him access to her mind.

There is a notebook entry dated about 1856, the time Price settled in Brooklyn and thus the most probable time that Davis and Whitman became friends. In it Whitman made notes about a poem he planned to write:

> A poem in which is minutely described the whole particulars and ensemble of a *first-rate healthy Human Body*—it looked into and through, as if it were transparent and of pure glass—and now reported in a poem—
>> Read the latest and best anatomical works
>> talk with physicians
>> study the anatomical plates
>> also casts of figures in the collections of design[4]

Paulina Wright Davis (1813–1876). Engraving by J. C. Buttre (Bullre?) of New York from a photograph by Manchester Brothers. Reproduced courtesy of The Schlesinger Library, Radcliffe College.

This notebook entry suggests an early working out of Whitman's ideas for "I Sing the Body Electric." Though I do not claim that Paulina Wright Davis had anything to do with Whitman's adding section 9 to "Body Electric," it is interesting that he added the section in 1856 to the second edition of *Leaves of Grass,* about the time that Whitman became acquainted with the Price circle.

Whitman could follow his own admonitions—"read," "talk," "study"—with publications like the *Water-Cure Journal,* with its numerous diagrams of the human skeleton and organs; he could also converse with physicians such as Lydia Fowler; and he could attend lectures such as those given by Paulina Wright Davis. He could examine collections of casts at places like the Fowler and Wells firm and review self-help medical books and articles. In fact, Whitman's notebook entry listing the sources for his anatomical study sounds much like a description of Paulina Wright's lecture procedure, described by newspaper editor William Elder in an 1846 issue of the *Water-Cure Journal:* "Provided with the best substitutes for actual dissection which art has been able to supply . . . [and] with the aid of that wonderful machine, the *modelle du femme,* capital life-sized plates, and such dry preparations as our anatomical museums afford, I regard her, for all purposes except practical surgery, as a complete anatomist."[5] In a positive sense, Elder's use of the word "machine" fits well with Wright's focus on the female body, for Wright took part in a substantial health movement in antebellum America, a movement whose members believed in noninvasive medicine, in caring for the body in ways opposed to such invasive "cures" as bloodletting, which was a primary practice of the allopaths. The noninvasive practitioners believed that healthy practices would keep the body in good working order as maintenance would a machine. Susan Cayleff, in *Wash and Be Healed: The Water-Cure Movement and Women's Health,* distinguishes between allopaths and reform-oriented sects: "Allopaths emphasized remedial drug intervention, whereas reform-oriented sects, operating out of a zealously guarded let-nature-take-its-course position, stressed (to varying degrees) preventive, patient-controlled, hygienic living principles, a different view of drugging, and, often, less intrusive therapeutics."[6] Paulina Wright's interest lay in seeing to it that the (female) body had the "maintenance" it deserved. She looked at the body as an entity, with each part affecting the next, none to be denied its purpose and significance. An announcement in a September 1848 issue of the *Water-Cure Journal* once more spoke of Davis's procedures: "Mrs. Paulina S. Wright is giving . . . a course of lectures on the subject of anatomy and physiology; illustrated by a fine French apparatus, an artificial female figure, anatomical plates, and perfect models."[7]

In 1851 the *Water-Cure Journal* ran an article by Paulina Wright Davis, "The Providence Physiological Society," describing the educational system used by the women who made up this society, a group started by Davis in 1850 to educate women about their bodies, its aim comparable to that of sex education classes today. The difference is that these women were adults, many of whom were already married, with children. Given Whitman's own method of self-education and his interest in health, possibly he read the article. The description of the Physiological Society reads: "The library numbers nearly or quite one hundred well-selected volumes. . . . We have also had the use of a fine French model, a set of Endicott's life-size engravings, with models of the eye, bronchial tubes, skeleton, &c. Dr. Preston, one of our first physicians . . . also presented several fine engravings of the vocal organs, and some other articles useful to students. Several other physicians have presented books to our library."[8] Davis furnished many of the books, models, and engravings used by the society, taken from her own private library.[9] She also wanted to know the human body, to "look into and through" it, "as if it were transparent and of pure glass." Her mode of communicating her commitment to physiology was that of the lecture and, on a local level, the Providence Physiological Society, which, thanks to her, did what Whitman admonished himself to do: the members read and studied the latest and best anatomical works, they brought physicians in to lecture to them, they studied plates, casts, and the modelle du femme. Davis wanted that "wonderful machine," the human body, to work and work well, but she concerned herself specifically with the female body.

The body, then, links Whitman, Davis, and their culture. Though Abby Price also spoke of the body, most specifically when she agitated for dress reform, the prevailing connection between her, Whitman, and her times is her understanding of the role that space plays in a person's sensibility. Price's arguments often center, finally, on the absurdity and danger of the separate spheres ideology. Thus poems such as "Song of the Broad-Axe," with its passages about women assuming their place in public space, and "Song of the Open Road," with its invitation for women as well as men to join the persona in his discoveries, come to mind when reading Price's speeches. She wanted a larger family than the nuclear family; she wanted home to be more than the isolated one-family home. (Whereas the primary connection between Whitman and Davis is that of the body, the primary connection between Ernestine L. Rose and Whitman is the theory of democracy.) Price's use of spatial tropes makes her arguments for breaking down the separate spheres ideology effective. Davis also adroitly uses tropes, calling on pre-Darwinian evolutionary theory to support her points.

Whitman's celebration of the aesthetics of the body and his celebration of sex, however, contrast with Davis's focus on the body's

social implications, that is, the cost of ignorance. The lack of knowledge regarding birth control and first aid, indeed the lack of knowledge about how to stay healthy in general, had life-and-death consequences for women.[10] Whitman and Davis come together, however,
in their perception of the body as a democracy: they both maintained that the body itself has rights. It is, after all, inextricable from
the soul. (Speaking of "I Sing the Body Electric," Betsy Erkkila says,
"The divine and sexually charged body that Whitman celebrates becomes the platform from which he launches an attack on race and
class attitudes in America.")[11] Through Whitman's ability to concretize the body, he embodies the abstraction of freedom.

Though sheer aesthetics—love of *Leaves of Grass* as sound and
rhythm—may have prompted Paulina Davis in June 1875 to mail a
copy to Mary Gove Nichols, another radical reformer who, like Davis,
spoke publicly on women's issue prior to the 1848 Seneca Falls Convention, I think not.[12] Rather, these women read *Leaves of Grass* as a
text supporting their own texts. Aware that the very term "woman"
had to be redefined and new images of women instilled into public consciousness, activists such as Davis saw at work what Whitman
called his image making, and they recognized its potential, its power.
By juxtaposing *Leaves of Grass* and woman's rights texts, represented
in this chapter by Paulina Wright Davis, we can see the dialogue
between *Leaves of Grass* and the woman's movement during the years
when the first three editions were written and published. Such a juxtaposition creates, in our minds, a new text and reshapes our present-day critical readings of *Leaves of Grass*. Such a juxtaposition
makes it difficult to fault Whitman for ideological stances because
many of these stances, problematic to some feminists today, were
held by some of the most radical woman's rights activists of his time.

Paulina Kellogg's parents, Ebenezer and Polly Saxton Kellogg,
died before Paulina reached seven. Raised by an aunt in a strict Pres-
byterian church, she married Francis Wright in 1833. Wright, a successful Utica businessman, shared her reformist consciousness.
Their convictions prompted them to leave the Baptist church they
were attending in Utica because of its proslavery stance. In addition
to working in the abolitionist cause, Paulina Kellogg Wright was active in the Female Anti-Slavery Society, the Female Moral Reform
Society, and the Martha Washington Temperance Union while she
lived in Utica.[13] In 1836, she and Ernestine L. Rose canvassed the

state eliciting signatures for a bill supporting married women's property rights.

Francis Wright died in January 1845. Though his death filled Paulina Wright with "desolation,"[14] she did not let it constrict her life. She decided against living off the estate Francis Wright willed to her, though she did use it to care for her adopted parents. Rather she chose to support herself by giving lectures, telling a friend, "I dared not have other resources than my lectures would give me for I am indolent by nature and might fall back if there was a chance."[15] There is no evidence of indolence in her life. She was an ambitious and assertive woman who saw the connection between economics and independence and between language and activism.

The 1 June 1846 issue of the *Water-Cure Journal* carried a letter from William Elder recommending her lectures. Elder, the editor of the *Philadelphia Republic*, outlined her speaking activities: "Mrs. P. S. Wright, who has been lecturing to female classes on anatomy and physiology during the past winter, in Harrisburg, Trenton, Baltimore, and other places in East Pennsylvania, Maryland, and New Jersey, is now in New England, with the intention, I believe, of lecturing during the summer."[16] Elder praises Wright's skill as a teacher and unique position as a female health specialist: "She is now one of the very few women in the United States who are technically acquainted with anatomy, physiology, and the general principles of medicine." The editors of the *Water-Cure Journal* seconded Elder's recommendation: "From personal acquaintance with this lady, we are convinced that the friend who writes us above, has in no wise overrated her qualifications as a teacher upon the important subject of human health. We design . . . to give a general view of the plan of these lectures."[17] Announcements of her lectures appeared regularly in the *Journal*.

In April 1849, Paulina Wright married Thomas Davis, an antislavery Democrat and successful manufacturer of jewelry who served in the Rhode Island Senate from 1845 to 1853 and in the U.S. House of Representatives from 1853 to 1855 and continued to be active in state politics thereafter. He died in 1895. Biographers of Elizabeth Buffum Chace, a leader in the antislavery and woman suffrage movements, describe Paulina Wright Davis's status in Providence, where she lived after marrying Thomas Davis: "Mrs. Davis dwelt like a sort of foreign princess in Providence. She was too much of a reformer for adoption into the 'society' set of the city, too alien in purpose to suit its great cotton manufacturing families, and too heretical for its college folk,—but nevertheless she was a radiant figure in its circle of literary, artistic and reformatory people."[18]

Paulina Davis's accomplishments ranged widely. She initiated the national woman's rights conventions; she wrote and published a history of the first twenty years of the movement; she organized the 1870 conference called to celebrate twenty years of woman's rights activity; she wrote numerous articles, letters, and speeches agitating for woman's rights; she founded and maintained the *Una* for three years of publication; she studied painting in Europe; she lectured on women's anatomy and by extension on birth control and rape prevention; and she founded local organizations to work for antislavery reform, women's rights, and women's health reform. One such local organization was the Providence Physiological Society.

The minutes for this society's meetings contain repeated references to the contributions Paulina Davis made to its success. To put into practice the object of the society—sex education—she lent twenty-two of her own volumes on health and related subjects for the members to read and circulate among themselves. Minutes from a 19 September 1851 meeting read: "Mrs. Davis has from the organization of the society given it essential aid by donation of valuable books, lectures, influences, together with her very agreeable presence. It is often spoken of by the members in their friendly intercourse and perhaps needs not the corroboration of my testimony."[19] She spoke before the society regularly and recommended that it order books from Fowler and Wells and thereby form its own library. She also recommended that the society subscribe to the *Water-Cure Journal* and the *American Phrenological Journal,* which could then announce the society's business in their pages. The minutes of the society provide us with information about nineteenth-century white middle-class women's culture and add to our understanding of women's access to medical, anatomical, and scientific knowledge. Readers of Whitman will be quick to note the relationships between Davis's interests and Whitman's.

No public involvement meant as much to Davis, however, as the *Una.* She spoke of it as her child, just as Whitman spoke of *Leaves of Grass.* For three years it dominated her life, from the first issue in February 1853 to the last in October 1855. The story of Davis's struggle to keep the *Una* going reveals her priorities: she wanted to promote writing that she felt worked directly on her readers to bring about change, and as to genre, she preferred autobiographical writing over fiction. With Paulina Wright Davis listed as president, the following announcement for the second National Woman's Rights Convention articulates the stance of the *Una* as well as declares the charge for the second National Woman's Rights Convention: "The work contemplated is no child's play. It wars directly with the thought, so deeply rooted and so hoary, that woman is only an appendage, and not an integral part in the fabric of human society. It is in full conflict with the world's teachers, its preachers, its lawyers, its poets, and its painters. It stands opposed to those soul blighting usages of society which have consigned women to an aimless and objectless existence; and have baptized a life so unworthy as peculiarly fitting and graceful for women."[20]

The position of editor appealed to Davis, but the enormity of the job eventually wore her down, that and the lack of financial and institutional support from the national woman's rights movement. Though Davis had set into motion the National Woman's Rights Conventions by organizing the first one, privately she said that she tired of conventions, and by 1852, she began to criticize their effectiveness. She considered her real contribution to the cause to be the *Una.* After financing, editing, and seeing to its publication for two years, she asked for help from the Convention: "I proposed to the Convention to take the Una with my subscription list, the paper I have on hand, the heading &c and that I would give all the labor I should have health to perform, and one hundred dollars per year, this they declined."[21] She felt that "the Convention women do not want the paper to live, a few of the talkers are jealous of everything practical." A year later, she said much the same thing: "I wish the women in our cause could be made to see what an efficient agency this might be if established—It is sometimes a hard struggle for me to stand where I do, almost unrecognized by the party and proscribed in the circle where I am expected to move. I say unrecognized because so few have given any sympathy to this practical work."[22]

After two years of publication, Davis wrote in the *Una* that she would have to stop publication. The next month, however, she wrote that with the help of Caroline Healy Dall as coeditor and the move to the Boston publisher S. C. Hewitt, the *Una* would continue. The letters in the Dall Papers from Davis to Dall document what came to be a bitter demise for the *Una.* According to these letters, Davis

viewed Dall as using the *Una* as an outlet for her own writing and
translation; Dall wanted it to be a "literary" journal. Davis, however,
had founded it as a reform journal. She wanted everyday women's
voices in it: "We must awaken woman to her own necessities, give
her a chance to speak for herself. One letter in print from some worn
and weary spirit does more to develope and help woman out of her
weakness than ever so many private complaints."[23] She published letters from women recounting their experiences; she felt the con-
sciousness-raising provided by these letters to be of infinitely more
value in making women think than "tales continued from month to
month."[24]

In June 1855, she told Dall that the paper must not lose sight of
its first aim, which was reform: "No one now disputes woman's literary ability, we are not at work to establish that point."[25] Dall used
Bronson Alcott to support her own views, Davis said:

> Mr. Alcott is in no way authority for me either in literature art or
> reform. A single opinion from his honest earnest practical wife
> would be worth to me more than all his pseudo visions and fancies.
> He was here a week not long since and harped perpetually on the
> same string. We each judge from our own standpoint of observation.
> You are connected with the Literati of Boston, I with no set, sect, or
> clique, having friends among all classes. . . . I would give more for
> one genuine utterance [from readers] than for any quantity of Mr
> Alcotts poetry—the truth has power though if told in a homely way.
> I do not wish to be understood as deprecating literary merit and a
> high tone, nor do I underestimate your articles. Your biography
> sketches are interesting but a paper of them would not answer long.[26]

Davis wanted the *Una* to educate. She wanted women to feel a
sense of self-pride, to help them establish a point of view that would
enable them to see outside the dominating partriarchal ideology
that many women themselves defended. She told Dall that "Women
must be educated up to their wants, and we must remember that it
is not crowding in but the drawing out that performs this work so
doubly needful now."[27] In another letter, she reiterated this point: "I
am not disposed to shut [*Una* subscribers] out if they wish to speak.
Education is not crowding in but the drawing out of the powers."[28]
She wanted the *Una* to provide an opportunity for dialogue among
women that would cut across class lines: "I write what is called out

by letters and what I judge is the want of the general class of readers."[29] The *Una*, Davis said, had "been a voice to many who could
not have uttered their thoughts through any other channel."[30] She
printed a letter sent to her by a subscriber that recounted Henry
Ward Beecher's censure of the female voice, thus channeling this
letter to her readers. Beecher said in a lecture that "he had heard
some of the best of female speakers, and he felt that women could
talk in the domestic circle, but that they were not fitted for public speakers . . . had he a mother, wife, or daughter, that were gifted
to speak, he would not hinder, but he prayed that mother, wife, or
daughter, of his, might never be thus gifted."[31]

The controversy between Dall and Davis became increasingly
heated. Davis felt that the new publisher and Dall, as coeditor of the
Una, ignored her submissions and her editorial philosophy. When
Whitman's 1855 *Leaves of Grass* went on sale in July, Davis's journal
the *Una* had only three remaining months of life. Davis discovered
that Dall's translation of George Sand's *Spiridion* would fill the November 1855 issue, and she withdrew her financial support. The en-
thusiasm she voiced in January 1853—"I am very happy in my work,
it is all new to me, I never corrected a proof till two days ago, it is
much less tedious than I anticipated"[32]—had turned into bitterness:
"I have lost faith in womanhood to that extent that I will never un-
dertake any enterprise that depends in the least upon her to sustain.
I must work in the future in some other way."[33] There was no November 1855 issue. The *Una* ceased publication. Davis never published or edited another journal, but she did continue to work for
woman's rights.

Several years after Whitman published the 1856 *Leaves of Grass,*
Paulina Davis gave a speech in Providence entitled "On the Renting
of a Hall for Woman's Rights Meetings" and quoted from Whitman's
poem "Unfolded Out of the Folds." The unpublished manuscript of
her speech is in the Vassar Library and is undated. In this speech,
Davis speaks of the day when women in Providence will own, not
rent, their building. She lists some of the rooms the building will
have: a library, a laboratory, a game room, and a gymnasium "with
all of the means for the physical culture of womanhood, thus securing to the State a strong sweet race of mothers, for remember that
from the 'noblest mothers are unfolded the noblest men,' and to
make great women they must be educated . . . for the State and by
the state." The "noblest mothers" passage paraphrases a line from

Whitman's 1856 "Poem of Women," which he later titled "Unfolded Out of the Folds." Whitman's line actually reads: "Unfolded only out of the superbest woman of the earth is to come the superbest man of the earth."[34]

Davis uses in this speech the Republican mother argument. Linda K. Kerber, in her article "The Republican Mother," shows how revolutionary women used the socially approved role of women as nurturers and early educators of their children (sons, in this case) to acquire a political voice. According to Kerber, "those who opposed women in politics had to meet the proposal that women could—and should—play a political role through the raising of a patriotic child. The Republican Mother was to encourage in her sons civic interest and participation. She was to educate her children and guide them in the paths of morality and virtue. But she was not to tell her male relatives for whom to vote. She was a citizen but not really a constituent."[35] Davis uses the expediency argument in her speech, but in Whitman's poem the word "mother" is never mentioned. The point of Davis's speech is the point she repeatedly makes: that women's inferiority—and Davis does mean inferiority—comes from the restrictions imposed upon them by male-controlled society. It is not that Davis avoids indicting patriarchy for the hypocrisy of society; she does indict it. She blames patriarchy for the laws that denied women opportunities and thus reduced their potential for development, and she blames mainstream society for its perpetuation of the "true woman" ideal, whose effects polarized domestic space and the workplace and intensified economic inequality. But both Davis and Whitman use the mainstream argument that strong women (mothers) create strong and virtuous citizens. Whitman, however, factors in a new dimension in "Unfolded." In his use of vulval imagery, he speaks, indirectly, against the culturally sanctioned mainstream view of the sexless and ineffective woman ("aimless," to use Davis's term).

It comes as no surprise that Davis chose to quote from this poem. It supports her point of view; it textually concretizes women's bodies; it counters culturally sanctioned, debilitating views of women; indirectly, through the Republican mother argument, it argues for women's self-development and consequently for a society that enables such development; it valorizes women. On the other hand, because Whitman so frequently used "man and woman, female and male," the use of only "man" in this poem to name the unfolded being reifies sexist hierarchy. Or so it seems to readers now. Davis had no problem here. More so than Price and Ernestine L. Rose, up until the late 1860s, Davis kept practical considerations in her mind and advocated a pragmatism of sorts in her speeches. She said in her keynote address before the 1850 convention: "A creed of abstract truths, or a catechism of general principles, and a completely digested list of grievances, combined, are not enough to adjust a practical reform to its proper work, else Prophets and Apostles and earnest world-menders in general would have been more successful, and left us less to wish and to do." Her sense of audience combined with her awareness that the reforms she sought were radical reforms aligns her with Whitman, who knew his audience well enough to realize that anything but his "indirect rather than direct" aesthetics would relegate his poetry to the failed work of prophets and apostles referred to by Davis. In her 1850 speech, Davis spoke of reform work in practical terms; she spoke like a rhetorician: "It is one thing to issue a declaration of rights or a declaration of wrongs to the world, but quite another thing wisely and happily to commend the subject to the world's acceptance, and so to secure the desired reformation. Every element of success is, in its own place and degree, equally important; but the very starting point is the adjustment of the reformer to his work, and next after that is the adjustment of his work to those conditions of the times which he seeks to influence." When *Leaves of Grass* appeared five years later, she may well have seen Whitman's image-making work, to use his term, as an "adjustment" to the times, a way to say what the society refused to hear spoken when it was said overtly. Though she called for rhetorical sensitivity, she was well aware of the radical nature of her goals: "The reformation which we propose, in its utmost scope, is radical and universal. It is not the mere perfecting of a progress already in motion, a detail of some established plan, but it is an epochal movement—the emancipation of a class . . . a conforming re-organization of all social, political, and industrial interests and institutions. . . . Its intended changes are to be wrought in the intimate texture of all societary organizations."[36]

Davis ended her speech as she had begun it, calling for prudence, a word and concept highly valued by Whitman: "We can help ourselves to much of the prudence and some of the knowledge we shall need, by treating the prejudices of the public as considerately as if they were principles, and the customs of society as if they once had some temporary necessity, and so meet them with the greater force for the claim to respect which we concede to them."[37] Whitman's *Leaves of Grass* shared with Paulina Wright Davis's speeches a honed rhetorical awareness and a call to reorganize society radically, yet Whitman worked with language in a way foreign to Davis, though she saw its power.

In the 1856 edition of *Leaves,* "Poem of Women" directly follows "Poem of Walt Whitman, An American," later titled "Song of Myself."[38] The prominence of the 1856 placement of "Poem of Women," later titled "Unfolded Out of the Folds," is one more example bearing out my contention that the 1856 *Leaves of Grass* is a more activist text than its predecessor in the area of woman's rights and that Whitman's enhanced awareness of woman's rights came from his association with women such as Price, Davis, and Ernestine L. Rose.[39] In the same way that "Song of Myself" illustrates the concepts voiced by Whitman in the 1855 Preface, "Poem of Women" illustrates one of the main points that Whitman made in the 1856 Preface, which was more particularized in terms of its discussion of sexuality than its predecessor.

The 1856 letter/preface that Whitman wrote to Emerson, which Whitman put in the appendix of the 1856 *Leaves of Grass,* actually has little to do with Emerson and everything to do with Whitman's theories of American literature. In it, Whitman boldly states the role of sexuality in literature. He links democracy with freedom from sexual repression. He calls upon American writers to "recognize with joy the sturdy living forms of men and women of These States, the divinity of sex, the perfect eligibility of the female with the male." The "lack of an avowed, empowered, unabashed development of sex," he says, accounts for "the remarkable non-personality" of literature. He calls the refusal to address sexuality explicitly in literature a "filthy law" that, unless repealed, would block great reforms: "Of women just as much as men, it is the interest that there should not be infidelism about sex, but perfect faith. Women in These States approach the day of that organic equality with men, without which, I see, men cannot have organic equality among themselves." Whitman calls for the use of specific words to speak of sexuality: "To me, henceforth, that theory of any thing, no matter what, stagnates in its vitals, cowardly and rotten, while it cannot publicly accept, and publicly name, with specific words, the things on which all existence . . . all of woman and of man . . . all friendship . . . all immortality depend."[40] Though "Unfolded" does not use "specific words," vulval imagery dominates the poem:

Unfolded out of the folds of the woman man comes unfolded, and is always
to come unfolded,

Unfolded only out of the superbest woman of the earth is to come the
superbest man of the earth,

Unfolded out of the friendliest woman is to come the friendliest man,

Unfolded only out of the perfect body of a woman can a man be form'd of
perfect body,

Unfolded only out of the inimitable poems of woman can come the poems
of man, (only thence have my poems come;)

Unfolded out of the strong and arrogant woman I love, only thence can
appear the strong and arrogant man I love,

Unfolded by brawny embraces from the well-muscled woman I love, only
thence come the brawny embraces of the man,

Unfolded out of the folds of the woman's brain come all the folds of the
man's brain, duly obedient,

Unfolded out of the justice of the woman all justice is unfolded,

Unfolded out of the sympathy of the woman is all sympathy;

A man is a great thing upon the earth and through eternity, but every jot of
the greatness of man is unfolded out of woman;

First the man is shaped in the woman, he can then be shaped in himself.[41]

This inscription of female sexual imagery into poetry is one of the radical aspects of "Unfolded." It is important to keep the vulval imagery in mind, since Whitman's imagination is so often regarded as "spermatic."[42] If insemination is the poet-persona's vital act in *Leaves of Grass,* birthing is the female correlative. Of the two, Whitman stood in awe of the latter perhaps even more than of the former.

By inscribing the female body into text and stressing its generative power, the poem works against the notion of female passivity. The poem adroitly mixes the polarized characteristics accepted unquestionably as "natural" by mainstream antebellum Victorians. The woman giving birth enables the child—the male child—to possess the qualities of friendliness and sympathy, qualities denoted in the culture as feminine. In turn, the woman also possesses qualities the culture relegated to the male—the perfection of the body itself, strength, arrogance, intellectuality, and justice.[43]

In the poem, personality traits (friendliness, arrogance, sympathy), biological traits (strength, well-muscled brawniness), intelligence, and justice pass from the mother to the child. Underlying the hereditary transferal of personal character traits laid out in the poem is a Lamarckian view of evolution holding that acquired characteristics could be passed on to one's offspring. Whitman came to his views of science and evolutionary theory through a popularized understanding of Robert Chambers, Lamarck, and theorists who thought along the same lines.[44] Paulina Davis's study was more systematic. Her activities in the Providence Physiological Society and the articles announcing her lectures attest to her extensive reading in the field. Evolutionary thinking certainly contributed to the kinds of authority woman's rights activists used to advance their cause; in that respect, the role that the environment played in pre-Darwinian evolutionary theory offered them a perfect argument as they fought for improved conditions for women. They were able to make the pre-Darwinian analogy that just as the environment shaped organisms, so did society shape individuals (women).

Pre-Darwinian evolutionary ideas furnished concepts and tropes central to Whitman and activists like Davis. Davis was especially adept at using tropes from the developmental hypotheses, or pre-Darwinian evolutionary theory, to lend scientific "truth" to her arguments. Since her articles and speeches were readily available beginning with her 1850 keynote address, Whitman had ample opportunity to hear her, and others, employing developmental hypothesis language to support her argument for woman's rights. "Unfolded" sounds as if it comes out of those many articles Davis wrote. It is useful to note, as well, that by introducing the role the environment played in creating change, essentialist views, whatever their origins, were tempered. Woman's rights activists chose a dramatic and concrete example to support their argument that environment controlled, or at least greatly influenced, development. That example was the early nineteenth-century foundling Caspar Hauser. They argued by analogy that just as Caspar Hauser was kept confined and thus emerged at the age of fifteen or sixteen illiterate and foolishly naive, so too were women, through their restricted lives, dependent and vulnerable (illiterate and foolishly naive).[45] Women as individuals would not change, develop, and grow until societal institutions changed. The poem "Unfolded" illustrates the kind of woman such changes would create.

The adverb "only" is used in the poem six times. It is *only* out of the superbest woman that the superbest man can come; it is *only* out of the woman with a perfect body that a man with a perfect body can come. It is only out of her poems (her language, her body) that the poet-persona's poems can come (his language, his body); it is only from the strong and arrogant woman that the likewise strong and arrogant man comes. It is from the folds of her brain that the man's brain unfolds in a "duly obedient" fashion. The poem stresses causality: *first* the woman possesses (or acquires) characteristics the poet-persona desires for the male; then the male is shaped inside the woman, and these characteristics are transmitted; finally, he can be shaped in himself. The desire for the healthy child/adult/citizen looked to individual perfectionism for its realization rather than to technology. With no recourse to the technology we know today, a premature birth, for example, meant death. The sounder the mother's body, the better chance she had for survival and the better chance for a successful birth. In turn, she passed on to her offspring her strength, acquired as well as genetic.

Davis and like-minded activists used another concept from pre-Darwinian theory as an analogy for their reformist arguments: the use/disuse theory. They employed this to argue against the privatization or domestication of women's sphere. The use/disuse theory—holding that organs grew or atrophied through use or disuse, thus accounting for change—permitted activists to argue that women had to be freed from existing laws, which confined them to the home, so that they could use and develop what they innately possessed—minds that handled scientific and artistic concepts, for example, and bodies that were not "naturally" passive. These scientific views offered women like Davis a framework to combat the culturally sanctioned view, that women's bodies limited women's possibilities, a framework that had authoritative status.

Davis describes the ideal interworkings between individuals and society as a process of unfolding. As she stated in her letters to Caroline Dall, education was not a matter of filling a student's mind with data; rather, it was a matter of enabling a student's interests and abilities to grow and develop. If allowed by society to use what she had, a woman would develop in ways that would benefit society at large. If not, she would be dependent, a drag on the nation and a less than positive force in her family.[46]

Six years before the unfolding poem, as early as her 1850 speech to the first National Woman's Rights Convention, Davis used the trope of unfolding. In this speech, she used it to call for equal opportunity, stressing the "unnatural" conditions that restricted women's development: "I ask only freedom for the natural *unfolding* of [woman's] powers, the conditions most favorable for her possibilities of growth, and the full play of all those incentives which have made man her master, and then . . . I ask that she shall fill the place that she can attain to, without settling any unmeaning questions of sex and sphere, which people gossip about for want of principles of truth, or the faculty to reason upon them" (emphasis added).[47] Using slightly different phraseology, but continuing to use the unfolding trope, she made the same point the following year, at the 1851 National Woman's Rights Convention: "We do not claim for woman parallelism . . . as against men, but we merely claim the freedom of her proper life, whatever that may prove to be, upon fair trial; we claim the privilege and the opportunity for *unfolding* all her powers . . . and the full play of all those hopes, incentives, and prospects, whose monopoly has developed man into her master, and enslaved and degraded her, in the proportion that they have been withheld from her" (emphasis added).[48] She did not attend the 1852 state convention at Westchester, Pennsylvania, but she wrote a letter. In this public letter she continues to develop the same theme—the need for a "natural" or fair environment to enable changes to unfold. In answer to the taunt "If women wanted more rights, then why didn't they take them?" she enumerates the societal institutions that denied women access, and thus credentials, such as medical schools: "Does a woman desire a *thorough* medical education, where is the institution fully and properly endowed to receive her?" There can be no harmony, she says, if there is class legislation (gender discrimination). Using spatial metaphors, she speaks of the cramped and narrow sphere to which women are arbitrarily assigned and calls for equal development: "This unrecognized *half* desires these factitious restraints removed, and to be placed side by side with the other, simply that there may be full, free, and equal development in the future. The moral life which urges this claim is the God within us."[49] Davis, then, uses the trope of unfolding to argue for societal change. Without a nation of strong women, there will be no strong nation. Whitman's poem argues for both.

The connections between Paulina Wright Davis's writings and Whitman's provide a new context for reading *Leaves of Grass*. At the same time, by familiarizing ourselves with Davis's work we increase our understanding of women's history and historicize our feminist critical readings. In an 1853 article, "Intellect of the Sexes," Davis once more uses the figure of unfolding: "Womanhood is to be unfolded and realized in the future. . . . the past is neither its measure nor its prophecy."[50] In an 1854 editorial, "Inequality of Women in Marriage," she uses the theory underlying pre-Darwinian evolutionary theory to the fullest extent:

> Men and women are in fact and effect, just what their accidental *developments* make of them. Deny the *unfolding*, and growth and excellence, that the faculties receive from all the functions of civil life-restrict the social liberties within the narrow compass assigned by custom to womanhood,—train her in youth to the restraints of semi-annihilation, and in marriage bar her out from all the larger and higher interests and offices, the trusts, sympathies, and experiences of the common life of the world around her, and what chance for the reciprocities of equality are left to him who looks to such a mutilated existence for the reflex of his own?[51]

Juxtapose this 1854 passage with a notebook entry written by Whitman. Edward Grier gives the following entry a probable date of the late 1850s. The notebook entry can be interpreted as a vindication for male homosexual love, free from heterosexual institutionalization. But it must also be read in light of its declared audience: women. If read within the context of female reformers' censure of (heterosexual) marriage, it sounds much like Davis's 1854 speech.

Lect. (To Women.

Why should there be modesties, and prohibitions that keep women from strong actual life—from going about there with men

I desire to say to you, and let you ponder well upon it that the fact that under present arrangements, the love and comradeship of a woman, of his wife, however welcome, however complete, does not and cannot satisfy the grandest requirements of a manly soul for love and comradeship.—The man he loves, he often loves with more passionate attachment than he ever bestows on any woman, even his wife.—Is it that the growth of love needs the free air—the seasons, perhaps more wildness, more rudeness? Why is the love of women so invalid? so transient?[52]

Davis's "mutilated existence" becomes Whitman's "invalid." Note also Davis's use of the word "unfolding." Whitman is saying, in the 1850s, exactly what Price, Davis, Rose, Stanton, and other reformers were saying. Women *had* to move out of the home. They had to take part in the human family, as Price said, rather than just the biological family. They had to control their movements. The "present arrangements" in the 1850s in terms of marriage meant for women what many saw as legalized prostitution. Women were legally subjects, victims, no more than legal chattel. Whitman's choice of the word "invalid" to describe the love of women puns on the very point women were making over and over—that women's health was endangered by the circumscription of their space, by childbirth, and by dress. Their legal and political status was not valid. They did not live under the same terms as men; the Declaration of Independence and the Constitution were not their texts. Women were made to be "in-valids." They were invalid as citizens, precisely because society did not allow unfolding, precisely because institutional structures such as educational and professional institutions barred them from entrance.

Whitman addresses women in this entry and writes from the point of view of a male who wants (within the context of the lecture, I stress) a relationship with a woman who could join him on equal terms, say, on the "open road." He wants a lover and a companion. Social codes at that time did not permit "the free air," "wildness," or "rudeness" for and in women, and thus—so ran the argument—women were not physically, psychically, or intellectually equipped to be companions on the "open road." Davis says as much: "The deference and submission of dependence, carried even to the length of abject self-abnegation, are certainly capable of pushing modesty to its superlative degree, but such subserviency may be unworthy, unnatural, and unprofitable to both the parties concerned in it." Under the present conditions, she argues, not only are women cheated of self, but also men are cheated of companionship: "His loves must go out and return to him on the place of a level reciprocity, or he is dragged down by the descent of his affections. How poor a cheat then he puts upon himself, by exchanging a large, generous, and complete appreciation, for a blind, meagre, and low toned idolatry!" Of course women could seize "wildness," but only at a significant cost. Frances Wright seized the lifestyle Whitman describes and paid for it, a fact well known to Whitman. Only an extensive reading of Price's, Davis's, and Rose's articles and speeches in the 1850s yields the full impact of activists' rejection of the marriage institution as it then existed. Davis said in her 1852 address to the National Woman's Rights Convention: "Marriage as it now exists is only a name, a form without a soul, a bondage, legal and therefore honorable. Only equals can make this relation. True marriage is a union of soul with soul, a blending of two in one, without mastership or helpless dependence."[53] Whitman's notebook entry "Lect. (To Women" can be read as his veiled address for male/male love, but it must also be read in light of the woman's rights movement. Davis's editorial makes it impossible not to do so. In the "Calamus" poem "Fast Anchor'd Eternal O Love!" it is as if Whitman had taken "Lect. (To Women" and turned it into a poem, this time clearly celebrating the persona's love for men. The 1860 version of the poem opened with the line, "Primeval my love for the woman I love." In 1867 that line was dropped and the poem read:

> Fast-anchor'd eternal O love! O woman I love!
> O bride! O wife! more resistless than I can tell, the
>   thought of you!
> Then separate, as disembodied or another born,
> Ethereal, the last athletic reality, my consolation,
> I ascend, I float in the regions of your love O man,
> O sharer of my roving life. (*Variorum*, 2:403)

Davis's numerous articles on marriage do not dispute the view offered by this poem.

In her 1854 editorial "Inequality of Women in Marriage," when Davis subscribes to the belief that circumstances play a major role in shaping the individual, we see the influence not only of pre-Darwinian evolutionary theory but also of early American communitarian thought. Also, Davis held tightly to the Englightenment belief in inherent rights. Individuals are socially constructed, to use current terminology; they are the "fact and effect" of their circumstances. Because patriarchy has prescribed a subservient role for women, and because women have lived this subservient position, "reciprocities of equality" in marriage are impossible. Under the present laws and conditions of marriage, Davis says, no one can find satisfaction in marriage. Love becomes invalid. But if people could *see* their sexism (racism, etc.), they would change and they would change their institutions. Her idealism led her to believe that ignorance or blindness caused people to misuse power. In an 1852 public letter to Caroline H. Dall, Davis wrote: "I would not resist taxation, but I would remonstrate with clear, cogent arguments, that would ultimately prevail; for truth is mighty, and though long restrained, it will . . . , when it breaks forth, sweep away all barriers, and accomplish its full purpose."[54]

In the editorial "Inequality," Davis is careful not to attack her audience: "We are the creatures of habit, and are skilful in discovering reasons for things that we habitually do, not only without reason, but against all reason, right and expediency." She realizes the difficulty in seeing outside ingrained ideologies: "When a system of opinions and usages is once completely incorporated with the general institutions of society, a sort of harmony results from the ordinary operation that prevents their inherent mischief from exposing itself."[55] She expresses here the ubiquity of sexism. The challenge for Davis was to get people to see the sexism. In this respect, Whitman's poetry appealed to her: it disturbed the "ordinary operation" and thus allowed the "inherent mischief" to expose itself. It provided readers a way to modulate or to alter that "harmony." Language used as Whitman used it would urge readers to question, to read their society with their own eyes, to reject inequities, or so she hoped. In an 1853 editorial Davis uses the unfolding trope to talk about reading. She asks the reader to take an equal role with the author in the production of textual meaning. In words complementary to those that Whitman used in his own calls for active readers, Davis states her belief in the text as mobile, of meaning as an unfolding taking place between the text and the reader: "It is in fact not unusual, and by no means impossible, that the receiver shall find more in a thought than was in the comprehension of the mind that evolved it."[56]

When in 1855 Davis read lines like the following passage from "Song of Myself," she recognized it as a validation of her views—that the mind's acuteness did not depend on size, no matter that the French anthropologist Paul Broca would "prove" the contrary in 1861[57] and that pride was an integral part of the woman's makeup just as it was part of a man's. The passage can also be read as an outline for the 1856 "Unfolded Out of the Folds."

> I am the poet of the woman the same as the man,
> And I say it is as great to be a woman as to be a man,
> And I say there is nothing greater than the mother of
> men.
>
> I chant the chant of dilation or pride,
> We have had ducking and deprecating about enough,
> I show that size is only development. [*Variorum,* 26–27]

This last line—"size is only development"—can be read in two ways: in the context of its own three-line stanza, it refers to the individual's developing her- or himself to the fullest extent. Historically speaking, it calls for an American citizenry that will never be subjugated to a foreign power. Here, however, size refers not to physical power or economic power or even moral power but rather to the individual's realization of self. While the emphasis appears to be on the individual and on her or his ability or willingness to better herself, put in the context of "Democratic Vistas"—on which Whitman was working in 1868 at the time of his visit to Davis's home—the line also reminds readers that individuation (development) depends on conditions (society, culture, environment). "Democratic Vistas" clarifies the role that the nation or the state holds for the individual citizen. The nation furnishes the culture, the seedbed, so to speak, from which the individual grows. The degree of selfhood reached depends on the fertility of the culture (nation).

Control over one's sexuality and access to the workplace, major issues for the contemporary feminist movement since the 1960s, were Davis's concerns, putting her well ahead of her time. Whitman, though he understood well the politics of sexuality, did not or could not envision women in the workplace to the extent that Davis, Price, Rose, and other activists could. He could conceptualize women outside the private sphere and create images of active women in diverse situations, but the actual concrete images of women as artisans or engaged in other kinds of wage-earning work scarcely exist in his poetry. Davis, however, had no trouble imagining female artisans and professionals. In a January 1854 article in the *Una,* "Pecuniary Independence of Women," she made the point that "the poor and illiterate, compelled by their sharp necessities, have already pressed into such avocations of business, as cheap wages and light responsibilities have opened to them; but this will never relieve the fate and fortunes of women; it will do no more for them as a class, than hod-carrying, barbering and coach-driving does for the free colored people." Davis, by this time, had no money problems herself, a fact that helps to explain how she had the time and freedom to work for reform in the first place. Her point here was that repressed people were not truly exercising freedom of choice when they took whatever job they could get in order to cope with the "sharp necessities" of their economic lives. She wanted women to have the same degree of choice that she attributed to middle-class men: "These employments must be taken up by those who choose them *with a purpose,* being free to choose, and not accidental resorts under difficulty, and in the same spirit a higher and better range of business callings must be undertaken. To name a few; daguerreotyping, chrystalotyping, drugstores, . . . clerkships in public offices, bookstores, printing, goldsmithing, the administration of descendant's estates, the study and practice of medicine and dentistry, law and divinity, . . . education and capital, all of which have been already tried with success, in a few instances, and all of which are waiting to engage and reward our energies."[58]

Whitman does not show women at work at any of these kinds of jobs in his poetry, though he does present images of women working in "Democratic Vistas" that moved beyond cultural inscriptions. In his poetry, women are almost always shown performing domestic labor, though there is the line in section 14 of "Song of Myself": "The clean-hair'd Yankee girl works with her sewing-machine or in the factory or mill."[59] Though he does image women as part of public life, he presents few concrete images of women working independently of men. The pattern I have already mentioned—the 1856 and 1860 editions of *Leaves of Grass* being the most radical in their creation of images of independent, public women—remains consistent with Whitman's *generalized* depiction of working women. The 1855 (untitled) poem that we know as "A Song for Occupations" became in 1856 "Poem of the Daily Work of the Workmen and Workwomen of These States." In 1860, the pattern breaks, however, for immediately in the third edition, the title becomes generalized: "Chants Democratic. 3." In 1867, women become even more marginalized as the title becomes "To Workmen." But even in the 1856 and 1860 editions of *Leaves,* Whitman did not include in the long catalogs of crafts anything approaching Paulina Wright Davis's list of specific jobs women could hold.

This shift from the 1856 title ("Poem of The Daily Work of The Workmen and Workwomen of These States") to the 1867 title ("To Workmen") clearly illustrates Whitman's shift from the more radical stance he took on woman's rights during the 1850s and in the 1860 edition to the increasingly generalized stance he took as he revised many of the political images of women into the image befitting his concept of Republican motherhood; in this instance, "workwomen" disappears altogether. The shift in *Leaves of Grass* parallels the shift in the women's movement as well; it was more conservative in 1870 than it was in 1850 as the movement splintered, a result of woman's rights marginalization, ostensibly necessary in order to secure full citizenship for black males. The Woman's Rights Movement, 1848–1861, became the woman's suffrage movement. Whereas the woman's rights movement fought for suffrage, it also agitated for reforming married women's property rights, liberalized divorce laws, education for women, freeing the workforce so that women held more than the lowest paid jobs, comparable worth, and equal pay. The Civil War put an end to the national woman's rights movement and initiated the split into two women's reform organizations: the more radical National Woman Suffrage Association (NWSA) and the more conservative American Woman Suffrage Association (AWSA). The radical arm of the movement, NWSA, led by Elizabeth Cady Stanton and Susan B. Anthony, and supported by Davis and Ernestine L. Rose, was forced to become more narrowly focused in order to be effective in the fight for suffrage. The AWSA, led by Lucy Stone and her husband Henry Blackwell, became a single-issue movement, fighting for suffrage. For twenty years, the two groups struggled on independent of each other. In 1890, they joined forces, and conservatism continued to hold more power within the movement. The Nineteenth Amendment was not ratified until 1920.

Like Whitman's own pattern of radicalism/conservatism, "workwomen" does not completely disappear from *Leaves of Grass,* though it disappears from the title of "Song for Occupations." Whitman rarely shows women as artisans in the many listings of crafts that appear throughout *Leaves of Grass,* but he does speak of workwomen in his poems. In "Song for Occupations" the fourth line reads: "Workmen and Workwomen!" "Workwomen" also appears, once more, near

the ending of the poem: "You workwomen and workmen of these
States having your own divine and strong life" (*Variorum,* 1:83–89).
In the 1856 "Salut au Monde," the "working-woman" appears, almost
as an afterthought: "You working-man of the Rhine, the Elbe, or the
Weser! you working-woman too!" (*Variorum,* 1:173). In the same
poem, he hears "the workman singing and the farmer's wife singing." He acknowledges the "women of the earth subordinated at
[their] tasks!" (*Variorum,* 1:163, 173). "Apostroph," which Whitman
mostly excluded after its appearance in the 1860 *Leaves of Grass,* contains the line "O workmen and workwomen forever for me!" (*Variorum,* 2:291). This line was not retained. "Song of Myself," in a remarkably contemporary phrasing, coins the term "workpeople":
"the loud laugh of work-people at their meals" (*Variorum,* 1:37).

An interesting omission occurs in his 1860 "Starting from Paumanok." In this poem, the following line appears (after line 266) in
1860 and then never again: "O to level occupations and the sexes!
O to bring all to common ground! O adhesiveness!" (*Variorum,*
2:289). The line calls for precisely the rights that activists like Davis
and Price called for: equal and free access to the workplace and inalienable rights for women as well as for men. Whitman's omission
of this line is another example of his toning down the radical call
for woman's rights. The use of "adhesiveness" here, however, suggests that more is at work. A passage such as this conflates Whitman's
homosexual orientation with his awareness of woman's rights (that
is, of their lack thereof) and suggests that it was not only the
woman's rights movement on his mind. The use of "adhesiveness" in
this line also suggests his own marginalization as a result of his sexual orientation.

Section 18 is composed of twelve long lines in which the poet
paints an ecstatic view of the past and of the future, naming and
accounting for the facticity of America. The point of view is that of
the poet looking *out.* Then, at the end of the penultimate line of
stanza 18, the point of view abruptly shifts: "See, lounging through
the shops and fields of the States, me well-belov'd, close-held by day
and night,. Here the loud echoes of my songs there—read the hints
come at last." The reader has been asked to turn her/his gaze away
from America and toward the poet. A space follows and then stanza
19. Here is stanza 19 as it appears in the final edition of *Leaves of
Grass,* with the exception of lines 2–5, which are the four lines appearing only in the 1860 *Leaves:*

O camerado close! O you and me at last, and us two only.

O power, liberty, eternity at last!

O to be relieved of distinctions! to make as much of vices as virtues!

O to level occupations and the sexes! O to bring all to common ground! O
adhesiveness!

O the pensive aching to be together—you know not why, and I know not
why.

O a word to clear one's path ahead endlessly!

O something ecstatic and undemonstrable! O music wild!

O now I triumph—and you shall also;

O hand in hand—O wholesome pleasure—O one more desirer and lover!

O to haste firm holding—to haste, haste on with me.

The abrupt shift of focus in the penultimate line of stanza 18
amounts to an assertion: by seeing all of the things America includes, you have to see that America includes me, the seer, sayer.
Section 19 then positions the reader to be the poet's comrades, or
at least voyeuristically to see and hear the poet and his comrade together as the poet takes the comrade with him, to hasten with him
along his open road. The line "O to level occupations" could be read
by women struggling with their culture's sexism and male or female homosexuals struggling with their culture's homophobia
(though there was no such term at the time): "O to level occupations and the sexes! O to bring all to common ground! O adhesiveness!"

The poem that comes closest to realizing Paulina Wright Davis's
vision of opening up the crafts and professions to women is, I think,
the 1860 poem "Mediums." For those believing in spiritualism, the
medium was the person through whom the dead spoke. Much
like Abby Price, Whitman had an in-and-out-of-the-game approach
to spiritualism. Though interested, he kept his distance, at least as
far as subscribing to any kind of doctrine. He speaks of a talk he had
with George B. Arnold about the popular medium Cora L. V. Hatch
in his 1857 letter to Sarah Tyndale. (Arnold had gone from Unitari-
anism to Spiritualism.) His comments in this letter succinctly sum-
marize his position: "I got into quite a talk with Mr. Arnold about
Mrs. Hatch. He says the pervading thought of her speeches is that
first exists the spirituality of any thing, and *that* gives existence to
things, the earth, plants, animals, men, women. But that Andrew

Jackson Davis puts *matter* as the subject of his homilies, and the primary source of all results—I suppose the soul among the rest. Both are quite determined in their theories. Perhaps when they know much more, both of them will be much less determined."[60]

In the poem, "Mediums," however, the mediums assume the role of the poet, the prophet, the teacher, or the orator.

> They shall arise in the States,
> They shall report Nature, laws, physiology, and happiness,
> They shall illustrate Democracy and the kosmos,
> They shall be alimentive, amative, perceptive,
> They shall be complete women and men, their pose brawny and
>   supple, their drink water, their blood clean and clear,
> They shall fully enjoy materialism and the sight of products, they shall
>   enjoy the sight of the beef, lumber, bread-stuffs, of Chicago the great
>   city,
> They shall train themselves to go in public to become orators and
>   oratresses,
> Strong and sweet shall their tongues be, poems and materials of poems
>   shall come from their lives, they shall be makers and finders,
> Of them and of their works shall emerge divine conveyors, to convey
>   gospels,
> Characters, events, retrospections, shall be convey'd in gospels, trees,
>   animals, waters, shall be convey'd,
> Death, the future, the invisible faith, shall all be convey'd. [*Variorum*, 2:313]

This poem empowers women as well as men to perform the prophet/teacher role Whitman himself performed, or aspired to perform, in *Leaves of Grass*. It empowered women as orators, a role Whitman ascribes to women in other poems, as well. Perhaps it is not odd that *Leaves of Grass* falls most short in depicting women as artisans. It was this class—white male artisans—that Whitman most defended and protected. It was here that his racism surfaced. It was not, however, difficult for him to create images of women as orators. He had in his actual view women who were consummate orators—Rose, most of all, but also Price and Davis and, in his youth, Frances Wright.

Possibly the kind of conflict Davis talked about in an October 1853 *Una* editorial was one reason Whitman did not depict women doing what had been considered men's work. This editorial, "Female Compositors, and Opposition of Interests," takes up the issue that

Christine Stansell talks about in *City of Women*—the troubled relationship between the labor unions (male) and female workers. Since
male laborers ultimately worked to keep women out of the market-
place, any support they gave female laborers was, in essence, pater-
nalistic and did not help women to gain economic independence.
Davis, in the editorial, did not mince words: "It is not a sentiment of
respect, and a desire to preserve the delicacy of the sex, that denies
us the liberties which the woman's rights movement is now claiming; and we rejoice that the facts of experience are rapidly opening
the eyes of sentimental conservatism, to the truth that it is *tyranny,*
and not *tenderness,* which opposes us."[61] Possibly Whitman feared the
competitive effect women would have on the workforce if they had
the chance to compete with males for jobs. (He worried about the
similar effects of the freeing of slaves, how black male labor would
devalue white male labor.) Whatever the reason, opportunities for
women to work outside the home were a priority for Davis and Price
that Whitman simply did not address with anything approaching the
intensity with which he addressed women's liberated physicality.

His address in this area, however, reached beyond the national
woman's rights conference circles. There is, for example, a letter to
Whitman in the Feinberg Collection from Elmina Slenker, a woman
who actively fought for sexual openness. Though Hal Sears, in *The
Sex Radicals: Free Love in High Victorian America,* says that Slenker did
not advocate pleasure as one of the bases for intercourse, Linda Gordon, in *Woman's Body, Woman's Right,* interprets Slenker's views differently. Gordon's point is that Slenker did not censure sexuality;
rather, she censured unrestrained heterosexual intercourse. She
wanted women to control their own bodies, and she was interested
in the production of healthy children and safe childbirth.[62] Slenker's
forthrightness in speaking about sexuality put Anthony Comstock
on her trail. In 1887 she was arrested for mailing private material in
sealed letters.[63] She frequently quoted from Whitman's poetry in her
numerous articles about sexuality and parenthood. When in 1888
Slenker heard he was ill, she wrote Whitman a letter:

> I hear thee is far from well. I want to send thee one more apprecia-
> tive greeting and to tell thee, thee has one appreciative worshipper
> way off here in Old Virginia.
>   One who has quoted from thy Leaves of Grass persistently ever
> since it appeared, and this, together with other hygenic sex work,

has robbed me of friends, husband, & perhaps of all the little savings
of a life time as Va. Law allows the man to sell all & the wife to be
turned from house & home till he dies, when she can get her third
of what *he* [underlined twice] does not squander.

I want thee to feel that thy work has done much for needed sexual
reform.[64]

Forthrightness in speaking about sexuality—the words one said and
where one said them—got Whitman in trouble with Comstock just
as it did Slenker, since Comstock's crusade against "vice" lay behind
Boston District Attorney Oliver Stevens's decision to ban the 1882
Leaves of Grass from the U.S. mail.[65]

Though a local organization and therefore not representative on
a national basis, the women of the Providence Physiological Society
had an attitude toward forthright speech about sexuality that comes
closer to Whitman's than to that of the "true" Victorian woman, our
present-day categorization of the mainstream white middle-class
woman. The minutes, 1850–1853, reveal an awareness of the implications involved when "false delicacy" dictated what could and could
not be said and thus what constituted knowledge. They also reveal
the Providence women's seriousness in their quest for knowledge.
The minutes give a sense of women well aware that the subject they
were dealing with often involved life-and-death situations or life-
long unhappiness. They reveal the women's intense curiosity to
learn about their own bodies. The following extract, not a public
document and therefore not something that Whitman would have
read, gives a sense of the Providence women's urgent curiosity: "Mrs.
Davis gave us the third lecture in her course. Subject: reproduction.
The origin of life, or lucid explanation thereof teems with thrilling
interest. It is the subject which of all others we most desire to understand, and of which we never get weary."[66] The subject teeming with
"thrilling interest" treated in the context of the society functioned
not only as a necessary means of educating for survival but also as a
way, simply, to talk about sex. In the minutes for the 11 April 1851
meeting, a Mrs. Johnson spoke on the "organs of generation" and
on "false delicacy":

[She began by saying that] the knowledge most needed by woman
is that on the diseases and functions of the generating organs. It is
a false delicacy that precluded attention to these subjects. The same

skill is exhibited in them as in the other organs & were it not for the taint of sin on the soul they would be examined with the same freedom as the other organs. Knowledge saves from suffering. She was sorry to say that some physicians are still opposed to the general dissemination of such knowledge. . . . The vagina, uterus, & fallopian tubes were separately & briefly described. It is the ovaries that give to woman her peculiarly feminine character.

The next month at the 22 May meeting, Paulina Wright Davis also spoke of the dangers involved when "false delicacy" kept women from controlling their bodies. Birth control is the subtext. "Mrs. Davis touched upon several points requiring moral courage with the prevailing ideal of delicacy. Women must take matters into their own hands and give the law on the subject."[67]

"False delicacy" is what Whitman countered in the "Children of Adam" cluster, first appearing as a cluster in the 1860 *Leaves of Grass*. Within Victorian middle-class white society, poems like "O Hymen! O Hymenee!" and "Spontaneous Me" spoke the unspeakable.[68] Mary Ryan, in *Cradle of the Middle Class*, referring to Utica's Protestant middle-class at midcentury, says, "Sexual matters had been relegated beyond the pale of polite conversation." She cites women's diaries as one of her sources and the *Oneida Whig* as another: "The *Oneida Whig* . . . let it be known that any attempt to educate women on these subjects, as proposed by the veteran moral reformer Paulina Wright [Davis] was an affront to femininity."[69] To this same mainstream middle-class citizen, Whitman's sex poems, one of which was "O Hymen! O Hymenee!" part of the "Children of Adam" cluster, fell into the same category. "O Hymen! O Hymenee!" is a short poem:

> O hymen! O hymenee! why do you tantalize me thus?
> O why sting me for a swift moment only?
> Why can you not continue? O why do you now cease?
> Is it because if you continued beyond the swift moment you would soon
>   certainly kill me? [*Variorum*, 2:363]

The poem itself more or less takes the definition of "hymen" given in the 1845 Webster's dictionary and puts it into narrative form: the dictionary first gives the mythological meaning; it then gives the anatomical meaning—"the virginal membrane." The dictionary also lists forms and usages from Pope and Milton, followed by the entomological meaning—"the hymenopters are an order of insects, having four membranous wings, and the tail of the female mostly armed with a sting." Joseph Worcester's 1860 dictionary is more explicit in its anatomical definition: "the virginal membrane at the outer orifice of the vagina."[70]

This is one of those short poems in *Leaves of Grass* that may slip by the reader. But as part of the reformist push for instilling into popular discourse a forthright sexual vocabulary, it deserves attention. The title first divides the god power between the female and male deities. This reapportionment changes the traditional initiator/receiver relationship. Conceivably, in the poem, Hymenee was as much the initiator as Hymen. In the first line of the poem, "hymen" and "hymenee" are not capitalized, allowing the meaning to slip from classical mythology to anatomy. In that first line, Whitman chooses the verb "tantalize," calling up the Tantalus myth. It is the lower-case "hymen/hymenee," however, that the "you" addresses. The persona appears to be addressing his or her own body, the "virginal membrane" or the penis. The poem can thus be read not only in the context of marriage—heterosexual marriage—but also in the context of autoerotic desire. Whitman's language in this poem, for a certain kind of reader, furthered the reform that women like Paulina Wright Davis fought for: to free women from the ignorance of their own bodies that Victorian society perpetuated; to inscribe a sexual vocabulary; to inscribe images of women's bodies as *forces,* as having, well, a sting. On the other hand, the poem can be read as participating in the culture's push to make male and female more different than alike, thus perpetuating the image reformers like Price and Rose, more than Davis, worked against.

In the 1856 poem "Spontaneous Me," the female does become the passive receptacle: "The hairy wild-bee that murmurs and hankers up and down, that gripes the full-grown lady-flower, curves upon her with amorous firm legs, takes his will of her, and holds himself tremulous and tight till he is satisfied" (*Variorum,* 1:258). This passage, like a similar passage in "A Woman Waits for Me," is the kind of passage that made Elizabeth Cady Stanton ridicule Whitman for his depiction of women's role in heterosexual intercourse. The depiction of male/female intercourse is displeasing to present-day sensibility because of the passivity of the female and the obliviousness of the male to her needs and reactions. Another way to look at it, however, would be to place it in the context of the nineteenth-century language of flowers. Images of the bee and the blossom occur over and over again in nineteenth-century texts. Louisa May Alcott used the image of the bee penetrating what looks like a morning glory on the title page of her novel *Work: A Story of Experience* (1873). Elaine Showalter speaks of Alcott's use of the image in *Work:* "[Christie's] gardener-husband seems to exist more to fertilize the ambitious flower than to complete her. Having given Christie a daughter/flower—Pansy—, David conveniently dies." Emily Dickinson used the image of the bee and the flower repeatedly in her poems. Elizabeth Stuart Phelps used the image in her novel *Avis.* The passage in "A Woman Waits for Me," also depicting penetration, does not, however, use analogy in its depiction.[71]

> I do not hurt you any more than is necessary for you,
> I pour the stuff to start sons and daughters fit for these States, I press with
> slow rude muscle,
> I brace myself effectually, I listen to no entreaties, I dare not withdraw till I
> deposit what has so long accumulated within me.[72]

Writing in her diary in 1883, Stanton said about the poem:

> I have been reading *Leaves of Grass.* Walt Whitman seems to understand everything in nature but woman. In "There is a Woman Waiting for Me," he speaks as if the female must be forced to the creative act, apparently ignorant of the great natural fact that a healthy woman has as much passion as a man, that she needs nothing stronger than the law of attraction to draw her to the male.[73]

Though Stanton has every reason to find the above passage objectionable, in this poem the following passage also occurs:

> They know how to swim, row, ride, wrestle, shoot, run, strike, retreat,
> advance, resist, defend themselves,
> They are ultimate in their own right—they are calm, clear, well-possess'd
> of themselves.

That passage had to have pleased Stanton; it sounds much like a passage in a public letter she wrote to be read at the Woman's Convention, held at Akron, Ohio, on 25 May 1851: "The childhood of woman must be free and untrammeled. The girl must be allowed to romp and play, climb, skate, and swim; her clothing must be more like that of a boy."[74]

One belief held at the time was that the more passive a woman was during intercourse, the more likely that impregnation would take place. Thomas Low Nichols, in his 1853 "treatise on the most intimate relations of men and women" *Esoteric Anthropology (The Mysteries of Man)*, listed a number of theories on reproduction that were based, he said, on a multitude of observations, one of which was the following: "It is not necessary that there should be any enjoyment of coition, on the part of the female. Women who have none, seem even more prolific than others. It may take place in *sleep,* or other *insensibility*" (emphasis added).[75] The point I wish to make here is that Whitman's depiction of male/female intercourse, lamentably, often followed popular medical thinking.

The poem "Spontaneous Me" depicts masturbation for the female as well as the male, and it thus inscribes a degree of control for the woman; the woman is controlling her own pleasure:

> The hubbed sting of myself, stinging me as much as it ever can any one,
>
> . . . .
>
> The curious roamer, the hand, roaming all over the body—the bashful
>   withdrawing of flesh . . .
>
> . . . .
>
> The like of the same I feel—the like of the same in others,
> The young woman that flushes and flushes, and the young man that flushes
>   and flushes. [*Variorum,* 1:257–59]

The female in control of her pleasure, to any degree, is missing from Whitman's depiction of male/female intercourse.

Possibly Whitman's intention in "From Pent-Up Aching Rivers" was to inscribe for the male/female relationship a kind of vitality that women, by and large, did not experience, as a rule, in antebellum America. Perhaps the poem is a gloss of sorts on his notebook entry "Lect. (To Women"—the part that reads: "Why should there be these modesties, and prohibitions that keep women from strong actual life—from going about there with men. Is it that the growth of love needs the free air—the seasons, perhaps more wildness, more rudeness? Why is the love of women so invalid? so transient?" The following eight lines offer an image of the female escaping into the ethereal regions with her lover analogous to that described in "Fast Anchor'd Eternal O Love.":

> The female form approaching, I pensive, love-flesh tremulous aching,
> The divine list for myself or you or for any one making,
> The face, the limbs, the index from head to foot, and
>   what it arouses,
> The mystic deliria, the madness amorous, the utter abandonment,
> (Hark close and still what I now whisper to you,
> I love you, O you entirely possess me,
> O that you and I escape from the rest and go utterly off, free and lawless,
> Two hawks in the air, two fishes swimming in the sea not more lawless
>   than we;) [*Variorum*, 2:354]

In the first four lines, the poet-persona uses phrases out of the sentimentalized diction of his society. Then there is the parenthetical statement in which the poet-persona speaks of another world. Here the female reader could imagine a life different from the one sanctioned by the Cult of True Womanhood, in which she was to base her existence on her home, her religion, her husband, and her children and not take into account her own desires and aspirations. The "tremulous aching," "divine list," and "mystic deleria" of the first four lines are subsumed by language that calls for the wildness and rudeness Whitman speaks of in his "Lect. (To Women." The free and lawless hawks in "From Pent-Up Aching Rivers" are enclosed in parentheses, an enclosure superbly appropriate, since the kind of freedom they represent—a different kind of male/female relationship or a male/male, female/female relationship—was not possible in society at large, was parenthetical to the main flow of the cultural syntax.

The animal images accumulate in the "Children of Adam" poems, tearing away the veneer of Victorian sentimentality that spoke of sex as only a spiritual act ("the spiritual influence of women, & sex—Mrs. Tyndale's theory"). In the "Children of Adam" poem "One Hour to Madness and Joy," a key line is dropped after 1860. This line advances the radical idea that women would be in charge of creating vital lives for themselves. They would be in charge (with the poet-persona's tutelage, however) of realizing for themselves a passional life. The two lines that precede the dropped line are:

O to return to Paradise! O bashful and feminine!
O to draw you to me, to plant on you for the first time the lips of a
    determin'd man.

The line that followed these two in the 1860 edition was: "O rich
and feminine! O to show you to realize the blood of life for yourself,
whoever you are—and no matter when and where you live" (*Variorum*, 2:356–57). The image of the woman realizing the blood of life
for herself furthers the view suggested in Whitman's notebook entry:
"Do you suppose you have nothing waiting for yourselves to do, but
to embroider, to clean, to be respectable and modest, and not swear
or drink?" But Whitman dropped this line after the Civil War when
he sought to accentuate the communal aspect of democracy, to use
the Mother as the prime image of cohesion, and thus to tone down
many of the more radical images that ask woman to realize her potential according to her wishes and not those of society or of another
person.

    Another interesting omission occurs in "Great Are the Myths."
In the 1855 version, a line (after line 37) reads "Great are marriage,
commerce, newspapers. "In the 1856 edition, the word "marriage"
no longer appears (*Variorum*, 1:158). By 1856, Whitman had heard
enough criticism of the marriage institution to reconsider this line.
The better acquainted Whitman became with Davis, Price, and other
woman's rights activists, the more conscious he became of the work-
ings of his own ideology regarding women in his poetry, and thus
we see the strengthening and compounding of the representations
of women starting in the 1856 and 1860 editions.

    The poet-persona tells us in the 1856 "By Blue Ontario's Shore"
that he will make new images for expressing the love for men and
women:

Underneath all is the Expression of love for men and women,
(I swear I have seen enough of mean and impotent modes of expressing
    love for men and women,
After this day I take my own modes of expressing love for men and
    women.) [*Variorum*, 1:206]

    As if responding to the illustrations in the *Water-Cure Journal*,
section 9 of "I Sing the Body Electric," added in 1856, far from being
a mere listing in what some think is exhaustive detail of the parts of

the body, comes exuberantly alive through the sheer mouthing of the words naming the body parts, through the force of the repetition as the words pile up, arranged so that they build up to a marvelous crescendo as the reader joins in with the writer's wonder and awe and ecstasy at this thing, the human body, "the human form divine," so feared by the Puritan forebears Whitman never chooses as exemplars of American democracy.

The second and third lines of section 9 of "I Sing the Body Electric," lines 131–32, form a compound/complex sentence: "I believe the likes of you are to stand or fall with the likes of the soul, (and that they are the soul,) / I believe the likes of you shall stand or fall with my poems, and that they are my poems." Lines 133–46 list the various parts of the body and thus "are" the poems, for example "Head, neck, hair, ears, drop and tympan of the ears" (line 133). Line 147, "All attitudes, all the shapeliness, all the belongings of my or your body or of any one's body, male or female," begins a new sentence, this time a periodic sentence with the noun phrases "all attitudes, all the shapeliness, all the belongings of my or your body" separated from the pronoun to which they refer by fifteen lines, numbers 148–62, which furnish concrete examples of what the poet means by "all attitudes, all shapeliness, all the belongings of the body." Line 163 finally gives the reader the complete sentence, a compound-complex structure: "O I say these are not the parts and poems of the body only, but of the soul, / O I say now these are the soul!"

Within these lines 148–62, the associations are arresting. Line 149 reads: "The brain in its folds inside the skull-frame." Departing from the pattern, now, of naming specific body parts, Whitman specifies the first of the "attitudes" he mentions in line 147 when in line 150 he speaks of "Sympathies."

> All attitudes, all the shapeliness, all the belongings of my or your body or
>   of any one's body, male or female,
> The lung-sponges, the stomach-sac, the bowels sweet and clean,
> The brain in its folds inside the skull-frame,
> Sympathies, heart-valves, palate-valves, sexuality, maternity,
> Womanhood, and all that is a woman, and the man that comes from
>   woman,
> The womb, the teats, nipples, breast-milk, tears, laughter, weeping, love-
>   looks, love-perturbations and risings,

The voice, articulation, language, whispering, shouting aloud,
[Ll. 147–53, *Leaves of Grass,* Comprehensive Reader's Edition, 100–1]

From the body comes the ability to form "attitudes," which leads the poet to sympathy, which in turn reminds the poet of the heart valves, valves then taking him to palate valves, to sex, to maternity—birthing. It is easy to see the relationship between the first two of this series of five, the relationship between "sympathy" and "heartvalves." It is also easy to see the relationship between the last two, "sexuality" and "maternity." Indeed, Whitman's linkage between the latter two poses a large problem for many contemporary women. Whitman also often links birthing to language, however, as he does here when he names women's reproductive abilities—"the womb, the teats, nipples, breast-milk" and moves immediately to "voice, articulation, language, whispering, shouting aloud." It is the image of the middle term, "palate-valves," that perplexes and arrests the reading.

First, "palate-valves" is an odd phrase, imaginatively linked to the heart through the association of the heart's two-sidedness, a dual-chambered pump. The visual appearance of the palate has, if one looks, two sides also, the uvula suspended from the center of the soft palate, above the back of the tongue, creating the soft palate into the shape, as popularly drawn, to represent the heart. Still, "palate-valves" was a term sufficiently odd to warrant etymological tracing. Through its Indo-European root, the word "valve" leads to the word "vulva." The vulva corresponds semantically and visually to the mouth: the word "labia" means "lips," the clitoris resembles the uvula, and the entrance to the vagina homologous to the throat. Here are the five lines as they appear in "Body Electric," the five lines that create the association between the body (the seen) and language or the soul (the unseen). The lines take the reader from the brain into the body and then back to the brain again, with language, the brain, and the body interwoven, with the female body the locus for the image melding the two:

The brain in its folds inside the skull-frame,
Sympathies, heart-valves, palate-valves, sexuality, maternity,
Womanhood, and all that is a woman, and the man that comes from
   woman,
The womb, the teats, nipples, breast-milk, tears, laughter, weeping, love-

> looks, love-perturbations and risings,
> The voice, articulation, language, whispering, shouting aloud.

Out of the womb and breasts come feelings, and feelings give rise to language. Language grows out of the female. The line describing male genitalia simply gives rise to a following line describing more body: "Hips, hip-sockets, hip-strength, inward and outward round, man-balls, man-root, / Strong set of thighs, well carrying the trunk above" (143–44). "Sympathy" occurs once more, directly followed with references to breath:

> The curious sympathy one feels when feeling with the hand the naked meat
>   of the body,
> The circling rivers the breath, and breathing it in and out. [Ll. 158–59]

M. Jimmie Killingsworth develops the connection between female genitalia and speech in *Whitman's Poetry of the Body*. His application of deconstructionist tactics to the 1856 poem "Unfolded Out of the Fold" enables him to discuss the vaginal images in the poem in a way that brings new life to "Unfolded" and also connects the images in the poem to Whitman's notions and images of creativity in general. He imaginatively links Whitman's inscription of vulval imagery to the insights that contemporary theory provides, citing Jonathan Culler's discussion of Derrida's concept of invagination and showing how this concept has, as Killingsworth phrases it, "a peculiarly Whitmanian ring."[76] Killingsworth brings into the discussion a notebook entry of Whitman's in which Whitman uses the words "enfolding," "effusing," and "hidden." This notebook citation and other Whitman poems lead Killingsworth to the following observation: "Enfolding and effusing—the actions of the female genitalia—become the model for ideal creative power, which Whitman would identify above all with artistic creation" (64). Killingsworth illustrates the way that for Whitman, "male creative power is thus thoroughly infused with femininity. Moreover, masculinity, as a model for creative power, is not as comprehensive as femininity with its deep enfolding" (64). Killingsworth closes his discussion of "Unfolded" by introducing Whitman's concept of interpenetration (61–65). Whitman uses the term "interpenetration" in his poem "A Woman Waits for Me": "I shall demand perfect men and women out of my love-spendings, / I shall expect them to interpenetrate with others as I and you interpenetrate now." Killingsworth's reading brings us a vital step forward in reading vaginal images as well as seminal in Whitman.

Line 151 in section 9 of "Body Electric" reads: "Womanhood, and all that is a woman, and the man that comes from woman." In its wording this poem is associated with the 1856 "Unfolded out of the Folds," the first line of which reads: "Unfolded out of the folds of the woman man comes unfolded, and is always to come unfolded." Other than aesthetics, Whitman's poetics offered activists like Davis the image-making faculty they were aware was needed in order to bring about reform, not through revolution, but through a change in public consciousness. Aware that the very term "woman" had to be redefined and new images of women instilled into public consciousness, activists such as Davis saw what Whitman called his image making at work, and they saw its potential.

With the opportunities that Whitman had to read Davis's work prior to meeting her, with the numerous occasions he had to talk with her at Price's home, and with their common interests, Whitman and Davis were in a position to benefit from each other's experiences and abilities. Then, in 1868, Whitman spent time with the Davises at their home in Providence. The visit was arranged while Whitman was staying at the Prices' home. True to her efficient self, Paulina Wright Davis made the arrangements: "Mrs. Paulina Davis has been here," Whitman wrote to William D. O'Connor, "& has, in her own & husband's behalf, kindly invited me, & indeed made the arrangements—I shall come on to Providence, to-morrow."[77] Thomas Davis met Whitman at the train with his carriage and took him to the Davis home. Whitman commented on the "hearty welcome from [Davis's] hospitable wife, & [the] family of young ladies & children." He described the Davis home to Peter Doyle as "a sort of castle built of stone, on fine grounds, a mile & a half from the town."[78]

While in Providence, Whitman divided his time between Jeannie and William Francis Channing's home and the Davises.[79] He joined the conversations held daily around his hosts' dinner tables. Conversations were very much part of the Davis household's regular pattern. Whitman wrote Doyle: "Evenings & meal times I find myself thrown amidst a mild, pleasant society, really intellectual, composed largely of educated women, some young, some not so young, every thing refined & polite, *not* disposed to small talk, conversing in earnest on profound subjects, but with a moderate rather slow tone, & in a kind & conciliatory manner—delighting in this sort of conversation, & spending their evenings till late in it. I take a hand in, for a change. I find it entertaining, as I say, for novelty's sake, for a week or two—but I know very well that would be enough for me. It is all first-rate, good & smart, but too constrained & bookish for a free old hawk like me."[80]

His description of the company—"pleasant," "really intellectual," "educated women," "refined," "polite," "not disposed to small talk," "conversing in earnest on profound subjects in a kind & conciliatory manner"—fits other descriptions of Paulina Wright Davis and, I imagine, her friends as well. It is not surprising that Whitman would not want to stay in such an atmosphere, especially at this point in his life, and it is not surprising that Whitman felt constrained at the Davis home. He was not comfortable staying at "grand" homes, or so he said when in January 1873 after his stroke he wrote in a letter to his mother that the Ashtons (J. Hubley Ashton was assistant attorney general) had invited him to convalesce in their home: "Mrs. Ashton has sent for me to be brought to her house, to be taken care of—of course I do not accept her offer—they live in grand style & I should be more bothered than benefitted by their refinements & luxuries, servants, &c—."[81]

Of the six extant letters that Whitman wrote while in Providence, five of them speak of the conversations he had with his friends. While he was there he made two new friends in Sarah Helen Whitman and Nora Perry, both writers. (Sarah Helen Whitman was a poet and longtime friend of William D. O'Connor, the same S. H. Whitman who at one time was engaged to Edgar Allan Poe. Perry wrote the 1876 article on Whitman that appeared in *Appleton's Journal*.) On the nineteenth, he wrote to Ellen O'Connor: "I have seen Mrs. Whitman, & like her—have seen her & talked &c. three times—have seen Miss Nora Perry—."[82] Two days later, Whitman wrote to Abby Price:

I am . . . at Mr. & Mrs. Davis's—Am treated with the greatest hospitality and courtesy every where. I have seen Mrs. Whitman—& like her. We had yesterday here to dinner & spend the evening Nora Perry, Wm O'Connor, Dr. Channing, &c—To-day Mrs. Davis had intended to take me out riding, but it is threatening rain, wind east, & skies dark—So it will have to be given up. I like Mr. Davis much.

I am very glad I made this jaunt & visit—Love to you, Helen, Emily, & all.[83]

On the day he left to return to Price's home in Manhattan, he wrote his friend John Burroughs a note, saying that he had "had a good time generally, in a quiet way—."[84] The women with whom Whitman had long talks at the Davis home in no way match the kind of woman Charles Eldridge said Whitman preferred: "old fashioned women; mothers of large families preferred, who did not talk about literature or reforms."[85] Davis had no biological children, and she did not adopt until she was in her forties. It is inconceivable that the group gathered around the Davis dinner table did not talk about reform and literature. Whitman's statement to Horace Traubel, late in life, clarifies the value he placed on women who were *not* known for being "old-fashioned" or the mothers of large families: "I had in mind the question, what is woman's place, function, in the complexity of our social life? Can women create, as man creates, in the arts? rank with the master craftsmen? I mean it in that way. It has been a historic question. Well—George Eliot, George Sand, have answered it: have contradicted the denial with a supreme affirmation."[86]

In December 1867, the *Galaxy* published "Democracy," the first of three essays Whitman wrote that in 1870 came together under the title "Democratic Vistas." In May 1868, the *Galaxy* published Whitman's essay "Personalism," the second essay of the three. The essay Whitman had yet to write was "Literature." Quite possibly the 1868 conversations that Whitman took part in while at Providence appear in some form in this essay. Women's rights activists were acutely aware of the gender-blind ideology that controlled their rights; to some degree, Whitman demonstrates his awareness of sexism in "Democratic Vistas."

Two years after Whitman's visit to Providence, Davis organized and ran the twenty-year celebration commemorating the first National Woman's Rights Convention and published a brief history of the movement.[87] Abby Price read a poem she had written for the occasion. The conference was held at Apollo Hall, 20 October. Whitman, in New York on leave, returned to Washington five days before the conference, on the fifteenth. *Democratic Vistas* was soon to go on sale. Whitman's intense years of productivity and the first movement for woman's rights in the United States were running on a parallel course—*Leaves of Grass* (1855) to *Democratic Vistas* (1870) and the first National Woman's Rights Convention (1850) to the Second Decade Celebration (1870).

By 1870, Paulina Davis had only six more years to live; Whitman, twenty-two. Davis's thirty years of public life—1846–1876—deserve a far more prominent place in history than they have been accorded. In terms of our reading of *Leaves of Grass,* they provide an insight to Whitman's knowledge of the issues surrounding woman's rights and thus a necessary contextualization.

Paulina Davis died on 24 August 1876.

In March 1874, Whitman wrote to Abby Price: "glad to hear about our friends Mrs. Davis & Mrs. Rein."[88] This kind of comment was typical, since Whitman and Price shared news and letters and had many mutual friends, Davis being one of their most treasured. Whitman's last reference to Paulina Wright Davis appears in a letter to Ellen O'Connor written a year and a half before Davis died: "Nelly, I just send you, (although one or two items confidential, sort o') Mrs. Price's last letter to me, two days since—read it, & destroy it—I also send Mrs. Davis's, she (Mrs. P) sent me, as you are interested in her."[89] It is a letter that once again suggests the interweaving of friends, the incessant exchange of ideas and news and affection.

4

Ernestine L. Rose

On 8 November 1890, Whitman wrote to his friend Maurice Bucke: "I am tickled hugely about the election ('Do you think the common people are logs or boulders' said a first rate lady friend Mrs. E L Rose to me once in N Y, anent old French Revo)."[1] Whitman repeated her words, slightly varied, in a talk with Traubel:

> The capacity of the true man for turning upon his oppressor is one of the glories of the race—its security, in fact. I remember Mrs. Ernestine L. Rose—the big, noble woman!—when speaking of the Revolution—the Frenchmen . . . her eyes would flash—and she would exclaim—"What!—to be trod down and not turn! Do you take the people to be of wood or of stone!" Oh! her eye, her cheek, her way, her half-rising from the chair—it was all fine. And the words are as strong, I put them there in my note-book—have kept them all these years. Perhaps I missed in giving them just now, but that is their substance.[2]

I have not found these words in one of the extant notebooks. But Rose's words are in *Leaves of Grass,* in a poem Whitman wrote in 1860, called "France, The 18th Year of These States." The poem commemorates the year 1794 and the French Revolution. The phraseology parallels Rose's words and gives evidence of Whitman's keen attentiveness to them:

Pale, silent, stern, what could I say to that long-accrued retribution?
Could I wish humanity different?
Could I wish the people made of wood and stone? Or that there be no
   justice in destiny or time?

O Liberty! O mate for me![3]

Twenty-two years after writing "France," Whitman set the stanza in which Rose's words occur in *Specimen Days,* in the section titled "Millet's Pictures—Last Items." Here Whitman tells of going to look at a collection of J. F. Millet's paintings. He admires the way Millet catches the everyday person and scene and comments on the "ethic purpose" in his work, which, Whitman says, he always looks for. He speaks of Millet's paintings in conjunction with the French Revolution, which then leads him once more to quote Ernestine L. Rose's words:

Could we wish humanity different?
Could we wish the people made of wood or stone?
Or that there be no justice in destiny or time?[4]

As well as leaving their imprint on Whitman, Rose's strong words, to use Whitman's phraseology, left their imprint on the woman's movement, a topic that she and Whitman had opportunity to discuss. The initial meeting between Whitman and Rose probably took place at Abby Price's home, where we know he visited with Paulina Wright Davis and Eliza Farnham. Ernestine L. Rose, like Abby Price and Paulina Wright Davis, attended the first National Woman's Rights Convention, held in Worcester in 1850. Rose and Price served and worked together in the movement until Price quit attending the meetings in late 1853. Price's and Rose's politics complemented each other in their radical stamp; there were, however, many differences between the women. Indeed, Ernestine L. Rose's very difference could be responsible for the continued lack of notable recognition given her in contemporary women's history.

In 1836 Ernestine L. Rose and her husband William chose to leave England and move to New York City. They based their choice on the egalitarianism promised in the Declaration of Independence. From 1836 to 1848, the date of the Seneca Falls Convention, Rose worked incessantly for broad-based reform, gradually focusing most

Ernestine L. Rose (1810–1892). Reproduced courtesy of
The Schlesinger Library, Radcliffe College.

of her energies on woman's rights. By the time she moved to the
United States, she had lived in Poland, Germany, Holland, France,
and England. She spoke the languages of these countries as well as
Hebrew. She was born in 1810 in Poland, an only child who because
of her own precociousness and closeness to her rabbi father received
from him a good education. Her mother died when she was six years
old. When she was sixteen, she left Poland, renouncing most of the
inheritance left to her by her mother. Her father had contracted a
marriage for her with a man much older than she. Freedom, she
said, was more important to her than money.

  After she moved to England, she associated with a circle of reformers that included Joseph Gurney, Elizabeth Fry, and, most important, Robert Owen, with whom she worked in the peace move-

ment and the Association of All Classes of All Nations. She met and married William Rose. William, a silversmith, and Ernestine shared the same political convictions and apparently had a happy marriage. They had no children.

Once she and William arrived in New York City, they associated with a group of freethinkers who banded together in an organization called the Society for Moral Philanthropists.[5] Ernestine Rose began speaking before this group. Yuri Suhl, her biographer, says that Frances Wright—writer, reformer, and admirer of Tom Paine—and Ernestine L. Rose "moved in the same free thought circles and, on at least one occasion, shared the same platform."[6] The Society for Moral Philanthropists was led by Benjamin Offen, who was, Sean Wilentz says in *Chants Democratic,* one of "an extraordinary collection of recent émigrés who had long been active in the clandestine enclaves of English deism."[7] They were bound together by their allegiance to the ideas of Tom Paine, another émigré, one of the three figures of early American history whom Whitman greatly admired and who, he said, "were either much maligned or much misunderstood. Paine, the chiefest of these: the other two were Elias Hicks and Fanny Wright."[8]

The mutual admiration of Thomas Paine and Frances Wright shared by Whitman and Rose meant that in important respects they also shared an ideological heritage. Whitman, who read a short piece in memory of Paine on the 140th anniversary of his birthday at Lincoln Hall in Philadelphia, in 1877, commented on that speech to his friend Horace Traubel: "The polite circles of that period and later on were determined to queer the reputations of contemporary radicals—not Paine alone, but others also—Fanny Wright, Priestley, for instance. . . . My speech on Paine at a Liberal League meeting in Philadelphia some years ago was only a sliver—a little bit of reverence done at a neglected shrine. I do not know that the audience cared at all, but I cared a good deal: it made me infinitely happy."[9] Of these three people, we have notes that Whitman made about two of them, Priestley and Wright. Significantly, in these notes, Whitman records the names of the people responsible for the information he is inscribing: George B. Arnold, in the case of Priestley, and Ernestine L. Rose, in the case of Wright, both connected with the Abby Price circle. Rose had begun speaking of her admiration for Paine at the annual Thomas Paine birthday celebrations soon after her arrival in New York, roughly forty years before Whitman's speech. The links between her and Whitman and their admiration of Paine and Wright speak for both Rose's and Whitman's belief in individual freedom as they worked to encode into their society a culture that lived up to its founding documents: that is, they wanted America's material culture to live up to the terms of its textual claims.

An October 1853 *Tribune* article reveals another ideological connection between Whitman and Rose. This article is one that Whitman would likely not have missed, for it speaks of a favorite stance of his, free trade. The *Tribune* writer, Horace Greeley, attacks Rose's article that had appeared in the *Evening Post* in which Rose had spoken against the *Tribune*'s support for a protective tariff on the grounds that it would help working women. Rose disputes this claim. The *Tribune* responds: "Mrs. Rose is a Free Trader, which we are not."[10] William Cullen Bryant, editor of the *Post*, charged the *Tribune*, and hence Horace Greeley, with hypocrisy. The *Tribune* writer attacks the *Post* as much as he attacks Rose, but the salient point here is the issue of free trade, which for Rose formed part of her larger ideological stance: removing arbitrary boundaries that regulated people's actions and infringed upon their freedom. In the seven volumes of *With Walt Whitman in Camden,* protectionism is one of the issues that consistently rankled Whitman. "I am for free trade because I am for anything which will break down barriers between peoples: I want to see the countries all wide open." "Why is everybody more interested in boundary lines than in unity?—in sects, parties, classes, hates, passions? What a humbug is our so-called civilization if it can't lead us the way out of the jungle! As for free-trade—it is greatly to be desired, not because it is good for America, but because it is good for the world." "I would wipe out all . . . tariffs—all bars whatsoever to freedom—everything, the last stone, or wave of any sea, that would serve as bar, impediment, to intercourse, concord of people."[11] Rose's and Whitman's belief in free trade is a manifestation of their underlying assumption that people have a basic turn for concord if left to follow their own desires, an assumption that the Civil War tempered.

The editors of the first three volumes of *History of Woman Suffrage*—Elizabeth Cady Stanton, Susan B. Anthony, and Matilda Joslyn Gage—view Rose as "the earliest advocate of woman's enfranchisement in America . . . next to Frances Wright."[12] She spoke in twenty-three states—at the Infidel Conventions, the numerous Tom Paine anniversary celebrations, state legislatures, the Hartford Bible Con-

vention of Free-Thinkers, the anniversary of the West Indian Emancipation, at almost every National Woman's Rights Convention from
1850 to 1860, and at countless state and local woman's rights conventions as well.[13] In 1863 at a meeting of the Woman's National
Loyal League, she spoke for total emancipation of slaves.

Morris U. Schappes—historian, author, and editor—wrote a tribute to Rose in March 1948. The occasion for the tribute was Inter-
national Women's Day. Schappes speaks of the range of Rose's interest: "Ernestine Rose was a lecturer of high rank. Men who came to
taunt stayed to listen, admire, and respect. Among her subjects were
"The Science of Government," "Political Economy," "Equal Rights
of Women," "Antagonisms in Society," and the wrongs of the op-
pressed, especially women, labor, and slaves." Schappes speaks in detail about the extent of her work:

> When traveling was difficult and the Erie Canal was still one of the
> wonders of the world, Ernestine L. Rose brought her messages into
> metropolis and hamlet far and wide. During her first year in our
> country, she lectured in New York City and upstate in Hudson,
> Poughkeepsie, Albany, Schenectady, Saratoga, Utica, Syracuse,
> Rochester, Buffalo, Elmira "and other places." In 1837 she also went
> to Pennsylvania, speaking in Philadelphia, Bristol, Chester, Pitts-
> burgh "and other places," and in Wilmington, Delaware. In 1842 she
> went up into New England, and was on the platform in Hartford,
> Connecticut, and in Boston, Charlestown, Beverley, Florence,
> Springfield, "and other points" in Massachusetts. In 1844 she lec-
> tured in Boston from the same platform as Ralph Waldo Emerson,
> William Lloyd Garrison and Charles A. Dana. That year she went
> westward to Ohio, and made public appearances in Cincinnati, Day-
> ton, Zanesville, Springfield, Cleveland, Toledo "and several settle-
> ments in the backwoods of Ohio, and also in Richmond, Indiana."
> In 1845 and 1846, she was in Michigan. In Detroit she gave two lec-
> tures in the Hall of the State Legislature, and was the first to broach
> the question of equality of women in public agitation in the State,
> not only in Detroit but in Ann Arbor and elsewhere. The following
> year, she went South, speaking in Charleston and Columbia, South
> Carolina.[14]

The biographical sketch of Ernestine L. Rose in *History of Woman
Suffrage* informs us of her activities in New York alone: "In the winter

of 1855, Mrs. Rose spoke in thirteen of the fifty-four County conventions upon woman suffrage held in the State of New York, and each winter took part in the Albany conventions and hearings before the Legislature, which in 1860 resulted in the passage of the bill securing to women the right to their wages and the equal guardianship of their children."[15] One has only to read the *New York Tribune* to know that Ernestine L. Rose's name was familiar to any dedicated newspaper reader. Whitman was just that.

Depending on the politics of the reporters, she became for readers a Polish Jew, a foreigner, an exotic, and, finally, the "queen of the company"—an ironic epithet, given her egalitarian politics. In the 19 May 1860 issue of Henry Clapp's *Saturday Press,* in a column next to an advertisement in bold type announcing the appearance of the 1860 *Leaves of Grass,* Ada Clare, a regular columnist for the *Press,* spoke of the effect Rose had on her: "A good delivery, a forcible voice, the most uncommon good sense, a delightful terseness of style, and a rare talent for humor, are the qualifications which so well fit this lady for a public speaker."[16] She was fearless and confident, knew the power of concision, and had a finely tuned analytical mind. She thought on her feet; many of her speeches were extemporaneous and so come to us through reports taken by stenographers. She had a strong theoretical grounding into which to place the social realities of her time. She believed in the power of language to effect social change: "We have often been asked, 'What is the use of Conventions? Why talk? Why not go to work?' Just as if the thought did not precede the act! Those who act without previously thinking, are not good for much. Thought is first required, then the expression of it, and that leads to action; and action based upon thought never needs to be reversed; it is lasting and profitable, and produces the desired effect."[17]

She did not limit herself to theory, however. She frequently mentioned her 1836 experience canvassing New York state for months to get women's signatures on petitions in support of Judge Thomas Herttell's proposal for married women's property rights legislation. She could get only five signatures. Women told her that they had rights enough. She realized then that Frances Wright's work, groundbreaking though it was, had not reached many women. At the tenth National Woman's Rights Convention, held at Cooper Institute, New York City, 10–11 May 1860, Rose said:

I went from house to house with a petition for signatures simply asking for our Legislature to allow married women to hold real estate in their own name. What did I meet with? Why, the very name exposed one to ridicule, if not to worse treatment. The women said: 'We have rights enough; we want no more': and the men, as a matter of course, echoed it, and said: 'You have rights enough; nay, you have too many already.' But by perseverance in sending petitions to the Legislature, and, at the same time, enlightening the public mind on the subject, we at last accomplished our purpose. We had to adopt the method which physicians sometimes use, when they are called to a patient who is so hopelessly sick that he is unconscious of his pain and suffering. We had to describe to women their own position, to explain to them the burdens that rested so heavily upon them, and through these means, as a wholesome irritant, we roused public opinion of the subject, and through public opinion, we acted upon the Legislature, and in 1848–'49, they gave us the great boon for which we asked, by enacting that a woman who possessed property previous to marriage, or obtained it after marriage, should be allowed to hold it in her own name.[18]

Interestingly, Whitman used the physician analogy ten years later in "Democratic Vistas," in a similar context, except that whereas Rose speaks of attempting to change public consciousness in relation to woman's rights, Whitman speaks more broadly of "our times" as the object of analysis. Whitman: "I say we had best look our times and lands searchingly in the face, like a physician diagnosing some deep disease."[19] There is a correlation between what woman's rights activists were doing as they worked to demarginalize women's position in their society and what Whitman was doing as he too attempted to bring into *Leaves of Grass* and thus into American society all sorts of marginalized persons: women, men like himself whose sexual orientation was male/male rather than male/female and, by extension, women whose sexual orientation also did not fit the norm, people of minority races, and social "outcasts."

Rose, an immigrant herself and therefore to some extent an outcast, learned from her fieldwork experience that she would have to work primarily on a cognitive level to bring about a shift in, to use Abby Price's phrase, the "false public sentiment," but her fieldwork never ceased and never ceased to be significant to her. Rose also

never failed to credit Frances Wright's groundwork and spoke often
of the insuperable odds that faced her: "Frances Wright was the first
woman in this country who spoke on the equality of the sexes. She
had indeed a hard task before her. The elements were entirely un-
prepared. She had to break up the time-hardened soil of conservatism. She was subjected to public odium, slander, and persecution."[20]
Like Abby Price, Frances Wright and Ernestine L. Rose were both
involved with reform communities. Wright actually organized and
financed one; Rose was a force behind the Skaneateles community,
a reform community in northwestern New York that lasted from the
fall of 1843 to the summer of 1846. Frances Wright provided an effective model of an activist, theorist, and orator. Sean Wilentz speaks
of Wright's electric presence: "To [her] defiant rhetoric, Wright
added an electrifying presence unmatched by any previous New
York deist speaker, and possibly unmatched by any American speaker
of the day."[21] Both Wright and Rose had what Whitman himself says
he yearned for: the ability to speak directly to the people, without
the mediation of the written word. Both women had the qualities
Whitman mentions in "Vocalism":

> After these and more, it is just possible there comes to a man, a woman,
>   the divine power to speak words;
> Then toward that man or that woman swiftly hasten all—none refuse, all
>   attend,
> Armies, ships, antiquities, libraries, paintings, machines, cities, hate,
>   despair, amity, pain, theft, murder, aspiration, form in close ranks,
> They debouch as they are wanted to march obediently through the mouth
>   of that man or that woman. [*Variorum*, 2:308–9]

Likely, Whitman had reformers like Wright and Rose in mind—
in addition to himself—when he wrote "To a Pupil," which first appeared in the 1860 *Leaves of Grass:*

> Is reform needed? is it through you?
> The greater the reform needed, the greater the Personality you need to
>   accomplish it.
> You! do you not see how it would serve to have eyes, blood, complexion,
>   clean and sweet?
> Do you not see how it would serve to have such a body and soul that when
>   you enter the crowd an atmosphere of desire and command enters

with you, and every one is impress'd with your Personality? [*Variorum*, 2:413–14]

Numerous people and newspaper accounts speak of Rose's magnetic presence as an orator. When she spoke at the 1854 Albany state convention and before the state legislature meeting at that time, one account, from the *Albany Transcript,* listed the names of various women speakers and noted each woman's oratorical skill; the reporter brought the summary to a close extolling Rose's eloquence: "But Mrs. Rose is the queen of the company. On the educational question in particular, she rises to a high standard of oratorical power. When speaking of Hungary and her own crushed Poland, she is full of eloquence and pathos, and she has as great a power to chain an audience as any of our best male speakers."[22]

Like Rose, Frances Wright also possessed "magnetism" and "tact," to use Whitman's words for her.[23] As a boy he would go to hear her speak at Tammany Hall: "She spoke . . . every Sunday, about all sorts of reforms. Her views were very broad—she touched the widest range of themes—spoke informally, colloquially. She published while there the Free Inquirer, which my daddy took and I often read. We all loved her: fell down before her: her very appearance seemed to enthrall us."[24] At another time, he said: "[Frances Wright] was one of the few characters to excite in me a wholesale respect and love: she was beautiful in bodily shape and gifts of soul."[25] In still another conversation, when he and Horace Traubel were looking at Wright's portrait in her book *A Few Days in Athens,* Whitman said: "She was more than beautiful: she was grand! It was not features simply but soul—soul. There was a majesty about her."[26] Traubel replied that he had never heard him speak so glowingly about any other woman as he did about Wright. "I never felt so glowingly towards any other woman," Whitman answered. "She possessed herself of my body and soul."[27]

Stanton, Anthony, and Gage, editors of the first three volumes of *History of Woman Suffrage,* list three immediate causes that led to the demand for equal political rights for women in America. Antislavery agitation was one; the drive to change the legal status of married women's property rights was another; and the third cause leading to the demand for women's political rights was the innovative work done by two women, Frances Wright and Ernestine L. Rose: "A great educational work was accomplished by the able lectures of

Frances Wright, on political, religious, and social questions. Ernestine L. Rose, following in her wake, equally liberal in her religious
opinions, and equally well informed on the science of government,
helped to deepen and perpetuate the impression Frances Wright
had made on the minds of unprejudiced hearers."[28] I suggest that
we take seriously Whitman's admiration of Frances Wright and Ernestine L. Rose; once we do so, we admit into our study of Whitman
a radical context for understanding women's role in Whitman's concept of American democracy.

It would be nice if we had numerous notebook entries and letters
to flesh out more fully the story of Whitman and Rose's friendship,
but we don't. We do, however, have a notebook entry documenting
a conversation that Whitman had with her about Frances Wright.
The story that Rose tells Whitman about Wright replays the plot that
Rose outlined time and again at conventions: women's forfeiture of
rights upon marriage. Whitman, then, heard, personally and directly,
Frances Wright's story from arguably the most radical woman's
rights activist at the time. (Because of her family responsibilities,
Stanton was not able to be as active in the movement at this time as
Rose was.) In a 9 February 1857 notebook entry, Whitman writes:
"Frances Wright Madame Darusmont (talk with Mrs. Rose Feb. 9th,
'57." He carefully notes what Rose told him about Wright's early days,
before she came to the United States, and Rose's account of Wright's
marriage:

> [The] noble, (but much scorned) woman—married D'Arusmont—
> the great error of her life—he coveted her property—thwarted
> her—kept exclusive possession of her child, a daughter; Frances had
> great wealth (Mrs. Rose says $150,000)—D'A. obtained all—Frances
> died somewhere about 1853—a heart-broken, harassed woman—all
> her philanthropic schemes and ideas, coming to nought.[29]

Beyond the documentary value of the entry (proving that Whitman
and Rose did meet and talk), it shows us Whitman *listening to* Rose,
one of the most theoretically astute and passionately dedicated
women's rights activists of his time, *talking about* the first woman's
rights activist to speak publicly in America on women's condition.
In addition to this notebook entry, there are three other entries
for Rose. The entries catalog her changes of address: "Mrs. Rose 72
White st. or 74—husband engraver name on the door"; "Mrs. Rose,

95 Prince"; "Mrs. Ernestine L. Rose 19 University Place cor 9th st N.Y. City/Mr. W. E. Rose, Silversmith 561 Broadway N.Y. city."[30]

Whitman's 1856 texts—*Leaves of Grass,* "The Primer of Words," *The Eighteenth Presidency!*—the notebooks he kept during the years 1850–1860, and the 1860 *Leaves of Grass* all indicate the close connections he had with Rose, as well as with Price and Davis. Once Whitman moved from New York, for whatever complex set of reasons, the effect Rose, Price, and Davis had on his reformist passages imaging female activists in *Leaves of Grass* slowly diminished, as he began to change some of the explicitly reformist or publicly political lines in *Leaves of Grass* to the representation best expressed as the Mother of All, stressing the community ("We") more than the individual woman ("I"). But certainly he had deeply felt these women's influence. We see and hear the effects of their influence just as we hear Rose's words in Whitman's poem "France."

Few of Rose's letters or private documents exist, and so in order to learn about her views, some of which we know she shared with Whitman, we must study the speeches she made. These speeches repeatedly emphasize the commitment Rose had to the principle of equal rights for all; these rights, she stated over and over again, were "natural" rights. Without these rights, women were not in actuality citizens of the United States at all. Without the vote, women were without rights.

Much of the early woman's rights activists' efforts went into educating women on their rights and persuading them that they could indeed act. Resolutions read by Rose at the opening of the 1856 National Woman's Rights Convention articulate in no uncertain terms the stance activists took regarding their noncitizen status:

> *Resolved,* That the present uncertain and inconsistent position of woman in our community, not fully recognized either as a slave or as an equal, taxed but not represented, authorized to earn property but not free to control it, permitted to prepare papers for scientific bodies but not to read them, urged to form political opinions but not allowed to vote upon them, all marks a transitional period in human history which can not long endure.
>
> *Resolved,* That the main power of the woman's rights movement lies in this: that while always demanding for woman better education, better employment, and better laws, it has kept steadily in view the one cardinal demand for the right of suffrage; in a democracy

the symbol and guarantee of all other rights.

Resolved, That the monopoly of the elective franchise, and thereby all the powers of legislative government by man, solely on the ground of sex, is a usurpation, condemned alike by reason and common-sense, subversive of all the principles of justice, oppressive and demoralizing in its operation, and insulting to the dignity of human nature.[31]

The resolutions call for women to *demand* what is already theirs: rights inherent to them by right of birth, and they recall Rose's own words set down by Whitman: "The capacity of the true man for turning upon his oppressor is one of the glories of the race—its security, in fact." The "transitional period" spoken of in the first resolution had come.

Whitman's 1860 poem "Starting from Paumanok" includes lines that speak to sentiments expressed in the resolutions. A line previously mentioned "O to level occupations and the sexes! O to bring all to common ground! O adhesiveness!" if read at the end of the twentieth century, does not speak startling sentiments. Read in 1860, within the agitation that the women's rights movement had provoked, it speaks radical sentiments. Work and sexuality, concerns that the radical woman's rights activists addressed, were to be shared equally by male and female. The line also insists that adhesiveness is shared by men and women alike. It can be read as meaning that adhesiveness or "friendship"—which, I repeat, had for its icon two women embracing—includes sexual love without distinction as to sexual orientation (female/female, male/male, female/male) and also levels the distinction between sexual and nonsexual relationships. Lines from another 1856 poem, in time titled "Song of the Answerer," also speaks of leveling:

> The words of the true poems give you more than poems,
> They give you to form for yourself poems, religions, politics, war,
>   peace, behavior, histories, essays, daily life, and every thing else,
> They balance ranks, colors, races, creeds, and the sexes. [*Variorum,* 1:143]

And in yet another 1856 poem, "By Blue Ontario's Shore," the inscription of equality and diversity is directly addressed: "Here the flowing trains, here the crowds, equality, diversity, the soul loves" (*Variorum,* 1:194).

The concept of adhesiveness provided the paradigm for the structure of the woman's rights movement, 1850–1860. At the 1852 National Woman's Rights Convention, held in Syracuse, New York, the subject of a national society was introduced. As a result of the discussion at this time, no more formal type of organization for the movement was instituted than the continuance of the central committee, "composed of representative men and women of the several states."[32] The function of this committee was to organize the yearly national conventions. To argue against a formal organization regulating the woman's movement a letter from Angelina Grimké Weld was read. Grimké Weld's comments on "the natural ties of spiritual affinity" sound much like Whitman's adhesiveness as articulated in "Democratic Vistas" and "Over the Carnage Rose Prophetic a Voice" and much like the organicism of Whitman's own poetics. Here are Grimké Weld's words:

> Organization is two-fold—natural and artificial, divine and human. Natural organizations are based on the principle of progression; the eternal law of change. But human or artificial organizations are built upon the principle of crystallization; they fix the conditions of society; they seek to daguerreotype themselves, not on the present age only, but on future generations; hence, they fetter and distort the expanding mind. Organizations do not protect the sacredness of the individual; their tendency is to sink the individual in the mass, to sacrifice his rights, and immolate him on the altar of some fancied good.
>
> Such an organization as now actually exists among the women of America I hail with heartfelt joy. We are bound together by the natural ties of spiritual affinity; we are drawn together because we are attracted toward one common center—the good of humanity. We need no external bonds to bind us together, no cumbrous machinery to keep our minds and hearts in unity of purpose and effort; we are not the lifeless staves of a barrel which can be held together only by the iron hoops of artificial organization.[33]

Such "natural ties of spiritual affinity" which Grimké Weld describes as women's, binding them together, are what Whitman hails for men in "Over the Carnage Rose Prophetic a Voice," a poem that first appeared in protoform in the 1860 *Leaves of Grass* but that Whitman altered and renamed and placed in the 1865 *Drum-Taps*. Though

Grimké Weld's letter did not appear in the *Tribune*'s coverage of the 1852 convention, it was printed as a tract.[34] Also, Lydia Fowler, convention secretary, could have shared its contents with Whitman. Whatever the connection between Grimké Weld's tract and Whitman's poem, and even if there are no direct textual connections, the similarities of imagery, diction, and concept are striking.

> It shall be customary in the houses and streets to see manly affection,
> The most dauntless and rude shall touch face to face lightly,
> The dependence of Liberty shall be lovers,
> The continuance of Equality shall be comrades.

> These shall tie you and band you stronger than hoops of iron,
> I, ecstatic, O partners! O lands! with the love of lovers tie you.

> (Were you looking to be held together by lawyers?
> Or by an agreement on a paper? or by arms?
> Nay, nor the world, nor any living thing, will so cohere.) [*Variorum*, 2:374]

But in "Starting from Paumanok," there is a line that particularly bears on suffrage, the issue that Ernestine L. Rose stressed more than any other. This line appears in "Paumanok" in the 1860 edition of *Leaves of Grass* only, following line 258. It reads: "See the populace, millions upon millions, handsome, tall, muscular, both sexes, clothed in easy and dignified clothes—teaching, commanding, marrying, generating, equally electing and elective."

This line is remarkable, given the historical context. Such a line in 1860 would place Whitman without question with the woman's rights advocates; it further enables us to read *Leaves of Grass* as a woman's rights text. The line starts with the imperative: "[You] see the populace." It tells the "you," the reader, just *how* she or he will see the populace, which is exactly the way Rose wanted the populace to be seen: both sexes strong; both dressed in the manner for which women agitated and the manner in which Whitman dressed in the 1855 *Leaves of Grass* frontispiece; both teaching, both sexes commanding, both marrying and generating; and, of utmost importance, both sexes electing and capable of being elected, an imperative for Rose, since she saw the ballot as the underlying power that would protect any and all other rights.[35] The image of women that this line suggests is far more radical than many of the images that remained intact in *Leaves*. It recalls the radicalism of "The Primer of

Words." Such a line, coupled with the images of women presented in "Mediums" and "Vocalism," does much to counter the notion that Whitman's images of women are always tied to the domestic.

Whitman kept lines in "Starting from Paumanok" that were not so topical in nature but that still aimed at gender equality:

> Here lands female and male,
> Here the heir-ship and heiress-ship of the world, here the flame of
>   materials,
> Here spirituality the translatress, the openly-avow'd,
> .   .   .   .
> Yes here comes my mistress the soul.
>
> .   .   .   .
> Democracy! near at hand to you a throat is now inflating itself and joyfully
>   singing.
> Ma femme! for the brood beyond us and of us,
> .   .   .   .
> And I will show of male and female that either is but the equal of the
>   other. [*Variorum*, 2:277, 282]

There are many other lines in "Starting from Paumanok" in which Whitman uses language that explicitly includes women as readers and inscribes equality, as in the line "And I will show of male and female that either is but the equal of the other." As this passage and countless others in *Leaves of Grass* indicate, passages in which both forms of the gender-marked pronoun forms are used, Whitman was acutely sensitive to the implications of gender-marked language. Part of this insistence on using both forms reflected Whitman's desire to leave no doubt as to his audience: he wanted women as well as men to believe that *Leaves of Grass* was addressing them. In the 1850s, woman's rights activists fought to have women *included* in the generic "man" and "men," thus including women in the body politic, thus arguing that when the Declaration of Independence said that all men were created equal, the meaning was that all people were created equal. Whitman uses the generic argument in a letter to a postmaster in Washington, D.C., which was probably written in 1872. In the letter, Whitman argues for an inclusive interpretation of the word "book," using "man" as analogy: "All *literary Mss.* are "Book manuscripts," and when printed, they become "Books"—and the law covers *all* (literary matter)—To contend otherwise would be same as to confine the meaning of the word *man* as used by metaphysicians and statesmen (by Jefferson in the Declaration of Independence for instance,) to mean a full grown *male person only*—while, of course, it is an ensemble and generic term, for both sexes, and all ages."[36] This statement makes Whitman's use of both gendered pronouns all the more self-consciously desirous of inclusivity. Since the culture read "man" not as "human" but as male, Whitman had to specify the terms of his address. Whitman also conceived of "Kosmos"—the word he used to delineate the *Leaves of Grass* poet-persona as "macrocosmic"—as masculine and feminine: "Kosmos, noun masculine or feminine, a person who[se] scope of mind, or whose range in a particular science, includes all, the known universe."[37] In yet another entry, he writes: "in Names—a suggestion. The woman should preserve her own name, just as much after marriage as before. Also all titles must be dropped—no Mr. or Mrs. or Miss any more."[38]

Along with this awareness of the inclusive generic, which of course is just what feminists have had to fight so hard to eradicate, now seeing it as detrimental, is Whitman's attempt to demarcate gender with his "-ess" suffix. He never resolved the problem of gendered language; at least the self-consciousness of the language indicates his continued awareness or concern. A notebook entry dating around 1856 shows his thinking on the issue:

> All through, a *common* gender ending in *ist* as—
> lovist
> hatist   both masc & fem
> hater   m
> hatress f   &c[39]

Whitman repeats this line of thought in another notebook entry:

> masc.} orator
>   oratist   both masc & fem.
> fem.} oratress
> m   reader
>   readist—both m & f
> fem.   readress[40]

Gender markings gave women trouble as well, as an article in the *Lily* demonstrates. The article reports on the fifth National Woman's

Rights Convention and mentions the *Una,* the journal published by Paulina Wright Davis, who is called "the Editress."[41]

The 1860 poem "Says," which Whitman eventually excluded from *Leaves of Grass,* speaks for cultivation of the intellect, against slavery, indirectly against property laws that controlled married women, for dress reform, against reading romances (which by and large inscribed female passivity), and, finally, for equal political rights for all—all points that Rose, Davis, Price, and other woman's rights activists made over and over.

2

I say nourish a great intellect, a great brain;
If I have said anything to the contrary, I hereby retract it.

3

I say man shall not hold property in man;
I say the least developed person on earth is just as important and sacred to
    himself or herself, as the most developed person is to himself or herself.

4

I say where liberty draws not the blood out of slavery, there slavery draws
    the blood out of liberty,
I say the word of the good old cause in These States, and resound it hence
    over the world.

5

.   .   .   .
And I say that clean-shaped children can be jetted and conceived only
    where natural forms prevail in public, and the human face and form
    are never caricatured;
And I say that genius need never more be turned to romances,
(For facts properly told, how mean appear all romances.)

6

.   .   .   .
I say discuss all and expose all—I am for every topic openly;
I say there can be no salvation for These States without innovators—

without free tongues, and ears willing to hear the tongues;
And I announce as a glory of These States, that they respectfully listen to
    propositions, reforms, fresh views and doctrines, from successions
    of men and women,
Each age with its own growth.

8

With one man or woman—(no matter which one—I even pick out the
    lowest,)
With him or her I now illustrate the whole law;
I say that every right, in politics or what-not, shall be eligible to that one
    man or woman, on the same terms as any. [Emphasis added][42]

This last line says just what Rose, Price, Davis, Mott, Stanton, and others kept hammering into the public consciousness. "Says" is the poetic rendering of those 1856 resolutions (and countless other resolutions) read by Ernestine L. Rose. It too issues a call. Listening to "propositions, reforms, fresh views and doctrines" meant listening to woman's rights activists whose fresh views followed on the heels of antislavery demands; it meant hearing that women were "eligible" to vote on the same terms as men. In this poem, antislavery and woman's rights are blended, as they so often were in the two movements themselves in the decade of the 1850s.

The "George Walker" notebook reveals Whitman thinking further about the word "eligibility."

Idea to pervade largely /
Eligibility—I, you, any one eligible to the condition or attributes or
    advantages of any being, no matter who,—.[43]

In another notebook entry, "All Others Have Adhered," Whitman wrote: "The foreign theory is that a man or woman receives rights by grant, demise, or inheritance. The theory of These States is that humanity's rights belong to every man, every woman, in the inherent nature of things, and cannot be alienated, or, if alienated, must be brought back and resumed.—"[44] This stripped-down two-sentence notebook entry expresses the substance of Whitman's belief in the ultimate rightness and eventual dominance of democracy as a system of government, founded on the belief in "natural rights." His poetry, indeed his life's work, was based on his belief in democracy. He used the word "feudalism" to stand for the concept expressed in the first sentence of his entry ("The foreign theory"); the word "democracy" stands for the concept expressed in the second ("humanity's rights belong to every man, every woman"). He made a poetry that attempted to represent that second concept.

With such theoretical grounding, words like those used in resolution 1 issued at the 1854 Albany state convention made it impossible not to include women as equal citizens under the law. (The Resolution itself, however, shows the inconsistencies of the times as it plays on the notion of divisiveness, making the distinction between mothers, sisters, wives, and daughters and aliens, criminals, idiots, and minors.) Resolution 1 reads:

> 1. *Resolved,* That the men who claim to be Christian Republicans, and yet class their mothers, sisters, wives, and daughters among aliens, criminals, idiots, and minors, unfit to be their coequal citizens, are guilty of absurd inconsistency and presumption; that for males to govern females, without consent asked or granted, is to perpetuate an aristocracy, utterly hostile to the principles and spirit of free institutions; and that it is time for the people of the United States and every State in the Union to put away forever that remnant of despotism and feudal oligarchy, the caste of sex.[45]

If Whitman had been so inclined to avoid the issue of woman's rights, as he was not, hearing words such as "aristocracy," "despotism," and "feudal oligarchy" would have made it nearly impossible for him to avoid confronting the issue of woman's rights (and slavery) and the fact that the United States had not, after all, succeeded in inventing a new world order.

The argument for human rights was the one most used by Rose in her many speeches before woman's rights conventions. In 1854 at the fifth National Woman's Rights Convention, Rose articulated this argument in an unusually rich manner. It was a line of reasoning that she elaborated again and again:

> There is one argument which in my estimation is the argument of arguments, why woman should have her rights; not on account of expediency, not on account of policy, though these too show the reasons why she should have her rights; but we claim—I for one

claim, and presume all our friends claim—our rights on the broad ground of human rights; and I for one again will say, I promise not how we shall use them. I will no more promise how we shall use our rights than man has promised before he obtained them, how he would use them. We all know that rights are often abused; and above all things have human rights in this country been abused, from the very fact that they have been withheld from half of the community.[46]

Rose kept attempting to make the concepts of the Declaration of Independence give birth to social realities, as in an 1860 speech: "By human rights we mean natural rights, and upon that ground we claim our rights, and upon that ground they have already been conceded by the Declaration of Independence, in that first great and immutable truth which is proclaimed in that instrument, 'that all men are created equal, and that therefore all are entitled to certain inalienable rights, among which are life, liberty, and the pursuit of happiness.' "[47]

As late as 1856, Whitman believed in the power of the Declaration of Independence and the Constitution to shape an actual nation, though as time went on he tempered this belief in documents with his theory of comradeship, or adhesiveness, and by 1871, in "Democratic Vistas," he makes it clear that documents form only the first step in nation building. The second step, that of setting up the material bases of a nation, must be followed by the third. He called this third step spiritual democracy, and by that he meant much the same thing as Angelina Grimké Weld when she spoke of the "natural ties of spiritual affinity," the human values needed for democracy. For Whitman, these values would come to the people through its national literature. In 1856, however, Whitman still spoke of America's great organic documents. He made one of the most precise statements explicating his belief in the power of the Declaration of Independence and the Constitution in his 1856 tract "The Eighteenth Presidency." In it he called the Constitution the second of the American organic compacts. The first was the Declaration of Independence with its proclamation "thenceforth to consider all men to be born free and equal into the world, each one possessed of inalienable rights to life and liberty."[48] After the war, Whitman found it difficult to remain optimistic about his country. After the war and after the Republicans, Democrats, Abolitionists, and some segments of the woman's rights organizations continued to deny women the vote and thus citizenship, Rose saw that it would be impossible for the woman's movement to maintain the momentum that it had achieved during the decade of the 1850s. After thirty-three years of activist work in the United States, she left to live in England.

Rose's departure came in 1869. In 1853, still very much the activist, she spoke at the anniversary celebration of the British West Indies emancipation. Accounts of this celebration as well as the text of Rose's speech appeared in numerous newspapers, including the *New York Daily Tribune,* the *National Anti-Slavery Standard,* the *Liberator,* the *New York Daily Times,* and the *New York Herald.* Though Whitman may not have joined the crowd of five or six hundred women and men who gathered at a grove in Brooklyn to celebrate the anniversary, he could hardly have avoided reading about the event and Rose's speech itself. At the end of her speech she spoke of the unfulfilled terms of the Declaration of Independence: "All women are excluded from the enjoyment of that liberty which your Declaration of Independence asserts to be the inalienable right of all. The same right to life, liberty, and the pursuit of happiness, that pertains to man, pertains to woman also. For what is life without liberty? Which of you here before me would not willingly risk his or her life, if in danger of being made a slave?"[49] As in "Says" when Whitman speaks of democracy ("the word of the good old cause in These States") and its absence in any slave-holding nation, Rose also speaks of liberty's absence in the United States. Both Whitman and Rose expand the logic of liberty to include equal rights for women (an issue of sexual equality) with the abolishment of slavery (a race issue). One needs go only to the next step to see that liberty is also denied those who are marginalized because of sexual orientation. In *Walt Whitman's Native Representations,* Ed Folsom speaks of the relationship between photography and Whitman's democratic poetics. "For Whitman, taboos were nothing but signals of resistant pockets of reality that had not yet been shown by the poet to fit into the ecstatic fullness and wholeness of life."[50] In 1856, in "The Primer of Words," Whitman said that we needed new words "to embody the new political facts, the compact of the Declaration of Independence, and of the Constitution." New words were needed, as well, "to answer the modern, rapidly spreading, faith, of the vital equality of women with men, and that they are to be placed on an exact plane, politically, socially, and in business, with men."[51]

The language of inalienable rights and belief in the "organic

compacts" were very much on Whitman's tongue in 1856. In his
1856 letter to Emerson, he said: "Women in These States approach
the day of that organic equality with men, without which, I see, men
cannot have organic equality among themselves."[52] Women, because
of their gender, were, however, "alienated." In the 1860 *Leaves of
Grass,* directly following "France," as if Ernestine L. Rose were still
on his mind, Whitman arranged a series of seven short poems he
called "Thoughts." "Thoughts. 4." addresses the theme of eligibility:

> Of Equality—As if it harmed me, giving others the same chances and rights
>   as myself—As if it were not indispensable to my own rights that
>   others possess the same;
> Of Justice—As if Justice could be any thing but the same ample law,
>   expounded by natural judges and saviours,
> As if it might be this thing or that thing, according to decisions.[53]

Whitman did not delete "Thoughts" from *Leaves of Grass,* but he
broke it up into three separate poems with other poems inter-
spersed. The final versions, because of the fragmentation, lose the
impact that the original poem has in the 1860 *Leaves of Grass,* the
impact that it had for the 1860 reader who would have had in mind
not only the issue of slavery but also woman's rights. To be eligible
to take part in a country's public life meant to be politically, socially,
and sexually equal.

The call for the seventh National Woman's Right Convention
illustrates the tactics that the activists were using by 1856. The seventh convention took place in October at the Broadway Tabernacle
in New York City; the call appeared on 3 September, the same month
that the 1856 *Leaves of Grass* went on sale. It helps to hear this language and to remember that Whitman also heard it. It creates a context for reading the more radical reformist poems Whitman later
deleted from *Leaves of Grass.* Here is the 1856 call:

> In this epoch of political and social excitement, the advocates of the
> Equal Rights of Woman find new reason to proclaim again their con-
> stant demand for a consistent application of democratic principles,
> for the emancipation not alone of one class or one nation, but of
> one-half the human race.
> We accordingly invite
> All who believe that Government derives its just powers from the
> consent of the governed;—

All who believe that Taxation and Representation should go together;—
All who believe in the right of all to a Trial by a Jury of their Peers;—
All who believe in a fair day's wages for a fair day's work;—
All who believe in the equal right of all children in the community to its public provisions for Education;
To meet in Convention at the Broadway Tabernacle,
New York, on the 8th, 9th, and 10th of October next, to consider whether these rights and principles shall continue to be popularly limited to one-half the members of the community.

In *Visionary Compacts,* Donald Pease says that the self-evident truths cited in the Declaration of Independence were not in jeopardy as long as they were part of the "cultural unconscious" and were made a subject of public talk only at celebrations of national holidays. "At the time Whitman wrote, however," Pease says, "the principles that should have remained unconscious were themselves the subject of a partisan debate destined to eventuate in the mass demonstration we commemorate as the Civil War."[54] The debate also took place in women's rights. Liberty, Pease says, "lost its value as an inalienable, self-evident truth" when it became used as a common means of talking about political disagreements—for example, when the South claimed the states were losing their rights (liberty) because slave-holding was threatened. For women, the "self-evident truths" of the Declaration of Independence had never been part of the cultural unconscious. Activists like Rose, Price, and Davis literally had to write and speak themselves into their culture's consciousness. They did so using numerous tactics. The call given above, drawing on the language of the Bill of Rights and the Declaration of Independence, was one way.

Whitman's 1856 "Poem of Remembrance for a Girl or a Boy of These States" was another means of cultural inscription. It almost answers the 1856 call. In this poem, Whitman commands his readers to remember the words of the "organic compact" that supposedly set forth the terms by which the citizens of the United States would live. The Union had disintegrated rapidly as fracture after political fracture foretold the coming war; the 1848 Seneca Falls Convention and the yearly National Woman's Rights Convention, as well as the numerous state and local conventions, brought great agitation in their wake. Set in the context of these events, the poem expresses Whitman's fears as he saw the nation's founding contractual words becoming less and less a reality and more a travesty. In some passages of "Remembrance," the lines seem an outgrowth of "The Eighteenth Presidency" and "The Primer of Words"; in other lines, Rose herself seems to be speaking.

In its 1856 form, Whitman used "Poem of Remembrance for a Girl or a Boy of These States" as the poem's title. In the 1860 edition, it reappeared as "Chants Democratic. 6." Whitman deleted the first twenty-one lines of the poem in the 1867 edition of *Leaves of Grass* and called the poem "Think of the Soul"; after the 1871 edition, he no longer included the poem in any form. The pattern recurs once again: the 1856 and 1860 editions of *Leaves of Grass* contain by far the most radical representations of woman's rights as articulated by the most radical woman's rights activists. These representations call for more than a glorification of motherhood. They call for women to claim their inherent rights and for the country to recognize the equality of men and women under the law. Not all of the women working for woman's rights during that first wave of woman's rights activism in the 1850s went as far as this poem goes in their demands. Price, Davis, and Rose did. These women were, I repeat, Whitman's friends.

The poem calls for the theoretical grounding of the Declaration of Independence to be remembered: "Remember, government is to subserve individuals." Whitman asks that the girl and boy of these states remember, recall, anticipate, shirk nothing, think of the soul, think of loving and being loved, think of the past. (The first line is an 1860 addition.) The poem begins:

> You just maturing youth! You male or female!
> Remember the organic compact of These States,
> Remember the pledge of the Old Thirteen thenceforward to the rights, life,
>   liberty, equality of man,
> Remember what was promulged by the founders, ratified by The States,
>   signed in black and white by the Commissioners, and read by
>   Washington at the head of the army,
> Remember the purposes of the founder,—Remember Washington;
>
> Anticipate when the thirty or fifty millions, are to become the hundred or
>   two hundred millions, of equal freedmen and freewomen, amicably
>   joined. [*Variorum*, 1:252]

This last line calls to mind the opening of "The Eighteenth Presidency!" In the second paragraph of that tract, Whitman breaks down the population numerically to show that in 1856 the United States was led not by the majority but by "limber-tongued lawyers, very fluent but empty, feeble old men, professional politicians, dandies, dyspeptics, and so forth, and rarely drawn from the solid body of the people."[55] In his breakdown of the population, he claims: "The States being altogether about thirty millions, seven tenths of whom are women and children" making the point that power was in the hands of the few. By using the terms "freedmen" and "freewomen," Whitman addresses race ("freedmen") and sex ("freewomen"). In the following lines, the poem focuses on women, on women and girls who do not sit (or lie) at home, passive. They claim the space which is theirs by virtue of life:

> Anticipate the best women;
> I say an unnumbered new race of hardy and well-defined women are to
> spread through all These States,
> I say a girl fit for These States must be free, capable, dauntless, just the
> same as a boy.

Assertion of personhood, however, does not mean separatism:

> The race is never separated—nor man nor woman escapes;
> All is inextricable—things, spirits, Nature, nations, you too—from
> precedents you come.

The poem ends with four lines mentioning the word "woman" five times:

> Think of womanhood, and you to be a woman;
> The creation is womanhood;
> Have I not said that womanhood involves all?
> Have I not told how the universe has nothing better than the best
> womanhood? [*Variorum*, 252–54]

The line "The creation is womanhood" states a principle that Whitman frequently treated indirectly, the connection that Whitman made between women's gestation and birthing capabilities and poetic creation.

Whitman's fusion in this poem of the primacy of the Declaration of Independence and the patriotic appeal of the Founding Fathers with woman's rights was a rhetorical device that Rose frequently used. That appeal structured her 1853 "Address on the Anniversary of West Indian Emancipation." Here she used the appeal to rights and to patriotism, an emotional appeal, to argue for the emancipation of American slaves, ending her address with her appeal for women's rights to life, liberty, and the pursuit of happiness, an appeal for gender equality as well as racial equality. In addition, just as Whitman began his poem with the appeal to patriotism, Rose began her address by referring to national celebrations: "I love to attend such anniversaries; I think the effect is very beneficial. Many such are celebrated in this country. New England celebrates the anniversary of the landing of the Pilgrim Fathers, and well she may." She moves from the Pilgrims to the Fourth of July, calling it the anniversary of the Declaration of Independence. Her speech uses many of the rhetorical strategies of Frederick Douglass's "What to the Slave Is the Fourth of July?" delivered a year earlier, on 2 July 1852, in Rochester, New York. This poem of Whitman's, "Remembrance for a Girl or a Boy of These States," fits into the Douglass-Rose rhetorical pattern.[56]

One of the strong structural patterns in "Drum-Taps" is Whitman's use of the Washington vignette. He portrays Washington and his troops besieged, with Washington reading the Declaration of Independence to his troops. But the "Drum-Taps" poet-persona calls on the memory of diverse Founding Fathers—Washington, Franklin, Jefferson, and Paine. Rose used this strategy as well in her West Indian Emancipation Address, but frequently she went further and also called on Frances Wright and other women who were known to at least some of her audience.

The line from "Remembrance" "Remember the pledge of the Old Thirteen thence-forward to the rights, life, liberty, equality of man" articulates the bedrock of Rose's argument, succinctly expressed in an 1852 National Woman's Rights Convention resolution: "*Resolved,* that we ask not for our rights as a gift of charity, but as an act of justice."[57] At the New York state 1853 convention, she said:

> This was termed a Woman's Rights movement. Alas! that the painful necessity should exist, for Women's calling a Convention to claim her rights from those who have been created to go hand in hand,

and heart and heart with her, whose interests cannot be divided from hers. Why does she claim them? Because every human being has a right to all the advantages society has to bestow, if his having them does not injure the right of others. Life is valueless without liberty, and shall we not claim that which is dearer than life? Oppression always produces suffering through the whole of the society where it exists; this movement ought, therefore, to be called a Human Right's movement.[58]

We see, once more, Rose's attempt to will social consciousness into the people. "With the present arrangement of society, social influence alone seems the only strong lever," she said. "Let the people be made right, and their representatives will speedily see the great truth."[59] At other times, she rested her faith in legality: "The laws of the country create sentiments. Our law-makers give the popular ideas of morality."[60] For her, electing public officials determined not only the laws one lived under but also the shape of a country's moral values.

The issue of authority came up in the 1852 National Woman's Rights Convention. Rose wanted complete separation of church and state; she saw ministers and lawmakers as the primary generators of oppression. She well knew the power of interpretation. Antoinette Brown, one of her sister activists, proposed a resolution, however, to authorize a "feminist" interpretation of the Bible. Brown, who was the first woman to be ordained a minister in the United States, offered the following: "*Resolved,* God created the first human pair equal in rights, possessions, and authority. He bequeathed the earth to them as a joint inheritance; gave them joint domain over the irrational creation; but none over each other." Ernestine L. Rose objected to Brown's interpretation. She said that she saw "no need to appeal to any written authority, particularly when it is so obscure and indefinite as to admit of different interpretations." She appealed to the example of the Founding Fathers: "When the inhabitants of Boston converted their harbor into a teapot rather than submit to unjust taxes, they did not go to the Bible for their authority; for if they had, they would have been told from the same authority to 'give unto Caesar what belonged to Caesar.' "[61]

Lucretia Mott agreed with Rose. Her Quaker belief in inner authority and her experience in the antislavery movement shaped her view. Rose, a Jewish secularist, and Mott, a Hicksite Quaker, professed a belief in the individual as the interpreter of texts, written or cultural, in preference to reliance on an official interpretation. When Whitman read newspaper accounts of views such as Rose's and Mott's, he heard them articulating his own stance.

Whitman, like Rose, felt that if the people could "read" corrupt lawmakers and sectarian religious leaders, they would have one more device to free themselves to live the life that the Declaration of Independence promised. His 1860 poem "Thought" puts into poetry the same thoughts that Rose put into prose:

> Of public opinion,
> Of a calm and cool fiat sooner or later, (how impassive! how certain and
>   final!)
> Of the President with pale face asking secretly to himself, *What will the*
>   *people say at last?*
> Of the frivolous Judge—of the corrupt Congressman, Governor, Mayor—of
>   such as these standing helpless and exposed,
> Of the mumbling and screaming priest, (soon, soon deserted,)
> Of the lessening year by year of venerableness, and of the dicta of officers,
>   statutes, pulpits, schools,
> Of the rising forever taller and stronger and broader of the institutions of
>   men and women, and of Self-esteem and Personality;
> Of the true New World—of the Democracies resplendent en-masse,
> Of the conformity of politics, armies, navies, to them,
> Of the shining sun by them—of the inherent light, greater than the rest,
> Of the envelopment of all by them, and the effusion of all from them.
>   [*Variorum,* 2:351–52]

This poem does not appear in the contents of the 1860 *Leaves of Grass;* in the book itself, it is entitled "Thought" and faces the "Children of Adam" cluster, like a frontispiece. The main point of the poem is that the inherent rights (in the poem, "inherent light") will be enacted by the people and that the institutions and officers of these institutions will have to take their cues from the people, rather than the other way around. In order for this to happen, Whitman and Rose knew, the people had to rely on their own interpretation of their world. They had to read with their own eyes. The 1856 persona of "Song of the Open Road" exhorted the great companions to join him to see (read) with their own eyes: "Allons! from all formules! / From your formules, O bat-eyed and materialistic priests"

(*Variorum,* 1:233). In "By Blue Ontario's Shore," also an 1856 poem, Whitman wrote:

> People's lips salute only doers, lovers, satisfiers, positive knowers,
> There will shortly be no more priests, I say their work is done.
>   [*Variorum,* 1:204]

In the 1855 "Song of Myself," Whitman said: "He most honors my style who learns under it to destroy the teacher" (*Variorum,* 1:76). When Lucretia Mott and Ernestine L. Rose called on the women at the convention to read with their own eyes and not to inscribe an official reading of the Bible as convention doctrine, they were in line with the cultural work that Whitman felt *Leaves of Grass* performed as it demanded from its readers active participation in the making of the poem. Rose rejected the control over individual minds that she felt organized religion enforced, and she called for each reader to be her or his own interpreter.

In addition to the argument for human rights on which Ernestine Rose focused, many activists claimed that moral superiority was grounds for changing laws and conditions. This argument, based in biology, held that women by nature were morally superior to men and that including them in the body politic would improve society (a version of the "greatest good" argument). Women's moral and emotional "nature" took its cue from women's biological makeup. The body, then, dictated women's roles and places in society. Women's bodies supposedly made gentle, moral, nurturing humans, a result of their reproductive capabilities. According to activists who used the moral superiority argument, gentleness and nurturing were precisely what society needed. The moral superiority reasoning, a form of essentializing, can be seen as an argument of expediency.

Rarely did the activists keep the human rights argument and the moral superiority argument separate, though indeed, logically, the human rights argument canceled out that of moral superiority. Activists contradicted themselves as they used one argument or another to achieve an end. In this respect, Ernestine L. Rose is unusual. Rose's wide exposure and experience in European and English reform circles before her arrival in the United States helped make her mind more finely tuned to the issues facing the activists than were most other activists' minds. Her mind worked theoretically, as her feet and hands walked and talked a pragmatic reform strategy. She believed that arguing only against the double standard—against specific injustices—amounted to seeking reform on too narrow a ground. She did not deny the effectiveness of or need for this reform strategy. She used it herself, though not as a primary rhetorical tool. She rarely used the moral superiority argument, however, since its alignment with biological determinism did not fit her rational mind-set and training. Mainly, she argued for what she saw as self-evident facts: that no one element in the species deserved special privileges at the expense of another—in the "nature" of things, that is. Whitman was not as consistent as Rose, nor were most of the other activists.

Different activists weighted their rhetoric one way or the other. Whether arguing for women's inherent rights that were denied them or against a double standard, both arguments frequently relied on the "greatest good" principle: what was good for women was good for men and ultimately for the country. Elizabeth Cady Stanton, however, saw a trap in the "greatest good" argument, and at the 1860 National Woman's Rights Convention held at the Cooper Institute in New York City, she rejected it: "In the settlement, then, of any question, we must simply consider the highest good of the individual."[62]

The 1860 National Woman's Rights Convention took place on 10–11 May, a week before Henry Clapp began running advertisements announcing the appearance of the third edition of *Leaves of Grass*. The letters written by women defending the new edition of *Leaves of Grass* that appeared in the June issues of Clapp's New York paper contained arguments and sentiments that were articulated at this convention, a convention known for Elizabeth Cady Stanton's strong call for legal reform in married women's rights and for an overhaul of the divorce laws. But Stanton and the 1860 convention had been preceded by ten years of agitation. From the beginning of the conventions in 1850, Rose, Davis, Price, Clarina Howard Nichols, and others had demanded reform of divorce laws, married women's property laws, inheritance laws, and child custody rights, to name a few. They had also decried prostitution—within marriage and outside it. Since the papers carried the proceedings of the conventions as well as the calls, Whitman was well exposed to the different arguments. Once the context of the woman's rights movement is foregrounded, poems such as the 1860 "To a Common Prostitute" and section 11 of "Song of Myself"—the twenty-ninth bather section—

can be seen as growing out of a specific cultural contextualization that places Whitman within the woman's rights reformist sensibility.

Many of the resolutions read and recorded at the conventions, for example, spoke of the subjugation that married women faced. Reformists made it clear from 1850 on that if a woman had property, she stood to lose it and other civil rights if she married. Once contemporary readers become aware that the debate about married women's rights was part of the cultural dialogue, passages such as section 11 of "Song of Myself" may be read in a new light. Though this passage invites divergent interpretations, it is not out of line to view it as an independent woman's answer to marriage laws that would take away privileges that her unmarried financial independence accorded her. Why, indeed, should she marry? (Why not become the voyeur?)

Twenty-eight young men bathe by the shore,
Twenty-eight young men and all so friendly;
Twenty-eight years of womanly life and all so lonesome.
She owns the fine house by the rise of the bank,
She hides handsome and richly drest aft the blinds of the window.

Which of the young men does she like the best?
Ah, the homeliest of them is beautiful to her.

Where are you off to, lady? for I see you,
You splash in the water there, yet stay stock still in your room.

Dancing and laughing along the beach came the twenty-ninth bather,
The rest did not see her, but she saw them and loved them.

The beards of the young men glisten'd with wet, it ran from their long hair,
Little streams pass'd all over their bodies.

An unseen hand also pass'd over their bodies,
It descended tremblingly from their temples and ribs.

The young men float on their backs, their white bellies bulge to the sun,
    they do not ask who seizes fast to them,
They do not know who puffs and declines with pendant and bending arch,
They do not think whom they souse with spray. [*Variorum*, 1:12–13]

Many married women were saying that marriage in no way cured
the loneliness mentioned in this passage, while staying single allowed
women some measure of control not permitted in marriage. At least,
if a woman was fortunate enough to have her own money and property, she did not run the risk of losing her financial independence,
as she did if she married. Placed in the activists' context of the
woman's rights movement, it is understandable why the twenty-ninth
bather went "dancing and laughing along the beach." The contrast
between the richness of Whitman's language and the starkness and
abjectness in many women's lives (signified by the legal tone of the
resolutions calling for change) permits a reading of this passage
of "Myself" such as I suggest: that it could be far preferable not to
marry, that it could be preferable to indulge oneself sexually as a
voyeur and to keep one's financial independence than to marry and
lose all rights (plus obtain the possibility of a grim sex life). Resolution 7, from the 1854 state convention in Albany, gives an idea of
the conditions married women faced. That such primary issues had
to be addressed as acquiring and holding property signals the depth
of the problem. "7. *Resolved,* That as acquiring property by all just
and laudable means, and the holding and devising of the same is a
human right, women married and single are entitled to this right,
and all the usages or laws which withhold it from them are manifestly
unjust."[63] Clarina Howard Nichols, newspaper editor and woman's
rights leader, who had written a series of articles as early as 1847 for
the *Windham County Democrat,* which she edited, spoke on married
women's lot at the 1852 National Woman's Rights Convention: "It
is worthy of remark that in no case is the right of the husband to
possess and control the estate which is their joint accumulation, set
aside; no, not even when the wife procures a divorce for the most
aggravated abuse and infidelity combined. She, the innocent party,
goes out childless and portionless, by decree of law; and he, the
criminal, retains the home and the children, by the favor of the same
law."[64] Usages and laws that withheld property and other civil rights
from women and that were "manifestly unjust" ruled. It is no wonder
the twenty-ninth bather stayed single and danced and laughed along
the beach as she began her seduction of the twenty-eight young men.

Likewise, the woman's rights movement provides a reformist
context outside the New York Female Moral Reform Society and New
York City politics in which to place such poems as Whitman's 1867
"The City Dead-House" and the 1860 "To a Common Prostitute."

Abby Price devoted a sizable portion of her time in her 1850 convention speech to the problem of prostitution. At the 1853 National Woman's Rights Convention, held in Cleveland on 6, 7, and 8 October, Ernestine L. Rose berated established religion for its role in subjugating women and its role in maintaining a moral double standard. She spoke of male privilege in controlling power structures such as the legislature and public spaces in general:

> The woman is admitted into no such places; the Church casts her out; and a stigma is placed upon her, for what is called the slightest "impropriety." Prescribed by no true moral law, but by superstition and prejudice, she is cast out not only from public places, but from private homes. And if any woman should take her sister to her heart, and warm her there again by sympathy and kindness, if she would endeavor once more to infuse into her the spark of life and virtue, of morality and peace, she often dare not so far encounter public prejudice as to do it. It requires a courage beyond what woman can now possess, to take the part of the woman against the villain.[65]

Whitman addresses the issue raised in the latter half of Rose's passage in his 1860 "To a Common Prostitute," in which he includes the prostitute as part of his circle, as possibly one of his lovers, as one of his readers, and, by extension, as part of the body politic. In this poem, he takes his "sister" to his "heart," and as a result, in 1882, this poem was one of two that the Boston District Attorney demanded that Whitman exclude in entirety. The first half of Rose's passage is addressed in his 1867 poem "The City Dead-House." ("The woman is admitted into no such places; the Church casts her out. . . . she is cast out not only from public places, but from private homes.") In "The City Dead-House" Whitman cites the three institutions that Rose cites as implicated, in some degree, in the prostitute's lifestyle and her death: the "capitol" (line 9), the "cathedrals" (line 9), and the "rows of dwellings" (line 8) (*Variorum*, 2:561–62). Rose spoke of prostitution in other speeches, as well.

In the 1860 poem "Our Old Feuillage," Whitman speaks of "The athletic American matron speaking in public to crowds of listeners."[66] His friends, Price, Davis, and Rose, had so spoken, with Rose the reformer who most excelled as an orator. Whitman's love for public events may have taken him to hear her speak, if not to a woman's rights convention, or perhaps to one of the anniversary celebrations honoring Thomas Paine. Whitman speaks frequently in his poetry and prose of the power that the spoken word held for him, just as he speaks of Rose's power to Traubel: "Her eyes would flash. . . . Oh! her eyes, her cheek, her way, her half-rising from the chair—it was fine. And the words are as strong, I put them in my note-book—have kept them all these years." In two poems, especially, Whitman treats the power of oratory. These two poems— "Chants Democratic. 12." and "Leaves of Grass. 21."—became, in revised form, by the 1881 edition, one poem, called "Vocalism." In its 1860 form, "Chants Democratic. 12" had for its first line: "To oratists—to male or female." In 1871, the title read "To Oratists." After 1871, Whitman dropped the first line and title. But he specifically includes women as speakers:

> After complete faith, after clarifyings, elevations, and removing
>   obstructions, After these and more, it is just possible there comes to
>   a man, a woman, the divine power to speak words;
> Then toward that man or that woman swiftly hasten all—none refuse, all
>   attend,[67]

In the spring of 1854, Susan B. Anthony and Ernestine L. Rose traveled together to Washington, D.C., and points south to speak for their causes: woman's rights, temperance, abolitionism. The diary Susan B. Anthony kept of this trip provides a rare insight into Rose's inner life. Anthony's 9 April entry uncharacteristically records in some detail a conversation between the two women. The entry, though long, is sufficiently revelatory to quote in its entirety:

> Mrs. Rose & myself were talking of the "*know nothing*" organizations, when she criticized Lucy Stone & Wendell Phillips with regard to their feelings toward foreigners. Said she had heard them both express themselves in terms of prejudice against granting to foreigners the rights of Citizenship.
>   I expressed disbelief as to either of them having that narrow, mean prejudice in their souls. She then said *I was blinded & could see* nor hear nothing wrong in *that clique of Abolitionists*. She thought she [less?] connected with no society or association [than Anthony], either in religion or reforms[, and thus] could judge all impartially,—& then ventured to say that Kossuths [non?] committed course while in this country, it seemed to me, she did not criticize

as she would an American—She thought she did, & could see reasons why he pursued the course he did. Yes said I you excuse him, you can see the causes why he acted & spoke thus, while you will not allow me to bring forward the probable causes of Lucy's seeming fault—It seemed to *me* that she could not ascribe *pure motives* to any of our Reformers, & while to her it seemed, that I was blindly bound to see no fault, however glaring—At length in the anguish of my soul, I said Mrs Rose, There is not one in the Reform ranks, whom you think true, not one but whom panders to the popular feeling— She answered I can't help it, I take them by the words of their own mouths. I trust all until their own words or acts declare them false to truth & right, & continued she, no one can tell the hours of anguish I have suffered, as one after another I have seen those whom I had trusted, betray falsity of motive, as I have been compelled to place one after another on the list of panderers to public favor— said I, do you know Mrs. Rose, that I can but feel that you place *me too* on that list. said she, I will tell you, when I see you untrue. A silence ensued, while I copied the verse from the hymn sung at Church this A.M., & inscribed Susan B. Anthony, for her dear friend Ernestine L. Rose, as I handed it to her, I observed tears in her eyes, Said I Mrs. Rose, have I been wicked, & hurt your feelings. She answered, No, but I expect never to be understood while I live"—. her anguish was extreme & too [illegible], for it filled my soul [with] anguish to see one so noble, so true (even though I felt I could not comprehend her) so bowed down, so overcome with deep swelling emotions.— At length she said, no one knows how I have suffered from not being understood. I know you must suffer & heaven forbid that I should add a further weight to your burdens.

Mrs. Rose is not appreciated, nor cannot be by this age—she is too much in advance of the extreme ultraists even, to be understood by them—[68]

Because Ernestine L. Rose was Jewish, because she publicly proclaimed her "infidelism," and because she was a "foreigner," she stands apart from the other reformers with whom she traveled. But her difference lies in other areas as well. She was, simply, a fearless woman who had a keen, logically tuned mind and felt the compulsion to use it. Though Paulina Wright Davis was far from the representative lady depicted in *Godey's Lady's Book,* for example, still she had many of the trappings associated with a *Godey's* lady. She had a fine home, for example, and liked to entertain, and she differed from Rose in preferring to couch her arguments in terms that the public would find at least somewhat palatable. Rose, though very skilled as a rhetorician, clearly and publicly voiced her complete rejection of the Puritanism that continued to inform cultural assumptions. Abby Price, though close to Rose's politics when it came to class, had the background of the Hopedale community, a practical *Christian* community. The great wonder is that Rose held the power she did. In a private letter (dated 23 August 1853) to the writer Caroline Dall, Paulina Wright Davis spoke of the convention that would take place the following month in New York City. In this letter, Davis urges Dall to attend the convention and says that she plans to nominate Dall for president if Dall attends. Davis does not want Lucretia Mott to preside, nor does she want Rose. "I care not much who does so if it is not [Lucretia Mott] or Mrs. Rose. Mrs. R has no position in NY."[69] Lucretia Mott was elected to preside over the New York convention, and in a later letter, Davis spoke of the good job she had done. Rose was elected president of the 1854 National Woman's Rights Convention.

In 1869 Ernestine and William Rose left the United States. She had come to the United States because it offered the most promising opportunity of any place in the world for freedom to become a reality in people's everyday lives. She had believed she would see the promise of the Declaration of Independence become a reality. She worked against the power of organized religion. She gave speeches. She worked to make the declaration a reality. The years of absorbing America's realities finally exhausted her spirit. The Civil War and its effects on the woman's movement added weight that finally became too heavy. When the war began, the National Woman's Rights Conventions no longer met. In May 1863, a new organization was formed in its place, the Woman's National Loyal League. Elizabeth Cady Stanton was the president, Susan B. Anthony the secretary, and Ernestine L. Rose served on the Business Committee. The problem that would eventually split the women's movement into two factions surfaced at this meeting. The problem came from Anthony's inclusion of the word "women" in the following resolution: "*Resolved,* There never can be a true peace in this Republic until the civil and political rights of all citizens of African descent and all women are practically established."[70]

Some women objected to the resolution on the grounds that the unpopular woman's rights movement and its association with eman-cipation would hurt the cause of emancipation. Rose answered the objections: "I for one object to the proposition to throw woman out of the race for freedom. And do you know why? Because she needs freedom for the freedom of man. Our ancestors made a great mis-take in not recognizing woman in the rights of man. It has been justly stated that the Negro at present suffers more than woman, but it can do him no injury to place woman in the same category with him. . . . It can do no injury, but must do good, for it is a painful fact that woman under the law has been in the same category with the slave."[71] Rose clarified her stance in her speech at the evening ses-sion. She did not adopt a conciliatory tone. And she made her stance toward emancipation clear: she called for immediate emancipation of all slaves, not just those in the South. "I speak for myself," she said. "I do not wish any one else to be responsible for my opinions. I am loyal only to justice and humanity. Let the Administration give evi-dence that they, too, are for justice to all, without exception, without distinction, and I, for one, had I ten thousand lives, would gladly lay them down to secure this boon of freedom to humanity."[72]

When the war ended, the issue of inclusion broke the woman's movement in half. There are many ways to look at the story of the split. Some feel it was inevitable that in order to make the Thirteenth Amendment work, women—black and white—had to wait their turn, as the phrase went. Others do not agree.

To buttress the Thirteenth Amendment, two more amendments were passed. The Fourteenth Amendment inserted the word "male" into the Constitution: "But when the right to vote . . . is denied to any of the male inhabitants of such a State . . . the basis of repre-sentation shall be reduced in the proportion. " The fifteenth read: "The right of citizens of the United States to vote shall not be denied or abridged by the United States or by any State on account of race, color, or previous condition of servitude."[73] The fourteenth stipu-lated that only males could vote, while the fifteenth did not mention gender. Women were enraged. Many used racist language in their attacks on the politicians, as did Cady Stanton when she remarked, "As the celestial gate of civil rights is slowly moving on its hinges, it becomes a serious question whether we had better stand aside and see 'Sambo' walk into the kingdom first."[74]

On 10 May 1866, woman's rights activists met to attempt to work out a strategy for survival. The leading male abolitionists had already defected from the woman's rights cause. Susan B. Anthony proposed the following resolution: "*Resolved,* That as the time has come for an organization that shall cover the broad ground of universal suffrage, we shall be known hereafter as the American Equal Rights Association."[75]

At an 1867 American Equal Rights Association meeting, Rose made it clear that in her eyes, the war had not changed the power structure of the United States. Her speech mocks the association's name. Her language shows how far removed the principles on which the United States was founded now seemed to her. The speech foreshadows her action in 1869 when she introduced the resolution that split the women's movement. The derision in her 1867 speech is obvious:

> Before this Republic could count a hundred years, it has had one of the mightiest revolutions that ever occurred in any country or in any period of human existence. Its foundation was laid wrong. It made a republic for white men alone. It discriminated against color; it discriminated against sex; and at the same time it pronounced that all men were created free and equal, and endowed with certain inalienable rights, among which are life, liberty, and the pursuit of happiness. It raised its superstructure to the clouds; and it has fallen as low as any empire could fall. It is divided. A house divided against itself can not stand. A wrong always operates against itself and falls back on the wrong-doer. We have proclaimed to the world universal suffrage; but it is universal suffrage excluding the negro and the woman, who are by far the largest number in this country. It is not the majority that rules here, but the minority. White men are in the minority in this nation. White women, black men, and black women compose the large majority of the nation.[76]

Whitman had made nearly the same point in "The Eighteenth Presidency!" The struggle became increasingly bitter. The rhetoric is now extremely painful to hear. The campaign became a class and race struggle. Educated white women were pitted against uneducated black men, immigrants, and people incapable of literacy. Few, very few—Sojourner Truth, for one—made the point that black women were all but forgotten in the fight.

By the May 1869 American Equal Rights Association meeting, Rose had ceased to believe that there was even a slim chance for universal suffrage. Since she did not think that suffrage for black men precluded suffrage for women of all colors, or vice versa, she made a decision. She submitted the following proposal: "I suggest that the name of this society be changed from Equal Rights Association to Woman's Suffrage Association."[77] She said that she did not intend to stop fighting for the rights of former slaves but that it was necessary to change the name in order to clarify the terms of the struggle. The woman's movement split at this time. The National Woman Suffrage Association was led by Stanton, Anthony, and Rose, with Paulina Wright Davis joining them, as well as others. The other group, the American Woman Suffrage Association, was led mainly by New England abolitionists, like Lucy Stone and her husband Henry Blackwell. Henry Ward Beecher became the group's president, the same Beecher who said in 1854 that women should not speak in public. When some of the National Woman Suffrage Association members wanted to exclude males from their organization, Rose demurred. She said that she would never be a member of any organization that excluded her husband. Her view prevailed. But all of the officers were female.

On 8 June 1869, Ernestine and William Rose sailed out of New York harbor for England; they gave her health as the reason for their departure. Although Ernestine had lived in the United States for many years and had channeled her energy into reformist causes, she had never become a United States citizen. She did so seventeen days before she and William left. Suhl regards the years that she spent in the United States without applying for citizenship as her "conscious protest against a government that denied woman her full legal equality."[78]

In September 1873 the Roses returned to the United States to sell their belongings before moving permanently to England. They spent eight months finishing their business and then left for good. On 4 July 1878, Rose wrote Susan B. Anthony a letter. The words "Anniversary of the Declaration of Independence" followed the date. Anthony had written Rose to inform her of a celebration to be held at Rochester, New York, to celebrate the thirtieth anniversary of the first woman's rights convention. Rose wrote back:

> Oh, how I should like to be with you at the Anniversary—it reminds me of the delightful convention we had in Rochester, long, long ago!—and in regard to woman—compare her present position in

society with the one she occupied 40 years ago, when I undertook
to emancipate her from not only barbarous laws, but from what was
even worse, a barbarous public opinion. No one can appreciate the
wonderful change in the social and moral condition of women, except by looking back and comparing the past with the present.

I will . . . only say to the friends, "Go on, Go on! halt not and rest
not. Remember that 'eternal vigilance is the price of Liberty' and
of Right. Much has been achieved; but the main, the vital thing, has
yet to come. The Suffrage is the magic key to the statute,—the in-
signia of citizenship of the Republic."[79]

On 25 January 1882, William Rose died. Ernestine L. Rose died
on 4 August 1892, four months or so after Walt Whitman. She and
William were buried in Highgate Cemetery in London. Through co-
incidence, their graves lie next to that of Karl Marx.[80]

Robert Ingersoll—secularist, lawyer, lecturer—spoke at Whitman's graveside. George Jacob Holyoke—secularist, author, socialist,
free-speech advocate—spoke at Rose's. There is an ideological parallel between the two men. Holyoke spoke of the passion that Rose
and Whitman shared: "Her passion was to see women possess civil
and social equality, and to inspire women and men with self-helping
sense, not taking religion, politics or social ideas second-hand from
their 'pastors and masters,' but choosing principles of belief, government and conduct for themselves."[81]

5

Responses of Some 19th-Century Women to the 1860 *Leaves of Grass*

Betsy Erkkila, in *Whitman the Political Poet,* argues, "If at times Whitman's work seems to reinscribe the conservative sexual ideology of his time, his poems had and still do have a galvanizing effect on women readers."[1] The words "at times" in Erkkila's statement are important. Even the most radical of the woman's rights activists—women like Elizabeth Cady Stanton and Ernestine L. Rose—would *at times* inscribe what is now considered to be conservative sexual ideology as they worked for change. Domestic fiction writers—such as Susan Warner and Maria Susanna Cummins—were much less outspoken about and critical of the status quo than were women like Stanton and Rose. As we speak now of the work of nineteenth-century female fiction writers, however, we do not say that it is or was disabling for women. Rather, we talk about contradictory discourses; we talk about subversive strategies. We give measure. Susan Coultrap-McQuin, for example, speaks of the swings in Elizabeth Stuart Phelps's work: "Despite the energy and self-affirmation of these works in the 1870s, other more conservative, somewhat contradictory topics continued to crop up in Phelps's work."[2] In Susan Harris's article "But is it any good?" Harris states: "Writers aiming for a popular audience had to observe, at least superficially, essentialist rules for inscribing female protagonists and for their narrators' attitudes towards their heroines' adventures."[3] Though Whitman's audience was not exactly the same as the popular audience spoken of here by Harris, still, Whitman wanted *Leaves of Grass* to be read by the everyday American citizen. Contradictions within nineteenth-century women's fiction, feminist critics often imply, do not necessarily mean that this fiction disempowered female readers, then or now. Whitman's own contradictions are no different in kind from those of his female contemporaries. Though Whitman envisioned a society radically different from what he saw, he also knew his audience.

Though Whitman was prudent, he was not so prudent that he deleted the "Enfans d'Adam" cluster, which Emerson advised him to do while the 1860 edition was going to print, nor did he subsequently edit out the poems that some people found offensive, though in 1882 his book was formally charged with obscenity. His prudence can be seen in his reaction in 1882 to two radical reformers who defended him and his poetry when the Suffolk County district attorney attempted to ban the 1882 *Leaves of Grass,* published by the Boston firm Osgood. Martin Henry Blatt, in *Free Love and Anarchism: The Biography of Ezra Heywood* (1989), assesses the contrary shifts in Whitman, that is, the play between his reformist desires and his "prudence." Blatt outlines the plot: that in 1881 the Boston publisher Osgood and Company brought out the sixth edition of *Leaves of Grass;* that with the urgings of Anthony Comstock, the morality czar at the time, Oliver Stevens, the district attorney of Suffolk County, advised Osgood that portions of the book were obscene. After letters back and forth between Osgood and Whitman, Whitman obtained the plates and contracted with David McKay, a Philadelphia publisher, to print the second issue. Ezra Heywood, anarchist, writer, and publisher of the *Word,* and Benjamin Tucker, anarchist, writer, and publisher of *Liberty,* challenged the charge. Heywood printed "A Woman Waits for Me" and "To a Common Prostitute" on a single sheet, which he called "The Word Extra," to be sent with his other mailings and also printed them in his paper, the *Word.* Tucker did not single out any poem but defended *Leaves of Grass* as a book and offered to publish it. Heywood and Tucker both wrote letters to Whitman, but as Blatt notes, Whitman reacted to them "very differently."

Whitman responded to Tucker and Heywood very differently. In a letter to his friend William O'Connor in which he enclosed Heywood's letter, Whitman wrote: "As to the vehement action of the Free

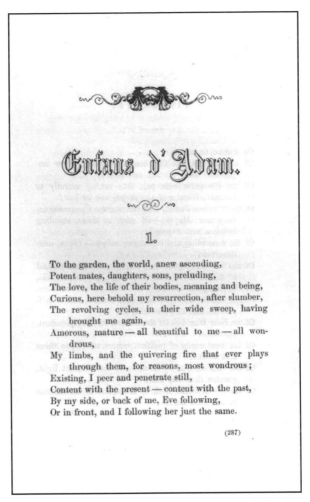

The first page of the cluster "Children of Adam" ("Enfans d'Adam") in the 1860 edition of *Leaves of Grass*. Reproduced courtesy of Special Collections, Texas Tech University Library.

Religious and lover folk, in their conventions, papers, &c in my favor—and even proceedings like these of Heywood—I see nothing better for myself or friends to do than quietly stand aside and let it go on. . . . I shall certainly not do anything to identify myself specially with free love." . . . In contrast, Whitman had great respect for Tucker, who had moderated his public pronouncements of free love quite a bit since his earlier days with the New England Free Love League. "I often feel," wrote Whitman, "as though I would like to see Tucker and have a long, long, long confab with him. . . . " Whitman did not "bank much on his anarchism . . . but on Tucker—well, he is a safe risk."[4]

Whitman's lines about contradicting himself in "Song of Myself" ("Do I contradict myself? / Very well then I contradict myself, / (I am large, I contain multitudes") need to be taken with more than a grain of salt. In 1855, for example, Henry Clapp's name was spread over the pages of the *Tribune* for his involvement in a New York Free Love League. Henry Clapp, like Heywood, radically departed from the norm. Yet Clapp's alignment with the Free Love controversy did not bother Whitman. What Heywood and Clapp declared publicly, Whitman spoke of in his poetry through images and wordplay. The 1855, 1856, and 1860 *Leaves of Grass,* overall, present a more daring Whitman than did the 1882 edition. In January 1889, in a private context, however, Whitman's words to Horace Traubel had a different tone:

Talking about "marriage forms" W. said to-night: "Some time they will have to yield—give way." I asked: "To what?" W. said: "I don't know to what—to something bigger than themselves." "Then you don't consider the present laws on the subject ideal." He laughed heartily: "Ideal? Far from it: far, far from it." Was it to go utterly—the system? Were we to have free love? He asked me: "What do you call free love? There's no other kind of love, is there? As to the next step—who knows what it means? I only feel sure of one thing: that we won't go back: that the women will take care of sex things—make them what they choose: man has very little to do with it except to conform." I laughed as I asked him: "What will become of the foundations of society if our mothers are mothers for love rather than for some other reason?" "You are cute—that is well said: yes: what will become of them? Why, the mothers are the foundations of society: mothers need no law." I asked W.: "When you and Emerson had that talk on Boston Common about the Children of Adam poems did the free love matter so-called come up?" "O yes! it did: Emerson said: 'For one thing you are in danger of being tangled up with the unfortunate heresy.' I told him that had already occurred: that worse heresies than that were charged to me: that nothing I could do now would mend matters." "Did Emerson appear to be shocked at the poems, or at free love, or at your defense of the book?" "Not at all:

he was calm, equable, agreeable: he was as he himself said only putting up a worldly argument: he wanted my book to sell—thought I
had given it no chance to be popularly seen, apprehended: thought
that if I cut out the bits here and there that offended the censors I
might leave a book that would go through editions—perhaps many
editions.[5]

The walk with Emerson occurred in spring 1860 when Whitman was
in Boston overseeing the printing of the third edition. On May 10
and 11, the tenth National Woman's Rights Convention met in New
York City, at the Cooper Institute, its proceedings recorded in the
pages of the New York papers. Whitman returned to New York probably on 13 May. Reports on the proceedings appeared in the 11 and
12 May issues of the *Tribune*. If we bear in mind Whitman's friendship with Price, Davis, and Rose, Whitman's interest in the subject
of sexuality, his recent talk with Emerson defending his "Enfans
d'Adam" cluster, it seems logical to assume that Whitman was curious about the convention, that he read newspaper accounts about it
after arriving in New York, and, most important, that he heard about
it from the circle of people who frequented Abby Price's brownstone.
Price was one on the few people whom Whitman wrote that spring
while he was in Boston. Surely, her letters to him contained news
about the convention. Surely, their discussions upon his return were
fired by the news of the convention as well as by his accounts of his
book.
    The issues discussed at this convention were hotly contested. The
most memorable was the controversy sparked by Ernestine L. Rose
and Elizabeth Cady Stanton concerning the "marriage question."
The rich speeches delivered by Stanton and Rose during the two
days of the convention provide a lesson for those who believe that
nothing was done for women's theory until the 1970s. (Rose began
her first speech talking about Frances Wright, moving smoothly into
her comments about women who deny that the past ten years of
woman's rights activism had accomplished anything.) On the second day of the convention, Elizabeth Cady Stanton proposed a list
of ten resolutions for the convention to adopt. These are radical
resolutions, using concrete language, opposing the marriage relation, as it existed at the time. No one resolution is unexceptionable,
but the following connect most directly with the defense of the 1860
Leaves of Grass that three women made the following month:

5. *Resolved,* That of all insulting mockeries of heavenly truth and holy law, none can be greater than that physical impotency is cause sufficient for divorce, while no amount of mental or moral or spiritual imbecility is ever to be pleaded in support of such a demand.

6. *Resolved,* That such a law was worthy those dark periods when marriage was held by the greatest doctors and priests of the Church to be a work of the flesh only, and almost, if not altogether, a defilement; denied wholly to the clergy, and a second time, forbidden to all.

7. *Resolved,* That an unfortunate or ill-assorted marriage is ever a calamity, but not ever, perhaps never, a crime—and when society or government, by its laws or customs, compels its continuance, always to the grief of one of the parties, and the actual loss and damage of both, it usurps an authority never delegated to man, nor exercised by God himself.

8. *Resolved,* That observation and experience daily show how incompetent are men, as individuals, or as governments, to select partners in business, teachers for their children, ministers of their religion, or makers, adjudicators, or administrators of their laws; and as the same weakness and blindness must attend in the selection of matrimonial partners, the dictates of humanity and common sense alike show that the latter and most important contract should no more be perpetual than either or all of the former.

9. *Resolved,* That children born in these unhappy and unhallowed connections are, in the most solemn sense, of unlawful birth—the fruit of lust, but not of love—and so not of God, divinely descended, but from beneath, whence proceed all manner of evil and uncleanliness.

10. *Resolved,* That next to the calamity of such a birth to the child, is the misfortune of being trained in the atmosphere of a household where love is not the law, but where discord and bitterness abound; stamping their demoniac features on the moral nature, with all their odious peculiarities—thus continuing the race in a weakness and depravity that must be a sure precursor of its ruin, as a just penalty of long-violated law.[6]

Stanton obesrves that if God made marriages, all would be happiness. But such is not the case, she says. Rather, "You all know our marriage is, in many cases, a mere outward tie, impelled by custom, policy, interest, necessity; founded not even in friendship, to say nothing of love; with every possible inequality of condition and development." Stanton addresses the concept of family: "The family, that great conservator of national virtue and strength, how can you hope to build it up in the midst of violence, debauchery, and excess? Call that sacred, where woman, the mother of the race . . . unconscious of the true dignity of her nature, of her high and holy destiny, consents to live in legalized prostitution?"[7] She makes an emotional appeal to parental ties: "What father could rest at his home by night knowing that his lovely daughter was at the mercy of a strong man drunk with wine and passion, and that, do what he might, he was backed up by law and public sentiment? The best interests of the individual, the family, the State, the nation, cry out against these legalized marriages of force and endurance."[8] She criticizes Horace Greeley who, in a discussion with Robert Dale Owen, said that "the ground has been all gone over and explored." Not so, Stanton says: "Let me assure him that but just one-half of the ground has been surveyed."[9] The Reverend Antoinette Brown Blackwell followed Stanton's address, offering her own resolutions, which made the marriage contract inviolable yet authorized women in destructive marriages to move away from the husband but not to divorce. Divorce, Antoinette Brown Blackwell claimed, was "naturally and morally impossible." Ernestine L. Rose followed Antoinette Brown Blackwell: "The question of a Divorce law seems to me one of the greatest importance to all parties, but I presume that the very advocacy of divorce will be called 'Free Love.' For my part (and I wish distinctly to define my position), I do not know what others understand by that term; to me, in its truest significance, love must be free, or it ceases to be love. In its low and degrading sense, it is not love at all, and I have as little to do with its name as its reality."[10]

Rose, like Stanton, attacked the fallacies of Horace Greeley's defense of the marriage institution. She then, in a biting reference to Antoinette Brown Blackwell's speech, spoke of "Fast Women" in the context of cause/effect (much as Whitman's poem "The City Dead-House" intimated seven years later):

> The Tribune had recently a long sermon, almost equal to the one we had this morning from our reverend sister, on "Fast Women." The evils it spoke of were terrible indeed, but, like all other sermons, it was one-sided. Not one single word was said about fast men, except that the "poor victim had to spend so much money." The writer for-

got that it is the demand which calls the supply into existence. But what was the primary cause of that tragic end? Echo answers, "what?" Ask the lifeless form of the murdered woman, and she may disclose the terrible secret, and show you that, could she have been legally divorced, she might not have been driven to the watery grave of a "fast woman."

Rose asks the question, "But what is marriage?" And answers, "A human institution." She calls for a divorce law. "I ask for a law of Divorce, so as to secure the real objects and blessings of married life, to prevent the crimes and immoralities now practiced, to prevent 'Free Love,' in its most hideous form, such as is now carried on but too often under the very name of marriage, where hypocrisy is added to the crime of legalized prostitution. 'Free Love,' in its degraded sense, asks for no Divorce law. It acknowledges no marriage, and therefore requires no divorce. I believe in true marriages, and therefore I ask for a law to free men and women from false ones."[11] Wendell Phillips spoke after Rose and moved that the resolutions not appear in the journals of the convention; they were, he said, out of order, since the purpose of the convention was to discuss the laws that treated women unequally. "We have nothing to do with a question which affects both sexes equally. Therefore, it sees to me we have nothing to do with the theory of marriage, which is the basis, as Mrs. Rose has very clearly shown, of divorce. One question grows out of the other; and therefore the question of the permanence of marriage, and the laws relating to marriage, in the essential meaning of that word, are not for our consideration."[12]

The convention voted Phillips down. Horace Greeley responded with a letter in the *Tribune,* on 14 May 1860, condemning the convention and Stanton for passing on the resolutions, indeed, for discussing the need for such a thing as divorce to exist. Stanton responded with her own letter to the *Tribune,* on 30 May, in which she documented her case, citing laws, one after another, using the background she had obtained in her father's law office. The year 1860 brought this debate on marriage and divorce to a public peak, but it had been going on in the conventions since the first National Woman's Rights Convention, in 1850, championed by Price, Davis, and Rose. Stanton had been engaged also but more on the state level, since she was often unable to leave her home and children to

attend the national conventions. In a 21 December 1855 letter to
Gerrit Smith, Stanton said:

> Did [man] ever take in the idea that to the mother of the race, and
> to her alone, belonged the right to say when a new being should be
> brought into the world? Has he, in the gratification of his blind pas-
> sions, ever paused to think whether it was with joy and gladness that
> she gave up ten or twenty years of the heyday of her existence to all
> the cares and sufferings of excessive maternity? Our present laws,
> our religious teachings, our social customs on the whole question of
> marriage and divorce, are most degrading to woman; and so long as
> man continues to think and write, to speak and act, as if maternity
> was the one and sole object of a woman's existence—so long as chil-
> dren are conceived in weariness and disgust—you must not look for
> high-toned men and women capable of accomplishing any great and
> noble achievement. But when woman shall stand on an even pedes-
> tal with man—when they shall be bound together, not by withes of
> law and gospel, but in holy unity and love, then, and not till then,
> shall our efforts at minor reforms be crowned with complete success.
> Here, in my opinion, is the starting-point; here is the battle ground
> where our independence must be fought and won.[13]

In March 1853, in a private letter to Susan B. Anthony, Stanton
wrote:

> I do not know that the world is quite willing or ready to discuss the
> question of marriage. I feel in my innermost that the thoughts I sent
> your convention are true. It is in vain to look for the elevation of
> woman, so long as she is degraded in marriage. I say it is a sin, an
> outrage on our holiest feeling to pretend that anything but deep,
> fervent love and sympathy constitutes marriage. The right idea of
> marriage is at the foundation of all reforms. . . . A child conceived
> in the midst of hate, sin, & discord, nurtured in abuse & injustice
> cannot do much to bless the world or himself. If we properly under-
> stand the science of life—it would be far easier to give to the world,
> harmonious, beautiful, noble, virtuous children, than it is to bring
> grown up discord into harmony with the great divine soul of all. . . .
> Man in his lust has regulated this whole question of sexual inter-
> course long enough; let the mothers of mankind whose prerogative

it is to set bounds to his indulgence, raise up & give this whole question a thorough, fearless examination. . . . I feel this whole question
of woman's rights turns on the pivot of the marriage relation, &
sooner or later it will be the question for discussion. I would not
hurry it on neither would I avoid it.[14]

In 1870 Stanton delivered a speech titled "On Marriage and Divorce" to a private club of men and women. Ellen DuBois says of this
speech: "The basic point of this speech—Stanton's criticism of the
external regulation of private affections either by law, 'dogmatic'
public morality, or mutual consent—clearly places her within the
tradition of free-love radicalism. She embraced this heresy by including an extended attack on the social conservatism of other women's-
rights leaders."[15]

Hearing what some of the most socially involved woman's rights
activists of the time said about issues of the day and about Whitman's
work as they responded to it makes it difficult to read Whitman's
sexual politics as reductive for women, problematic though specific
passages may be. The stories told in this chapter, of women for whom
Whitman's texts had galvanizing effects, to use Erkkila's term, form
a provocative new context for reading *Leaves of Grass* and, most specifically, the "Children of Adam" cluster. Put into the context of
women's history of the 1850s, for example, the "Children of Adam"
cluster becomes interesting on its own, rather than simply existing
as a pale companion to the "Calamus" cluster, as it is often read.

Here, then, I tell about the women who defended Whitman's
1860 edition of *Leaves of Grass.* This defense took place in June 1860,
in the pages of Henry Clapp's *Saturday Press,* one month after the
1860 National Woman's Rights Convention had met in New York, at
the Cooper Institute. The focus of the defense (and the attacks) was
the "Children of Adam" cluster, named in this edition "Enfans
d'Adam," which appeared for the first time in the 1860 edition.
Henry Clapp, Jr., a figure in Whitman's life who deserves more attention than he has yet received, published the first issue of his paper
on 23 October 1858; it ran until 15 December 1860, when Clapp ran
out of money to publish it. The paper resumed 5 August 1865 and
then folded once more on 2 June 1866. Clapp's iconoclasm and that
of the writers he attracted to his journal punctuated the cultural
dialogue with an acerbity that riled the mainstream press and its
readers. In Clapp's efforts to introduce the 1860 edition of *Leaves of*

Grass to the public, he put into full play his policy of printing negative as well as positive reviews and thus stirring up controversy and
attention. Regarding Clapp, Whitman told his friend Horace
Traubel, "Henry was right: better to have people stirred against you
if they can't be stirred for you—better that than not to stir them at
all."[16]

The story begins with the 2 June issue of the *Saturday Press,* in
which appeared a review of *Leaves of Grass,* signed Juliette H. Beach.
It's a familiar story now—that this article was not Juliette Beach's
work but rather her husband's. In this review, Calvin Beach charges
Whitman with writing filth, singling out the "Children of Adam"
cluster. Whitman's poetry, Calvin Beach says, calls up the feeling of
"brute nature [rather] than the sentiments of human love." Beach
says that Whitman sees women only as a means to propagate the
species and as an outlet for his own desires, that sex to Whitman is
a "purely animal affair, and with his ridiculous egotism he vaunts his
prowess as a stockbreeder might that of the pick of his herd."

In the next week's issue, Clapp printed a "Correction" explain-
ing the mixup, saying that the confusion was understandable, since
he had forwarded Juliette Beach a copy of the new *Leaves of Grass*
and therefore expected a review from her, not from her husband.
Implicitly the "Correction" says that Mr. Beach appropriated the
book and wrote his own review of *Leaves of Grass.* In this same 9 June
issue appeared the first of three reviews written by women. All three
allude to Calvin Beach's attack. Only one woman signed her full
name: "Mary A. Chilton, Islip, Long Island, June 5th, 1860." The
other two were signed "C.C.P." and "A Woman." Though it is not clear
how well Whitman knew Chilton, connections between the two existed—apart from her 1860 defense, that is. By knowing something
of her life, then, we may better understand the kind of women who
found *Leaves of Grass* sympathetic to their own lives and values. In
the process we further contextualize *Leaves of Grass.*

Whitman had written Mary Chilton's name down in his notebooks prior to her 9 June defense of him. She is mentioned in two
of his Brooklyn notebooks, which date to sometime between the
years 1857 and 1860. In one notebook—Whitman's "Dick Hunt"
notebook—Chilton's name and address seem to appear on the same
page as the addresses of Ernestine L. Rose and Abby Hills Price.[17]
In another, Whitman places next to Chilton's name and Manhattan
address the name and different Manhattan address of Theron C.

Leland, "an ardent convert to Fourierism. . . . With [Thaddeus Burr] Wakeman he conducted the [National Liberal] League organ, 'Man,' devoting all his daytime to that and the secretaryship, and supporting himself by teaching evening schools of shorthand."[18] As phonographer, he took down the proceedings of the fourth National Woman's Rights Convention, held in Cleveland in 1853. Chilton and Leland eventually married and had two daughters, Lilian and Grace. (In 1890, Lilian Leland published *Traveling Alone: A Woman's Journey around the World.*) Most likely, Mary Chilton and Theron C. Leland were part of Abby Price's circle. In addition to these connections and to Whitman's notebook notations, Whitman knew Chilton through her writing. An issue of the *Social Revolutionist,* the journal supporting free love/free thought for which Chilton wrote, is among Whitman's papers (now at Rutgers University). This issue—July 1857, slightly marked by Whitman—contains "Sexual Purity," one of Mary Chilton's articles.[19]

Put into contemporary terms, Mary Chilton was a radical feminist. George E. Macdonald, editor of the liberal journal the *Truthseeker,* who became Mary Chilton's son-in-law, described her as "another Frances Wright," a phrase frequently used to describe Ernestine L. Rose.[20] She believed in the rights of the individual and, most significantly for antebellum America, in the rights of the woman as an individual. Susan B. Anthony and Elizabeth Cady Stanton's 1869 *Revolution* carried "Suffrage," an article by Chilton. In it, Chilton sarcastically snips away at the idea of female passivity:

> Men have enjoyed the privilege of manning the ships of state for a long time; now, we want to have a chance to tug at the ropes. 'A storm is brewing,' help will be needed, let us lend a hand.
>
> Of course, men being gallant, will decline our assistance, but that is mere courtesy on their part; once we get fairly at work they will enjoy the change. Let us learn the art of voting, perhaps we shall find it as pleasant as croquet. It will take us out of doors for a walk, at least as often as once in a while. Then we will try what success we may have in making platforms; perhaps that will prove as profitable as making patchwork; and collecting customs, I am sure, will be quite to our liking. With their leave, or without it, let us go to work. Men like us at the opera, in the ball-room, at pic-nics, or in parlors; it is a mere whim, this pretending not to want us in the halls of legislation. If, however, after a fair trial, it should prove mutually

unsatisfactory, we can leave.

Let the *Tribune* trim its sails, let Dr. Lardner demonstrate the impossibility of navigating the ocean by steam, and let the English lord who engaged to eat the boiler of the first steamer that came to English shores digest the iron at his leisure; woman will, in defiance of all the 'scolding' and 'braying,' go hand in hand with her enfranchised father, brother, lover, or son, to the Polls, or to the Poles.[21]

In a society that censored women's public voice, Chilton spoke a radical message: she was an activist for women's rights, a proponent of free love, and a water-cure physician. Her quest for personal freedom led her to Modern Times, the Long Island community which became known in the early 1850s as a free love community, though it had many more ideological underpinnings than that, primarily the founder Josiah Warren's brand of individualistic socialism.[22] Modern Times became the destination of Fish and Seaver, the couple Abby Price counseled, which led to her public censure by the Hopedale morality committee. George E. Macdonald briefly sketches Chilton's life in his *Fifty Years of Freethought: Being the Story of The Truthseeker with the Natural History of its Third Editor.* He identifies Chilton as the wife of Theron C. Leland. Macdonald married Grace Leland in 1888. But before Grace and Lilian were born, Mary Chilton had led an extraordinary life. Moncure Conway—Unitarian clergyman, liberal leader, and writer—became acquainted with Chilton when he visited Modern Times, in the summer of 1857 or 1860. Taylor Stoehr, author of *Free Love in America: A Documentary History,* places her visit in 1857 and says the home where Conway stayed was Theron C. Leland's, that "Mrs. Leland" was Conway's hostess.[23] Conway includes his account of the Modern Times visit in his autobiography, in his novel *Pine and Palm* (1887), in an article he wrote for the *Cincinnati Gazette,* and in a *Fortnightly Review* article: "She [Chilton] was a woman I should say, a little over thirty years of age, and had an indefinable grace and fine intellectual powers, united with considerable personal beauty. She was a native of one of the Southern States,—Georgia, I believe,—where she had married. The marriage was unhappy, and on separation she considered herself, as I have heard, most cruelly treated by her husband and the law together, in being deprived of her children. She had studied medicine, and was earning her livelihood by medical practice. Her own experiences led her to sum up the chief evils of society in the one word *marriage.*"[24]

Macdonald dates Conway's visit to the summer of 1860 and cites the more amplified account of Chilton's life in the article Conway wrote for the *Cincinnati Gazette:*

> The Queen of Modern Times was in truth every inch a queen. She was a most beautiful woman, in the prime of life, who was born and reared in the cotton States. She had at an early age married a rich man and a tyrant. From him she separated, and the law which gave him her children gradually schooled her to sum up all the wrongs of society in the one word "marriage." If she was the champion of any popular cause Mary Chilton would be regarded as the leading female intellect of her country; and it would be impossible for anyone to see her in her inspired mood, and to hear her voice as it sweeps through the gamut of feeling, rehearsing the sorrows of her sisterhood, without knowing that she brings many momentous truths from the deep wells of nature.[25]

Conway gives the approximate date for his visit when he says in his 1865 *Fortnightly Review* article that he first heard of Modern Times "about eight years ago," while he was living in Cincinnati. If the visit was made in the summer of 1857, then it occurred during the period when Chilton was contributing articles to the *Social Revolutionist,* a monthly publication edited by John Patterson. If the visit came in the summer of 1860, then it coincided with. Chilton's *Saturday Press* defense of Whitman.

In the 1856–1857 *Social Revolutionist,* Chilton wrote three of the approximately twenty articles written by women. Not included in this count are the letters and brief notes that women contributed to the journal. The *Social Revolutionist,* a reform journal that ran from January 1856 through December 1857, stated in its prospectus that its goal was to further independent thinkers of every persuasion, claiming "always [to] welcome the radical thought and its brave and manly utterance. We shall refuse publicity to no opinion, whatever, for any difference between it and ours."[26] The journal was closely aligned with the Rising Star Association, which began functioning as a commune in 1853. Like the Long Island commune Modern Times, this Ohio community claimed that its stance on free soil, communal sharing, and free thought resulted in more freedom for the individual, not less. The *Social Revolutionist* focused on free love, however, perhaps more than on any other social concern.

What was meant by "free love" varied not only outside the movement but inside as well, as the November 1856 issue of the *Social Revolutionist* showed when the editor, John Patterson, listed five different free love views. John C. Spurlock, in *Free Love: Marriage and Middle-Class Radicalism in America, 1825–1860,* summarizes the findings of his study: "Free lovers helped to define a long tradition of radicalism that included antislavery activists, nonresistants, and feminists. An individual could be a radical, could adopt a consistent and socially unpopular version of any of these ideologies and not consider himself or herself a free lover. No one could be a free lover, however, without being a radical and therefore against the slavery of the black man and the married woman."[27] It is this latter point that occupied the minds and pens of the women who wrote for the *Social Revolutionist.* In fact, the first major article by a woman appearing in the *Social Revolutionist* was titled "Sexual Slavery," signed "Vivian Gray," though I am not sure if that was the woman's real name, since women who wrote often used pseudonyms.

Though women's writing in the *Social Revolutionist* did not actually take hold until the sixth issue, which came out in July 1856, from that point onward women's words appeared regularly. There are close to twenty essays arguing for the rights of women, and there are letters to the editor written by women as well. The constant in these writings is the charge against the institution of marriage. Most of these women do not talk of wanting multiple sexual partners, or even of wanting an "open marriage," to use a contemporary term. Rather, they talk about the harshly debilitating effects of marriage. Marriage is equated with slavery. The opposite of slavery, freedom, is mentioned time and again as the desired goal for women. In an April 1857 article, a woman who signed herself "Justicia" equates the term "Free Love" with "freedom for woman." In the last issue, C. M. Overton defined free love: "The distinguishing features of Free Love is, that it proclaims a woman's right to herself—to the control of her own body—the right to be let alone—to be free from personal abuse at the hands of force, legal or illegal—the first and most sacred of all rights, the right to her own soul and body—a right so plain and self-evident, that its denial by any man, but especially by the majority, is terribly significant of a barbarous age!"[28]

The precise reason why marriage failed as an institution was its *legalized* repression. Married women lost their names (as most women still voluntarily do today); they lost control of their bodies, wages, property, and children—legally. To use words current at the time, marriage enslaved women. The following list of phrases taken from the women's *Social Revolutionist* essays denotes women's contempt and fear of the marriage institution: "prostitution of wives," "marriage as a system of slavery," "ownership of women's bodies and hence souls," "the unquestioned access the husband had to his wife's body," "enforced marital prostitution," "Christian men and their lust," "scenes of pollution," "sham structure," "marriage-lottery," "trap," "bondage," "tyranny," "lust, rapine and murder," "infernal license for the unrestrained indulgence of lust," "miseries and slaveries of married life," "the marriage-bed a hot-bed of licentiousness," "seduction and rape," "legalized slavery," "legal lust," "prostitution for pay," "enforced maternities," and "spurious Christianity." Again and again women refer to law and public sentiment, or custom, as the causes for their enslavement. They saw these two forces maintaining a blind adherence to the subjection of women coupled with patriarchy's control of economics as the powerful forces that they indeed were.

These free love women spoke of the effects of marriage on women. Perhaps the most damaging effect at this time lay in its blow to the body itself. As a result of the laws and attitudes and lack of correct information concerning birth control, many women died in or as a result of childbirth; others suffered ill health and chronic fatigue; many lives were cut short because of excessive childbearing and complications going along with it. Marriage frequently brought anything but quality of life to a woman, nor did it allow her the right to the pursuit of happiness. Or so said the *Social Revolutionist* women. As damaging as marriage was to a woman's physical life, it was equally damaging to her concept of self or, to use a word frequently used in the articles, to her "soul." Over and over in these articles women speak of the abjection of women as they allow husbands unwanted sexual access to their bodies and thus often marriage damaged souls as well as bodies. Laws and usage succeeded in instilling in many women a damagingly low self-image, a dangerous resignation.

Three main arguments against marriage (in its nineteenth-century form) surface in the essays. The first argument is that of freedom. Here women speak of their exclusion from what was supposed to be the American citizen's birthright: that each citizen was equal in the eyes of the law. But of course there was no such equality, and these women felt their enslaved condition bitterly. They claimed the right to self. They rejected the position of the "femme covert." These *Social Revolutionist* women also used the argument of health in their attempts to convince society that their beliefs and for some their practice of a different relational structure were not harmful to society. They argued that marriage and unconditional access to the wife's body meant only harm to the family and, more pointedly, to the unborn children. Their third argument was that women's souls, supposedly equal with men's before God, were denied in the marriage relationship, which allowed the husband to control the wife's body.

The essayists used different strategies to argue their cause. The most common basis for argument was experience. The women used their own experiences, a case-study approach, personal experience based on the woman's status as a professional, the use of story to exemplify the representative woman, and two women told their mother's stories. Another strategy was argument based on theoretical awareness. The third strategy used language to expose the base nature of marriage laws and conventional attitudes. As for style, most of the essays followed the stylistic conventions of the journal and wrote in a relatively plain style. In fact, one woman was criticized for her "romantic" style, a criticism she in turn rejected as unfounded.

Chilton, in her three articles, creates a strong persona who speaks, she says, for the masses, for egalitarianism. She condemns the hypocritical society that pays lip service to a document like the Declaration of Independence yet openly supports and perpetuates enslaving institutions. She holds that freedom is an inherent right for all people. She scorns institutions in general, specifying the church and the institution of marriage in particular. She proclaims the naturalness of sexual feelings and expression and rejects the Calvinist notions of original sin and the depravity of the body. She argues that there is no distinction between the body and the soul. In addition to providing a context that invites new readings of passages in *Leaves of Grass,* Chilton's *Social Revolutionist* articles inform us of a cultural movement active at the time Whitman was writing the first three editions of *Leaves of Grass;* her articles inform us of her own specific politics; and they indicate ways that her views parallel Whitman's.

"Who Are the Martyrs," an article that she published in November 1856, criticizes reformers who advocate caution because "they say, the time has not yet come to realize Freedom in social relations." In this article, Chilton makes many of the same points that Whitman's "Song of the Open Road" illustrates, but her language is more direct than Whitman's in naming the objects of her critique. Though she avoids using the term "sexual relations" and instead uses the more conventionally acceptable terminology "social relations" or "most intimate relations," she is outspoken in her charges against the institution of marriage as it existed: people form legal bonds out of "selfish, mercenary, bread and clothes considerations" and as a "protection against poverty, combined with a purely selfish fear of the condemnation of the world, should the lovers follow their intuitions and obey the dictates of their hearts by simply remaining lovers." Like many free-lovers, her central goal was to change the laws and assumptions governing the institution of marriage rather than to have multiple sex partners. Chilton ends her article by urging her readers to study the picture she presents and, as a consequence, to work for reform. Using the argument prevalent in diverse reform movements at the time, she says that forced or nonconsensual sexual unions result in unhealthy, diseased children. She sees people locked in marriage with little hope for divorce as the real martyrs:

> Oh! cautious and conservative reformer, look about you and see the careworn faces of your respectable married friends; listen and hear the sighs and groans of heartbroken sufferers! What does all this sickness and misery mean that we see everywhere? Are not these prudent people really the martyrs, and not the brave and fearless, who leave home and friends, and position and luxury, for the love of Freedom and the freedom of love? Not they the martyrs; no, you will find the martyrs among the respectable and those deemed comfortable, and certainly cared-for portion of the community. Could you look behind the scenes, you would find manacles on arms that in secret are raised to Heaven . . . you might see the vinegar-soaked sponge of respectability, tauntingly offered in mockery, to the fevered lips.

Interestingly, the last half of section 13 in "Song of the Open Road" (1856) makes many of the same indictments as Chilton. The parallel between the two texts is significant when we consider the reception given Whitman's poetry in his own time; it helps to explain why in 1860 Mary Chilton, and others with similar views, defended *Leaves of Grass*. Knowing about Chilton's life, her views, and her defense of *Leaves of Grass* also guides us today in contextualizing our own readings of Whitman's representations of gender and in contextualizing our politics, which influence these readings.

Section 13 of "Song of the Open Road" speaks of living a life of deception, of conforming to popular mores and thereby denying one's authenticity. Though marriage, and I mean here heterosexual marriage, is not mentioned by name, certainly a reader like Chilton would immediately supply the term to the poem's indictment, as would others who did not subscribe to the culturally encoded valorization of marriage in antebellum America. Whitman calls to the reader, using his much repeated phrase "Whoever you are" in order to ensure inclusivity:

> Whoever you are, come forth! or man or woman come forth!
> You must not stay sleeping and dallying there in the house, though you
>   built it, or though it has been built for you.
>
> Out of the dark confinement! out from behind the screen!
> It is useless to protest, I know all and expose it.
> . . . .
> Inside of dresses and ornaments, inside of those wash'd and trimm'd faces,
> Behold a secret silent loathing and despair.
> . . . .
> Home to the houses of men and women, at the table, in the bedroom,
>   everywhere,
> Smartly attired, countenance smiling, form upright, death under the breast-
>   bones, hell under the skullbones,
> Under the broadcloth and gloves, under the ribbons and artificial flowers,
> Keeping fair with the customs, speaking not a syllable of itself,
> Speaking of any thing else but never of itself.[29]

Whitman's picture of couples "smartly attired, countenance smiling, form upright, death under the breast-bones" fits well with the picture that Chilton creates of "the careworn faces of your respectable married friends," both chipping away at the conventional view of the sanctity of marriage (and class), exposing instead a picture of couples living lives of deception. Both reject custom and reject silence, which functions as a safeguard of custom. Both passages speak to people who reject the principle that societal boundaries are inherent, to people who believe that through changes in custom and law—such as divorce laws—lives can become more fully realized.

Chilton's June 1857 article "Do We Need Marriage?" argues that legal marriages work against living a fully realized life. Marriage, she says, is instituted and regulated by the few to control the many. Marriage, then, must be demystified. Individuals must see the controls placed on their personal lives by the "arrogant few": "If I took a 'leap in the dark,' and in the despair of great suffering saw greater light, and found it good and life giving, that does not prove that life and happiness might not have been mine years sooner had I not been blindfolded by those self-righteous interpreters. I would not compel or enforce my code of morals or freedom on any one; but say cut the cords, loose the bonds, break the manacles which now hold the masses forcibly subservient: to a false and infernal system."[30] Though not with the same amount of righteous indignation, section 5 of "Song of the Open Road" also calls for the individual to see outside of ideology—outside the codes considered "natural" but which are in fact socially constructed:

> From this hour I ordain myself loos'd of limits and imaginary lines,
> Going where I list, my own master total and absolute,
> Listening to others, considering well what they say,
> Pausing, searching, receiving, contemplating,
> Gently, but with undeniable will, divesting myself of the holds that would
>   hold me.[31]

The cultural resonance between these texts helps us to understand the acceptance—indeed, the galvanizing effect—that *Leaves of Grass* had for readers in 1860 like Mary Chilton; it is also significant that Whitman knew women like Mary Chilton, that the years 1856–1860—a period of intense creativity for Whitman—were marked by his acquaintance with women active in reform movements, especially the woman's rights movement but also the associationist movement (Fourier and other communal attempts), the abolitionist movement, and the free love movement.

The July 1857 issue of the *Social Revolutionist*—the marked issue found in Whitman's papers—contains the article "Sexual Purity." This article makes many of the points already enumerated; it speaks of the debilitating effects of marriage when the relationship is not that of reciprocity and the harmful effects on children from such a relationship. But mainly in this article Chilton argues for the sanity of sexual pleasure. Cleverly, she titles this article "Sexual Purity." Her point in this article is that it is wrong to deny what she calls "the electric spark of energizing health" and "the thrilling power of vital force." It is wrong to deny the sensory pleasure of sexual attraction. Chilton, arguing the politics of sex, says that forced sex in marriage is nothing more than legalized prostitution.

These articles show us Chilton's celebration of sensuality—significantly for her time, of female sensuality—which explains one of the attractions that *Leaves of Grass* held for her. Hearing her views of sexuality can sensitize us to passages in Whitman's work. In fact, the opening section of her 1857 "Sexual Purity" can be read as a prose gloss on six lines of Whitman's 1855 "Faces," the "full-grown lily" passage:

> This is a fullgrown lily's face,
> She speaks to the limber-hip'd man near the garden pickets,
> Come here, she blushingly cries. . . . Come nigh to me limber-hip'd man
>   and give me your finger and thumb,
> Stand at my side till I lean as high as I can upon you,
> Fill me with albescent honey. . . . bend down to me,
> Rub to me with your chafing beard..rub to my breast and shoulders.[32]

Chilton writes:

> A fine, healthy, manly man meets a lovely, womanly woman. The look of recognition calls the color to face and neck. He speaks, and in her heart are awakened echoes never before dreamed of, making sweeter music than wind-kissed Eolian, or sweet voiced nightingale ever prophecied or foreshadowed. Has he done wrong in expressing by that look the involuntary admiration he felt on seeing her? Was it wrong to ask for the cup of cold water or the way to the next town? The needle is not more surely attracted to the pole than her heart to his. He takes her hand in parting. Why does she grow pale and lean against the casement, overcome with emotion. He would pass on his way, but a sweet spell binds him. Call it "sensual," brand it "bestial," denounce it as "lust," base "selfishness," anything an impure imagination can suggest; but ever will nature vindicate the purity of that admiring, reverential look, the purity of those manly

tones, the truth and inspiration of that electric touch; and, unless the most cruel wrong is done, the holiest feelings of womanhood outraged, the beauty, the truth, the love of that hour will be incarnated in Human Form Divine.[33]

She is saying here much the same thing that Whitman said in poem 15, the last of the 1860 "Enfans d'Adam" cluster, which became titled "As Adam Early in the Morning." She is saying, "Be not afraid of my body":

> Early in the morning,
> Walking forth from the bower, refreshed with sleep,
> Behold me where I pass—hear my voice—approach,
> Touch me—touch the palm of your hand to my body as I pass,
> Be not afraid of my body.[34]

Chilton's articles serve as preparation for reading her 1860 defense; they help to explain why Chilton publicly authorized herself as she wrote that defense; they create for us lines of connection between Whitman and serious, incisive, radical female activists like Mary Chilton.

In Chilton's 1860 defense of *Leaves of Grass,* she uses the same rhetorical strategies that she uses in her articles in the *Social Revolutionist.* She takes culturally loaded terms and shades or skews their meanings to create her own reformist view. In the 1857 "Sexual Purity," she uses "purity" to mean desire; to act in a "pure" way means to act on that desire. It most explicitly does not mean intercourse submitted to "purely" because of the marriage vow. In the *Leaves of Grass* review, she couples purity with religion, calling Whitman the "apostle of purity" and then the "poet of sexual purity." In 1857 she uses the term "vital force" when speaking of sexual attraction; in 1860 she calls Whitman "the teacher of the most vital, and hence the most Divine truth." She uses religious terminology in speaking of sexuality, thus conflating the body and soul and defusing the Calvinist belief in the duality of the psyche, just as Whitman did throughout *Leaves of Grass* and in "Song of Myself," in section 5. She argues for sexuality on the basis of organicism—that the parts of the body work to create the whole and that therefore no one part can be out of place, or vile. Those, however, who assert the doctrine of total depravity (alluding to Calvinism and to Calvin Beach's article)

must, she says, "find some part of the person too vile to think of."
Her review defends Whitman's poetry, but it also boldly defends
sexuality, a defense made by a woman in a society that worked to
silence women and to deny them control of their bodies.

On 10 June, one day after the *Saturday Press* ran Chilton's defense, an article by Adah Menken titled "Swimming Against the Current" appeared in the *New York Sunday Mercury,* in which Menken
defended Whitman. Menken—the actress and writer who in 1860
was married to the prizefighter John Heenan and who Lillian Faderman says in *Surpassing the Love of Men* was "undoubtedly not a
stranger to lesbian sex"—knew Whitman and admired his poetry.[35]
His influence can be seen in her own poetry. Charles Reade, the
English dramatist and novelist best known for *The Cloister and the
Hearth,* met Menken when she went to London in 1864 to perform
there. He said of her: "A clever woman with beautiful eyes—very
dark blue. A bad actress, but made a hit by playing 'Mazeppa' in
tights. . . . Menken talked well and was very intelligent."[36] Menken,
who like Whitman spent time at Pfaff's, in the 10 June *Sunday Mercury* article praises individuals who she feels have been courageous
in asserting their originality and who have gone against the taste
and mores of their culture to create a distinctly individual voice. The
list she gives of those who "swim against the current" is an eclectic
list: "Seward, Jefferson Davis, Sumner, Lovejoy, Wendell Phillips,
Beecher, Theodore Parker, Garrison, Walter Whitman, Mrs. Hatch,
and perhaps some few more." She singles Whitman out for his courage and perceptive reading of his culture: "Look at Walter Whitman,
the American philosopher, who is centuries ahead of his contemporaries, who, in smiling carelessness, analyzes the elements of which
society is composed, compares them with the history of past events,
and ascertains the results which the same causes always produced,
and must produce." His contemporaries, she says, "cannot comprehend him yet." R. H. Newell, the *Mercury* editor, who eventually married Menken, wrote a disclaimer to her article: "We are far from
endorsing all its sentiments, and are astonished to observe that Mrs.
Heenan indulges in a eulogium of that coarse and uncouth creature,
Walt Whitman. The lady is entitled to her own opinion, however,
though in the present expression of it she is certainly 'Swimming
Against the Current.' "[37]

Lillian Faderman's *Surpassing the Love of Man* provides a useful
source for nineteenth-century scholars interested in understanding

just what did constitute "love" between women. In addition, Faderman provides Whitman scholars with especially interesting insights
in her discussion of Charlotte Cushman, an actress Whitman admired (and whom Abby Price also admired), her remarks about
George Sand, and her brief comments on the friendship between
Menken and Sand. Throughout his life, Whitman speaks of George
Sand in almost rapturous terms; he speaks often of his admiration
of Cushman, whom he saw act; and he actually knew Menken. Like
the woman's rights activists whom Whitman knew, these women defied the model of the Cult of True Womanhood Woman. These
women do not image the Mother. They problematize our understanding of nineteenth-century sexuality. Faderman succinctly voices
the problem facing scholars today when she says that our difficulty
in understanding pre-twentieth-century sexual behavior lies in our
"assumption that what is true of behavior and attitudes today has
been true at all times."[38]

Six days after Menken's article, on 16 June, a long review blasting
Whitman appeared in the *Springfield Daily Republican*. The article,
titled " 'Leaves of Grass'—Smut in Them," was written in response
to Chilton's defense. Like the editorial voice of the *Mercury*, which
dissociated itself from Menken's approval of Whitman, the editorial voice of the *Springfield Republican* maintained that it had not intended to "notice" the new edition of Whitman's poetry but that
"certain of the soft heads, on the shoulders of men and women in-
discriminately, have conceived that it is a pure book. In the last number of the New York Saturday Press, Mary A. Chilton gives her ideas
of Walt Whitman's poetry generally, and especially of his smut; and
to show the public how far into degradation certain new lights are
ready to be led, we quote a portion of her letter, simply italicizing
such sentences as we wish to call special attention to." The editor
was especially incensed that the book had "respectable" credentials—a "respectable publisher—the author a writer for the Atlantic
Monthly—'for sale everywhere'—in very respectable type and binding." He goes on to note the attacks against Christianity that he sees
Leaves of Grass making, principally its appeal to nature as an authority rather than to "Christianity." He disparages Chilton's term "poet
of sexual purity." And he notes what he sees as the book's attack on
the institution of marriage: "The very first social institution that falls
into contempt after Christianity as a revelation is discarded is Christian marriage, and of all the 'teachings' in the world, we know of

none that so inevitably lead to impurity as those attributed to 'Nature.' " And Walt Whitman, he says, is "*par excellence* the 'poet of nature.' " The word "smut" in the title of the review leaves no doubt about the reviewer's scorn toward Whitman and *Leaves of Grass*. Emily Dickinson, a close friend of the *Springfield Republican* editors Samuel Bowles and Josiah Holland, would write two years later to her friend Thomas Wentworth Higgingson (25 April 1862): "You speak of Mr Whitman—I never read his Book—but was told that he was disgraceful."[39] A regular reader of the *Springfield Republican* as well as friend of the editors, Dickinson could hardly have missed this review with its condemnation not only of Whitman but of Mary Chilton as well.

One week after the *Springfield Republican* review, on 23 June, two more defenses of *Leaves of Grass* written by women appeared in the *Press* in response to the controversy that the poems provoked. One article was signed "A Woman" and one, "C.C.P." Gay Wilson Allen says that the review signed "A Woman" "seemed designed to counteract Mr. Beach's attack, and this may have been Mrs. Beach's belated review." Justin Kaplan calls the review "Juliette's own article . . . , signed 'A Woman.' " Betsy Erkkila also credits Juliette Beach as the author of the review.[40]

The particulars of Juliette Beach's and Whitman's relationship are not clear, but by examining the written evidence we have of their friendship, the following can be ascertained: Beach, a writer for Clapp's *Saturday Press,* had made her admiration of Whitman's work known to Clapp prior to the 1860 *Leaves of Grass,* so Clapp told Whitman to send her a copy of the 1860 edition to review: "You should send copies at once to Vanity Fair, Momus, The Albion, The Day Book, The Journal of Commerce, Crayon—also to Mrs. Juliette H. Beach, Albion, N.Y., who will do great justice in the S.P. (for we shall have a *series* of articles."[41] In spite of the furor that resulted over the 1860 publication and reviews, Beach and Whitman kept up some sort of friendship, which likely ended around 1871, except for Whitman's mention of her, though not by name, to Traubel in 1889: "There was a woman up there, a marvelous woman, who did some writing for the Press: she wrote about Leaves of Grass: there was quite a stew over it: some day I'll have to unbosom so you may know the ins and outs of the incident."[42] John Burroughs—the naturalist, writer, and friend of Whitman—said of her review (though not mentioning Beach by name): "The most pertinent and suggestive criticism of [*Leaves of Grass*] we have ever seen, and one that accepted it as a whole, was by a lady—one whose name stands high on the list of our poets. Some of the poet's warmest personal friends, also, are women of this mould."[43]

Clara Barrus, a physician and a friend and biographer of John Burroughs, says that Whitman wrote his 1865 poem "Out of the Rolling Ocean the Crowd" for Beach and that Beach had written "many beautiful" letters to Whitman that Burroughs had tried but failed to get her to publish.[44] Ellen O'Connor, Whitman's close friend from the time he moved to Washington until his death, mentions Beach to Whitman in three 1864 letters to him. In the original draft of Ellen O'Connor's article on Whitman, which appeared in the 1907 *Atlantic,* O'Connor claims that Whitman felt great sympathy, affection, and admiration for Beach. The Juliette Beach story is omitted in the published version of O'Connor's article.

Ellen O'Connor is another woman who had a life outside the home, though that life had not been mentioned in Whitman scholarship until Florence Freedman's 1985 *William Douglas O'Connor* documents Ellen O'Connor's interests and achievements. Most significantly, Ellen O'Connor wrote a book, published in 1885 by Houghton Mifflin, that tells the story of the school founded by Myrtilla Miner in 1851 "for the education of free Negro girls."[45] From 1850 to 1853, Ellen Tarr (O'Connor) was the governess of Gamaliel Bailey and Margaret Lucy Shands Bailey's children. At that time, Bailey was the editor of the *National Era,* the official voice of the Organization of American and Foreign Anti-Slavery Societies.[46] Ellen O'Connor attended the 19 September 1855, Woman's Rights Convention in Boston, where Paulina Wright Davis served as president. At this convention, reports were presented on the laws regarding women's property rights in the states of Rhode Island, Vermont, and New Hampshire. O'Connor presented the report on New Hampshire's laws, which read in part:

> The husband and wife are considered as one person, and her legal existence lost or suspended during the union.
>
> The husband becomes entitled, upon marriage, to all the goods and chattels of the wife, to the rents and profits of her and, becomes liable to pay her debts and perform her contracts.
>
> She has no legal power to contract.
>
> Thus we see, that while, in law, the "husband and wife are consid-

ered as *one person,"* that one is *the husband*—the wife is legally a *non-entity.*[47]

In 1911, two years before Ellen O'Connor's death, Sara M. Algeo featured Ellen O'Connor in the Sunday column of the *Providence Journal* "Equal Suffrage Notes," a column that represented the Rhode Island Woman Suffrage Association. Algeo writes:

> Whitman has left us the following description of [Ellen O'Connor]: "A superb woman, without shams, brags; just a woman. Ellen does not write; that gives her more time to get at the essentials of life." Words which have not remained wholly true, for Mrs. Calder's "Reminiscences of Walt Whitman," written but a few years ago for the Atlantic Monthly, and her contributions to the Una, edited by Paulina Wright Davis for the cause of suffrage, show much literary ability.
>
> When asked why she is an equal suffragist, Mrs. Calder says she was one at birth, and has seen or heard no valid arguments against equal suffrage since. To her it is simply "justice," and her faith in its value needs no defense. As an active worker in the early suffrage movement of the 60s, she was associated more or less closely with the leaders of the movement. Among them being Paulina Davis of Providence, Susan B. Anthony, Phoebe Cozens, Lucy Stone, Harriet Beecher Stowe and her sister, Isabella Beecher Hooker.[48]

Algeo also mentions that Ellen Tarr had at one time worked on Garrison's *Liberator.* There are letters from O'Connor in the Myrtilla Miner Collection at the Library of Congress, and there is an 1883 letter from Frederick Douglass to Ellen O'Connor in the Douglass Papers, also at the Library of Congress.

Reading Ellen O'Connor's original draft of her article on Whitman alerts us, once more, to the difficulty of determining Whitman's stance on the many issues he addresses in *Leaves of Grass.* Whitman's views evolved over time. Also, there is Whitman's dissimulation. Ellen O'Connor speaks in this article of Whitman's attitude toward free love. "He gave it no quarter, said that its chief exponent and disciple—Stephen Pearl Andrews—was of the type of Mephistopheles."[49] This free love discussion is not in O'Connor's original draft. It is also of interest to note that in an 1866 letter to Abby Price, Whitman tells her that he would be glad to meet Mrs. Andrews,

whom Miller footnotes as "possibly the wife of Stephen Pearl Andrews."[50] In her many letters to Horace Traubel after Whitman's
death, Ellen O'Connor would now and then allude to things that
she said she would discuss with Traubel but about which she would
not write. What she did write but what was edited out of her *Atlantic*
article is the following short sketch of the friendship between Whitman and Juliette Beach:

> He had met a certain lady and by some mischance a letter revealing
> her friendship for him fell into her husband's hands, which made
> this gentleman very indignant and jealous, and thereupon, in the
> presence of his wife and another lady, he abused Walt. All that ex-
> acted Walt's sympathy for the lady, over and above the admiration
> and affection he felt for her, so that in telling us about it he said, "I
> would marry that woman tonight if she were free." Correspondence
> was kept up between them for some time after that, the only instance
> I have known where he was strongly attracted toward any woman in
> this way. It was this lady for whom he wrote the little poem in "Chil-
> dren of Adam," beginning "Out of the rolling ocean, the crowd."
> Describing this lady to me, he said that she was quite fair, with brown
> hair and eyes, and rather plump and womanly and sweet and gentle,
> and he said that she bore herself with so much dignity and was so
> keenly hurt by what her husband said, that I think it drew him to
> her more. (This was in '64?) In connection with the above: the idea
> he conveyed to me was that he did not think it would have been well
> for him to have formed that closest of ties. He was so fond of his
> freedom, he so reacted from any restraint that I think he thought it
> would have been a great mistake if he had ever married. He said to
> me many times that he did not envy men their wives but he did envy
> them their children. He often used this expression: "Well, if I had
> been caught young, I might have done certain things or formed cer-
> tain habits."[51]

If Whitman did write the 1865 poem "Out of the Rolling Ocean the
Crowd" for Beach, it had to be as a rejection or consolation, to re-
assure her that though separated physically, spiritually they were not
separated, they would come together in the great scheme of things
(air, ocean, land), in time. In this context, it reads as a kind rejection,
or at least as kind as a rejection can be.

Ellen O'Connor mentions Juliette Beach in her 5 July 1864 letter to Walt: "In the hurry & suddenness of your leaving I forgot to give you Mrs. Beach's notes, shall I trust them to the mail, or keep them for you till you come back?" Beach may have been writing Whitman through Ellen O'Connor, in order to keep the correspondence from her husband. In the 18 August 1864 letter, Ellen O'Connor writes: "Have you seen a pretty little poem by Juliette H. Beach called *Claire?* It was published in the Leader? I infer that she has a new baby, a girl too." And finally, in her 30 November 1864 letter she wrote: "Enclosed I send you the little poem that we spoke of by Mrs. Beach." It is not surprising that Whitman valued Beach's friendship, for she had what many other women had who figured in Whitman's life—an independent mind and personal courage.

Juliette Beach was known to readers of the *Saturday Press,* since she contributed poems to the paper and occasionally wrote articles as well. Her work also appeared in other New York papers. Her review calls Whitman the long-awaited American poet; it argues for the acceptance of the body and the soul equally, denying, as Chilton had, the Calvinist rejection of the body; Beach argues for Whitman's (and God's) egalitarianism, again in contradistinction to Calvinism; she embraces Whitman's innovative style, speaking of the blend of prose and verse, and stresses the role of the reader. This last point distinguishes Juliette Beach as a critic and reader and marks her contemporaneity. In essence, she theorizes the role that the reader plays in the formation of textual meaning, anticipating (as did Whitman) our current interest in the reader's role. The parallel between Beach's and Whitman's interest in reader empowerment suggests reasons, beyond content, for Beach's interest in Whitman's poetry. It is possible, as well, that her articulation of the reading process helped Whitman to formulate his own articulation of the reader's role ten years later in the closing pages of "Democratic Vistas": "Books are to be call'd for, and supplied, on the assumption that the process of reading is not a half-slip, but, in highest sense, an exercise, a gymnast's struggle; that the reader is to do something for himself, must be on the alert, must himself or herself construct indeed the poem, argument, history, metaphysical essay—the text furnishing the hints, the clue, the start or frame-work."[52] In 1860, Beach sees Whitman's book doing what Whitman's "Democratic Vistas" advocated. She sees *Leaves of Grass* acting as a primer theorizing the role of the ideal democratic citizen, "men and women worthy a broad, free country," but in order for the book to be read and comprehended, she calls for educated readers: "If our sons and daughters were educated so that they could appreciate this book, we should in the next generation have men and women worthy a broad, free country." Here Beach's and Whitman's stances most directly coincide, with Whitman saying in 1871: "Not the book needs so much to be the complete thing, but the reader of the book does. That were to make a nation of supple and athletic minds, well-train'd, intuitive, used to depend on themselves, and not on a few coteries of writers." Beach says, however, in 1860 that most readers would read *Leaves of Grass* "literally only, and blindly, and therefore condemn the whole."[53]

Prior to Beach's review of Whitman's *Leaves of Grass,* she voiced her theoretical approach to criticism in a 26 November 1859 article in the *Saturday Press* discussing Augusta Jane Evans's novel *Beulah.* In response to an article written two weeks earlier by the *Press's* regular columnist Ada Clare, in which Clare called Evans's book a total failure, Beach argues against this kind of blanket condemnation of the book, looking at the writer's purposes in the book and analyzing the differences in the reading and writing cognitive processes. She views reading as a holistic process that defuses the sequential nature of language; writing, however, she considers determined to a great extent by time, by the sequential working out of the language and of the characters, both of which are influenced by the changes in the writer's own circumstances over time. By the time Beach wrote this review, Whitman's *Leaves of Grass* was already showing the evolving process and circumstantial effects that Beach defends. Beach also sees the role that an individual writer's point of view plays, calling an author's book "his dialect." For Beach, then, writers cannot distance themselves from their writings as readers (ideally) can. Beach's attempts at theorizing regarding the cognitive processes that go into reading and writing and her recognition of the role that ideology plays in language make her an unusual critic for her time.

Beach's notion of point of view—the author's "dialect" and, by extension, ideology—in a writer's work parallels in importance Whitman's notion of historical grounding. The ending paragraph of Whitman's 1876 Preface spells it out: Whitman tells us that he wrote out of his own distinct times and that his readers must factor in the history of the times in reading *Leaves of Grass:* "In estimating my Volumes, the world's current times and deeds, and their spirit, must be first profoundly estimated. Out of the Hundred Years just ending, (1776–1876) . . . , my Poems too have found genesis."[54]

Interesting though these parallels are, two letters that Juliette Beach wrote to Clapp, one on 7 June and one on 13 August, are even more so. As if to answer Calvin Beach's charge of Whitman's "ridiculous egotism," Juliette Beach tells Clapp in her June letter that she has the greatest faith in the book and that "its egotism delights me—that defiant ever recurring 'I,' is so irresistibly strong and good." Beach's statement is one key reason for considering *Leaves of Grass* a woman's book: the lack of a healthy ego in women was a common lament among women agitating for women's rights. Whitman's address to men and women and his stress on a healthy ego provided for women the "irresistibly strong and good" image that they needed.[55]

As in her review, Beach speaks of the role of the reader, or of *how* to read the book. She realizes that the proper *way* of reading the book would not be recognized as a component of the book itself but that it should be, that indeed *how* to read the book *should* be taken into consideration. She talks about the book's spirit, the need to take the book as a whole, and the influence that one's frame of reference has on her or his reception of the book. "It is useless," she writes Clapp, "in judging this book to draw dividing lines and say this is good, and this bad. It is to be accepted and examined and pronounced upon en masse." The book, she says, "is unfit to be read if read superficially, and not to be tolerated for an instant if viewed from the commonest social standpoints." She likes Whitman's rejection of what she calls "the vagueness of creeds" and says that Whitman is the poet that the age has waited for, an American original with a "fierce wild freedom from anything conventional."[56]

Beach's 7 June letter to Clapp speaks of her silencing: "I regret extremely that I have been obliged to deny myself the pleasure of writing at length and for publication, my view of Leaves of Grass. I feel sure that I could have reviewed the book in a manner worthy of it, and yet have been not misunderstood myself." She speaks of her inability to follow her own inclination to write to Whitman because she had promised not to. She speaks here, then, of her culture, which erected barriers for women's self-expression, and of her husband's possession of her self. In her 13 August letter, she speaks of her bitter regret that because she was a woman, she was denied the "happiness" of Whitman's friendship. "Outwardly," she writes to Clapp, "[*Leaves of Grass*] has caused me more pain and trouble than I have ever known before.—I do not deny that inwardly it has given me happiness and peace" (7 June letter).

"Being a woman, and having read the uncharitable and bitter attacks upon the book," the author of the other 23 June article, signed C.C.P., says, "I wish to give my own view of it." Because we know Whitman's record of self-reviewing and Clapp's practice of assuming personae, we may well wonder who wrote this review. Any of a large number of women who were Whitman's friends could have written the piece. Whitman's friend Abby Hills Price was one; Price had also been Clapp's friend since sometime in the 1840s. The *Press* columnist Ada Clare was another, as was Adah Isaacs Menken.[57] And then again, C.C.P. may not have been involved in any movement nor have been a writer or public figure at all. She may have been what is claimed in the review—a woman writing because she wished her voice, her view, to be heard.

C.C.P.'s review echoes points that Chilton and Juliette Beach made: the democratic or leveling effect that Whitman achieves in his poetry, the recognition of sex as a principle of life on a par with birth and death, the organic form of *Leaves of Grass,* and the force it holds in the creation of an American literature. C.C.P.'s review criticizes the current literature, calling it sentimental and hypocritical, as it assumes a "semblance of virtue." The review also indirectly comments on Calvin Beach's article, his singling out for censure the "Children of Adam" cluster and what he sees as the poetry's complete degradation of women. C.C.P., however, speaks of Whitman's regard for women: "a reverence . . . which holds the 'woman just as great as the man' and a mother 'The melodious character of the earth, the finish beyond which philosophy cannot go and does not wish to go.' "[58]

The controversy stirred by the publication of the 1860 *Leaves of Grass,* and specifically the "Children of Adam" cluster, has not ceased. In Whitman's time, Whitman was damned because he did not protect women by veiling their sexuality; in our time, some say that he protects women too much—makes too much of women as mothers, cannot see beyond timeworn gender stereotypes, does not see women as individuals. The "Children of Adam" cluster, which contained, according to the Boston district attorney, the largest number of offensive passages in *Leaves of Grass,* passages that needed to be excised because of their excessive sexual openness, is now seen, by some, as conservative.

The Boston district attorney's attempt to ban the sale of *Leaves of Grass* unless specific passages and poems were expurgated occurred in the spring of 1882. That June, Whitman's article "A Memorandum at a Venture," which addressed censorship and the treatment of sexuality in literature, appeared in the *North American Review.* The opening sentences frame the question as if in debate: "Shall the mention of such topics as I have briefly but plainly and resolutely broach'd in the 'Children of Adam' section of 'Leaves of Grass' be admitted in poetry and literature? Ought not the innovation to be put down by opinion and criticism? and, if those fail, by the District Attorney?"[59] Sexual passion, Whitman says, is part of life and thus must be treated in his poetry: "as the assumption of the sanity of birth, Nature and humanity, is the key to any true theory of life and the universe—at any rate, the only theory out of which I wrote—it is, and must inevitably be, the only key to 'Leaves of Grass,' and every part of it." The use of "sanity of birth, Nature and humanity" to argue for the inevitability of sex reiterates the same arguments made by the 1860 defenses of *Leaves of Grass* by women appearing in the *Saturday Press.* As if circling back to the 1860 controversy, Whitman then mentions the *Springfield Republican* and its attack on him. He also directly addresses the connection between women's rights and female sexuality: "To the movement for the eligibility and entrance of women amid new spheres of business, politics, and the suffrage, the current prurient, conventional treatment of sex is the main formidable obstacle. The rising tide of 'woman's rights,' swelling and every year advancing farther and farther, recoils from it with dismay. There will in my opinion be no general progress in such eligibility till a sensible, philosophic, democratic method is substituted."[60] In the 1850s, Price, Rose, Davis, and Stanton had argued for liberalized divorce laws, property rights for married women, women's entry into the professions, and equal educational opportunities.

In May 1860 three weeks before Calvin Beach's attack on Whitman appeared in the *Saturday Press,* Ernestine L. Rose and Elizabeth Cady Stanton had boldly called for liberalized divorce laws at the tenth National Woman's Rights Convention, held at the Cooper Institute in New York City. By 1882, in contrast to these two earlier periods, the women's rights movement had become more conservative, more of a one-issue movement. A woman like Mary Chilton would have a difficult time finding a representative voice in a movement with Frances Willard as one of its primary spokespersons. Frances Willard, though she accomplished her own victories for women's rights, was not a Frances Wright woman, as Whitman called women he admired, such as Anne Gilchrist or Mary Whitall Smith Berenson, and as the press in the 1850s (disparagingly) described Ernestine L. Rose. Willard first proposed that the Women's Christian Temperance Union (WCTU) support the suffrage movement in 1875. When she was elected in 1879 as president of the WCTU, suffrage became one of the organization's goals. Though she agitated for some of the same things Rose and Stanton did, she "attempted to justify these reforms on grounds that made them consistent with 'true womanhood' and acceptable to the evangelical Protestant culture from which most WCTU women came."[61] To some extent, there is a correlation, then, between the changes that the women's rights movement experienced and the changes Whitman made in his representations of women as *Leaves of Grass* evolved. Beginning with the 1867 edition of *Leaves of Grass,* Whitman's revisions accentuated the image of women as the Mother of All. Structurally, however, the cluster that Whitman called his "sex odes"—"Children of Adam"—remained intact and changed little.

Out of the original fifteen poems in the "Children of Adam" cluster, Whitman removed only one poem: "In the New Garden" appeared only in the 1860 edition. In terms of Whitman's sexual politics, the omission is significant. The editors of the Comprehensive Reader's Edition say that "In the New Garden" "in part resembles" the poem that opens the cluster, "To the Garden the World."[62] The endings of these two poems, however, differ dramatically in terms of gender politics. "In the New Garden" ends with the lines: "For the future, with determined will, I seek—the woman of the future, / You, born years, centuries after me, I seek" (*Leaves of Grass,* Comprehensive Reader's Edition, 594). The ending of the 1860 "To the Garden the World" reads: "By my side or back of me Eve following, / Or in front, and I following her just the same" (*Leaves of Grass,* Comprehensive Reader's Edition, 90). The coordinating conjunctions linking Eve and the Whitman/Adam poet-persona in "To the Garden the World" carefully play off the interchange of leadership positions. In the other poem, "In the New Garden," Eve is nonexistent, not yet evolved. This 1867 omission of "In the New Garden" is significant and is one of the few cases of a change that Whitman made in the 1867 edition that strengthens the image of women along the lines of the radical position in the woman's rights movement.

Eleven of the poems in this cluster were new to the 1860 edition. One, "I Sing the Body Electric," appeared in the 1855 edition. Two poems—"A Woman Waits for Me" and "Spontaneous Me"—appeared in the 1856 edition. Two poems were added after 1860: "Out of the Rolling Ocean the Crowd," which first appeared in *Drum-Taps*, 1865, and "I Heard You Solemn-Sweet Pipes of the Organ," which first appeared in the 1865–1866 "Sequel to Drum-Taps."

A trope running through much of the cluster occurs in the first poem, "To the Garden the World": "Curious here behold my resurrection after slumber" (*Leaves of Grass*, Comprehensive Reader's Edition, 90). The cluster, as a whole, turns on the idea of awakening, of seeing the world anew (and sexually) once the individual strips off societal frames of reference. The law that the persona sees, then, is the law of unity, the conflation of body and soul rather than the Calvinist (and transcendentalist) elevation of the soul over the body—a hierarchical relationship—and rejection of the body's essential goodness, thus fragmenting the psyche.

"We Two, How Long We Were Fool'd," the ninth poem in the "Children of Adam" cluster of sixteen (in the 1891 edition), holds a central position in both the 1891 and 1860 editions of *Leaves*. Like "To the Garden the World," "We Two" plays on the idea of awakening, though in this poem the awakening involves recognizing false consciousness and shedding it. The entire poem revolves around the trope of transmutation. The change or transmutation is seen positively in that the "we" of the poem awaken to desire, but there is also a tonally bitter reading as the two recognize the deceit that existed in their lives prior to their awakening. Here are the first eleven lines of the 1860 version of the poem:

> You and I—what the earth is, we are,
> We two—how long we were fooled!
> Now delicious, transmuted, swiftly we escape, as Nature escapes,
> We are Nature—long have we been absent, but now we return,
> We become plants, leaves, foliage, roots, bark,
> We are bedded in the ground—we are rocks,
> We are oaks,—we grow in the openings side by side,
> We browse—we are two among the wild herds, spontaneous as any,

We are two fishes swimming in the sea together,
We are what the locust blossoms are—we drop scent around the lanes,
    mornings and evenings,
We are also the coarse smut of beasts, vegetables, minerals,[63]

The use of the word "spontaneous" within this cluster and in this poem aligns this poem with the language used, on a regular basis, by the free-lovers to validate so-called natural attraction and to link attraction with nature. The argument ran, among some free love advocates, that attraction was something that just "happened" and that thwarting its expression was an "unnatural" act. Laws that regulated the expression of this "natural" attraction should be repealed or changed. The acts of shedding false consciousness and awakening to one's essence are societal and personal acts that take for a model in the natural world a popularized notion of the Lamarckian concept of evolution. This pre-Darwinian reading of evolution takes into account the role that the environment plays in bringing about an organism's change, but it also posits an Enlightenment twist when it views the organism as playing a role in its change. The popularized view of Lamarck took what Lamarck called "sentiment interieur" and saw in this concept an organism's "right" (or will) to develop unfettered. Woman's rights activists like Paulina Wright Davis and Abby Hills Price substituted "right" society for environment and the inherent rights of women (and men) for Lamarck's notion of "sentiment intérieur" to argue by analogy that a society that obeyed "natural" laws would allow individuals to develop unthwarted.[64] In such a society, women would have equal rights with men. The two in "We Two," then, are to cast off society's (false) projections and to become what their ("natural") selves desire. Once society's restrictions are removed, the "two" unfold to their desired essences.

We are Nature, long have we been absent, but now we return,
. . . .
We have circled and circled till we have arrived again, we two.[65]

When read by free love advocates, this poem confirms the principles that the movement supported: love must grow out of attraction, and love, like nature, must be allowed conditions for growth and change. Marriages, then, should not be irrevocable. When read by women working within the woman's rights movement, the poem creates an image of perfect equality—the two of "we two" are equal twos—and read in this way, the poem argues for the kind of active participation by women that the more radical women in the movement promoted. When read by gay men and lesbians (terms that did not exist in 1860), the poem confirms the authenticity of their desires as it rejects models imposed by society. Throughout the poem, the scientific basis of change or evolution undergirds its argument.

Since this poem appears in the "Children of Adam" cluster, most readers expect the "we" persona to be male and female—male and female plants, fish, hawks, suns. If it is read in this way, then we can see that by 1860 Whitman had made the move that Harold Aspiz claims he has made: according to Aspiz, Whitman's notion of sexuality became more a matter of reciprocity as his own ideas evolved. Aspiz says that Whitman "sometimes employs the premise (particularly in the early editions of *Leaves of Grass*) that the male is the sole transmitter of the electric spark of life and that the female is the source chiefly of the life-giving sustenance."[66] Aspiz cites Dr. Edward Dixon and Dr. Russell Trall as authorities for Whitman. Aspiz then cites lines from the 1856 "Poem of Procreation" (later titled "A Woman Waits for Me"), lines that Whitman deleted in the 1860 *Leaves of Grass:*

> O! I will fetch bully breeds of children yet!
> They cannot be fetched, I say, on less terms than mine,
> Electric growth from the male, and rich ripe fibre from the female are the
>   terms.[67]

Aspiz feels that through the deletion of these lines, "the principle of electric maleness which animates the Adamic persona in *Leaves of Grass*" has been blurred.[68] Thus, if the "we" in "we two" is read as male and female, the poem becomes a model of egalitarianism.

Likewise, blurring takes place in the following line from "We Two": "We are two resplendent suns, we it is who balance ourselves orbic and stellar, we are as two comets."[69] If indeed the "we" personae in this poem were read by Whitman's contemporaries as including both a male and a female, then the two equal suns cut away at any notion of polarized heavenly bodies, one more energized than the other. The blurring of the polarized male/female essences creates conditions of equality between male and female in Whitman's poem, but the blurring also creates the possibilities of same-sex unions. The "we," cleverly on Whitman's part, is never named a "he" and a "she." Thus, depending on the readers, the "we" could be two "he's," two "she's," androgynous "he's" or "she's," or, more conventionally, a heterosexual coupling. Gender typing that was conventional for the times is blurred throughout the poem: "We are what locust blossoms are. . . . We are also the coarse smut of beasts. . . . We prowl fang'd and four-footed. . . . We are two clouds. . . . We are what the atmosphere is, transparent, receptive, pervious, impervious." These two "we's" slide in and out of gender-marked associations, gleefully. They are not naive, however, for they know the issue in the gender debate—whether society or biology is the primary determinant of gender: "We are each product and influence of the globe." They know balance: "We it is who balance ourselves orbic and stellar, we are as two comets." Finally, the use of "you" in the first line, a line that appeared only in the 1860 edition, directly addresses the reader, ensuring that the reader becomes intimately part of the "we," sharing the possibilities it suggests, sharing the blurring of gender demarcations.[70] Blurring, blending, fusing—all are words Whitman favored, especially the latter two. The concept of the one and the mass, the individual and the union, the individual body and the fused body of sexual intercourse can be traced as a thread running throughout *Leaves of Grass,* a seemingly simple concept but one that continues to dominate political discourse. The idea of inclusivity, of variety yet equality, of tolerance, of difference—race, sexual orientation, spiritual acceptance—yet a cohesive society, was, for Whitman, the riveting question.

The whole premise of this poem—how long we were fooled—claims, then, that arbitrary social and legal structures have denied the we-personae their desired essence, whether that essence is a radically different heterosexual relationship from what society endorsed and enforced or a homosexual one—female-female or male-male. The actual lives of Mary Chilton, Adah Menken, and Ada Clare rejected the arbitrary structures that this poem challenges, and the more radical of the woman's rights activists challenged their antebellum societal structures in public words, written and spoken. These women spent time with Whitman; he considered them his friends.

Once we know that Whitman had numerous women as friends

and that these women lived highly politicized lives, Charles Eldridge's assessment of Whitman—the letter in which Eldridge said that "[Whitman] delighted in the company of old fashioned women; mothers of large families preferred, who did not talk about literature and reforms"[71]—simply fails to make its case. Whitman's mother does not neatly fit that description, nor do Chilton, Beach, Clare, Menken, Price, Rose, and Davis, not to mention Frances Wright, whom Whitman greatly admired, and many other women whom I have not mentioned. The facts of Whitman's life invalidate Eldridge's interpretation, which can be used to argue that Whitman's representation of women in his poetry and prose was reductive.

Eldridge, however, was not the only friend to misinterpret Whitman's view of women's rights and gender sensitivity. On the evening of 4 July 1889, Horace Traubel walked over to Whitman's Mickle Street house to pick up the revisions that Whitman had made in Traubel's manuscript, which was to become *Camden's Compliment.* Traubel mentions some of Whitman's changes:

> [Whitman] proposed speaking of "army hospitals" instead of simply "hospitals," and "secession war" instead of "war," and "the *person* Walt Whitman" instead of "the *man*" Walt Whitman"—certainly this last, a radical improvement in musicalness; suggested also "His love for the *aggregate race*" instead of "for the whole race of *man*." [Emphasis added][72]

Whitman was seventy years old at the time; Traubel, thirty-one. But Whitman's awareness of the political power of language far exceeded that of his progressive young friend. Whitman's concept of American democracy demanded gender equality, and so "musicalness" was not in Whitman's mind when he changed "man" to "person" and "race of man" to "the aggregate race." Rather, Whitman's awareness of his audience prescribed the change, his awareness of the role language played both in terms of his own poetic program—to address all of America—and his belief in the role poetry played in creating the kind of democracy that he believed the future held for the United States. Women took part in this democracy.

Conclusion

What kind of women, then, does Whitman envisage in his ideal democracy? For an answer we might look in Whitman's 1871 "Democratic Vistas." In this remarkable work, Whitman addresses the issues of gender, parentage, and women's rights in ways that are radical for his time, and, in some cases, for our own time as well. Still, "Democratic Vistas" can cause problems for female readers, as when Whitman occasionally uses the word "man" seemingly to mean the biological male only. Whitman says, for example: "Intense and loving comradeship, the personal and passionate attachment of man to man—which, hard to define, underlies the lessons and ideals of the profound saviours of every land and age, and which seems to promise, when thoroughly develop'd, cultivated and recognized in manners and literature, the most substantial hope and safety of the future of these States, will then be fully express'd." He footnotes the passage: "It is to the development, identification, and general prevalence of that fervid comradeship, (the adhesive love, at least rivaling the amative love hitherto possessing imaginative literature, if not going beyond it,) that I look for the counterbalance and offset of our materialistic and vulgar American democracy, and for the spiritualization thereof."[1]

When Whitman says "adhesive love," does he mean only male-male love? And what, finally, does "love" mean? If Whitman means by "adhesive love" same-sex love, then how do we account for his exclusive focus on males when in the culture of his time same-sex attachments among females were the rule, not the exception, and these attachments were defined in multiple ways, not exclusively by genital contact, as in our culture? Is Whitman's focus a result of a glaring absence in his culture, the result of Whitman's need to inscribe what he saw as lacking but what he believed necessary—a lack in the culture of generosity of spirit in male relationships? By the end of 1870, when Whitman was putting the closing words to "Democratic Vistas," two important movements were underway in the United States: Reconstruction and the intensified swing to corporate capitalism, which created a period now called the Gilded Age. In the footnote to "Democratic Vistas" that I have quoted above, Whitman goes on to talk about "manly friendship," describing it as "fond and loving, pure and sweet, strong and life-long." In the context of Whitman's time, it is difficult to imagine that a more anachronistic terminology could be used to describe adult male relationships.

One year later, in a letter dated 16 January 1872 to Rudolf Schmidt—the Danish poet, editor, and champion of *Leaves of Grass* in Denmark—Whitman outlined for Schmidt what he called the "object" of his poetry: "The main object of my poetry is simply to present—sometimes by directions, but oftener by indirections—the Portraiture or model of a sound, large, complete, physiological, emotional, moral, intellectual & spiritual *Man,* a good son, brother, husband, father, friend & practical citizen—& *Woman* also, a good wife, mother, practical citizen too—adjusted to the modern, to the New World, to Democracy, & to science." On 18 January, he wrote Edward Dowden—professor of English literature at the University of Dublin, Shakespeare scholar, and admirer and critic of *Leaves of Grass:*

> I would say that . . . the spine or verteber principle of my book is a model or ideal (for the service of the New World, & to be gradually absorbed in it) of a complete healthy, heroic, practical modern Man—emotional, moral, spiritual, patriotic—a grander better son, brother, husband, father, friend, citizen than any yet—formed & shaped in consonance with modern science, with American Democracy, & with the requirements of current industrial & professional life—model of a Woman also, equally modern & heroic—a better daughter, wife, mother, citizen also, than any yet.[2]

In these two lists of relationships, Whitman includes as a part of the model of a sound woman the role of the citizen, which speaks for his positive stance regarding woman's rights. What is strangely and disturbingly lacking, however, is his inclusion of women as friends, a quality that both lists require for the model man. I am not sure how to account for this disparity, but given the importance of phrenology to Whitman (and his culture), where adhesiveness was always represented by two women, I keep thinking that the explanation lies in what was in the cultural consciousness and what was not. Whitman's Utopian project required him to inscribe what he could not find there, and male-male affection was absent as a representation.

Whitman makes it clear in "Democratic Vistas" that when he speaks of individuality as "the pride and centripetal isolation of a human being in himself—identity—personalism" he means that women share in this kind of pride, as well as men. In "Democratic Vistas," for example, he speaks of "a single person, male or female," of a "full-grown man or woman," of "self-hood—female and male," and "American personalities . . . male and female." He announces the potential strength of "the women of America" and criticizes cultural and gender coding:

> Democracy, in silence, biding its time, ponders its own ideals, not of literature and art only—not of men only, but of women. The idea of the women of America, (extricated from this daze, this fossil and unhealthy air which hangs about the word *lady*,) develop'd, raised to become the robust equals, workers, and, it may be, even practical and political deciders with the men—greater than man, we may admit, through their divine maternity, always their towering, emblematical attribute—but great, at any rate, as man, in all departments; or, rather, capable of being so, soon as they realize it, and can bring themselves to give up toys and fictions, and launch forth, as men do, amid real, independent, stormy life. [*Prose Works 1892*, 2:389]

The movement of the prose reveals Whitman's own mind processing the implications of the new woman and the changes she would inaugurate. Democratic women will become (will be "*raised* to become") "robust equals and workers"; that much is declaratively stated. But Whitman qualifies the next statement, demoting women: "it *may* be" they will "even" become "practical and political deciders with the men." In the next breath, however, promotion occurs.

American women will become "greater than man . . . through their divine maternity, always their towering, emblematical attribute." The capacity for childbirth, then, tips the scale, making women superior to men, a proposition that Eliza Farnham developed in *Woman and Her Era* (1864). In the next statement, Whitman equalizes the field: "great, at any rate, as man, in all departments"; he then qualifies again, "or, rather, capable of being so." The rest of the passage could have been said by Price, Rose, or Davis, who repeatedly criticized the cultural valorization of the "lady," seeing it as a trap for women, as a way to keep women powerless, passive. They too used the image of woman as toy. They too wanted women out in the "real, independent, stormy life." Whitman's use of the word "fossil" in connection with the word "lady" expresses his belief that science—and specifically evolution—had rendered obsolete governments that were based on hierarchical distinctions of class—"feudalism"—and religions that defined themselves narrowly and exclusively. Evolution rendered obsolete disembodied women, "ladies."

In another passage in "Democratic Vistas," Whitman once more speaks of women. The two areas in American society most lacking, he says, were "moral conscientious fibre" and "the appalling depletion of women in their powers of sane athletic maternity." Once more, he speaks of maternity as women's "crowning attribute . . . , making the woman . . . superior to the man": "I have sometimes thought, indeed, that the sole avenue and means of a reconstructed sociology depended, primarily, on a new birth, elevation, expansion, invigoration of woman, affording, for races to come, (as the conditions that antedate birth are indispensable,) a perfect motherhood. Great, great, indeed, far greater than they know, is the sphere of women. But doubtless the question of such new sociology all goes together, includes many varied and complex influences and premises, and the man as well as the woman, and the woman as well as the man" [*Prose Works 1892*, 2:372–73].

Whitman's sense that the issue of an empowered motherhood was complex shows in this last sentence, in which he says in effect that he knows motherhood (ideally, parentage) *should* empower women but that he does not know how to change society to enable it to do so, though I do not know what to make of the last sixteen words. Perhaps they say that the confusion is equal to both sexes. No doubt Whitman would have no trouble agreeing with the version of the story of human evolution advanced by Nancy Tanner and

Adrienne Zihlman and reported and expanded by Ruth Bleier in *Science and Gender:*

> One important value of Tanner and Zilhman's viewpoint is that it does not begin with the assumption of woman's passivity and dependence as a basis for scenario-building of human evolution. It recognizes, unlike other evolutionary scenarios, that such a premise finds no supporting evidence from any species of animals nor, with only rare and historically recent exceptions, from human cultures. Their view attaches great importance to women's childbearing and lactation, as do other biosocial theories. Unlike other biosocial theories, however, they do not see reproduction as a force leading inevitably to helplessness and dependence. Rather, they view it as a social force leading to selection for innovativeness, sociability, and cooperativeness, since they consider early foraging mothers with dependent children as being highly motivated to increase their food-gathering capabilities, to invent tools and carriers for that purpose, and to be the protectors of their young against predators.[3]

If our culture privileged parentage in the way that Whitman did, and if parentage as a role had fiscal backing and therefore had "currency" in our society, then the privileging that Whitman gave motherhood (and fatherhood—that is, parentage) would make sense to us, given the standards that determine "success" in mainstream America (namely money). If the private role of parenting had public status backed by fiscal independence for the mother, then I would feel no discomfort when I read Whitman praising motherhood. As it is, Whitman's respect for motherhood is often maddening or embarrassing, maddening because of the common assumption that motherhood means self-sacrifice, at the ultimate expense of the mother, and particularly when motherhood means economic dependence. All too often, women have taken the role of the mother seriously indeed, only to find a divorce on hand or a spouse disabled and no means of supporting a family, since, indeed, their priority had been the job that Whitman privileges: caring for the children. Or a reader might not be angered by the glorification of Motherhood so much as embarrassed, embarrassed for Whitman, regarding him as a mere sentimentalist, seeing him glorifying an abstraction, an empty object of the male's fantasy—the Mother providing all that is needed (for everyone but herself), economically dependent, providing the culture, the seedbed, so to speak, into and out of which males move.

Betsy Erkkila speaks of Whitman's view of motherhood much as Abby Price did when she said that the private, isolated home unjustly limited possibilities, that the home should include the entire family of "man." Erkkila closes *Whitman the Political Poet* with a discussion of Whitman's view of the mother as the figure that "challenged a political economy based on the separation of female and male, private and public, home and world, by placing the values of community, equality, creation, and love at the center rather than at the margins of democratic culture." Erkkila quotes Whitman's poem "America," written in 1888:

> Centre of equal daughters, equal sons,
> All, all alike endear'd, grown, ungrown, young or old,
> Strong, ample, fair, enduring, capable, rich,
> Perennial with the Earth, with Freedom, Law and Love,
> A grand, sane, towering, seated Mother,
> Chair'd in the adamant of Time.[4]

Whitman, Erkkila says,

> had little patience with the Christian benevolent model of female behavior propagated by Catherine Beecher in *A Treatise on Domestic Economy* (1842). His mothers do not exist as wives in relation to individual husbands, nor are they pious, pure, domestic, or self-sacrificing in any limited sense of the terms. Like feminist works ranging from Margaret Fuller's *Woman in the Nineteenth Century* (1845) to Charlotte Perkins Gilman's *Herland* (1915) to Adrienne Rich's *Of Woman Born: Motherhood as Experience and Institution* (1976), Whitman sought to remove motherhood from the private sphere and release the values of nurturance, love, generativity, and community into the culture at large. Exceeding the bounds of home, marriage, and the isolate family, Whitman's "perfect motherhood" is motherhood raised to the height of solicitude for the future of the race.[5]

It is the motherhood Price calls for: "Say not to [women] you have done all you may do, keep your minds and attention within that narrow circle, though your nature and ripened intellects would fain be interested in whatever concerns the larger family of man, and your affections, strong in a healthful growth, yearn towards the suffering and the afflicted of every country."[6]

For many women, to give birth is to experience empowerment, power in a positive sense. The stripping of power comes afterward when marriages go bad or spouses die and women are faced with the sole financial responsibility of young children. For males in to-day's world, children are frequently also lost through divorce. The balance for which Whitman calls, so deceptively simple sounding, has not yet been achieved today. The "new sociology" to which Whit-man referred still lies in the future.

It is true, however, that Whitman at times glorified motherhood in terms of the female's biological role. He too was at times mired in his culture's ideology. But it is inconceivable to me that Whitman saw the body as in any totalizing way demarcating the possibilities of a person's life. Whitman envisioned not a homosexual, heterosexual, or bisexual world but rather, I think, to use James E. Miller's term, an omnisexual world. When Whitman depicted male/female sex, however, women all too often became objects, acted upon (no matter the cultural explanations), as in "A Woman Waits for Me." Further-more, there is no cluster of poems in *Leaves of Grass* that speaks of women's sexual love for women. But there are many other images of women. If we do not see these other images, and if we fail to read the images of women within their cultural context, we will fail to see the ways in which Whitman pushed his own notion of gender roles beyond what he was initially used to and comfortable with, beyond what was tolerated by the mainstream culture.

He could see beyond the arbitrary boundaries attributed to the body and on some level see that "motherhood" was not gender bound, just as the possibilities of sexual intercourse were not bound by male/female coupling. When we read in *With Walt Whitman in Camden* that Whitman fixed lunches and sent them to the sick girl who lived next door to him, what was he practicing here?[7] Mother-hood? Fatherhood? Or to use a term Whitman uses in "Democratic Vistas," "parentage"? For the most part, Whitman wanted to break down arbitrary barriers between people, to legitimate possibilities that in his culture were considered "unnatural": "I am for anything which will break down barriers between peoples."[8] In the democracy Whitman envisioned, he demanded "a programme of culture, drawn out, not for a single class alone, or for the parlors or lecture-rooms, but with an eye to practical life, the west, the working-men, the women also of the middle and working strata, and with reference to the perfect equality of women, and of a grand and powerful motherhood." To achieve the kind of citizen he envisioned, he called for forethought: "Parentage must consider itself in advance. (Will the time hasten when fatherhood and motherhood shall become a science—and the noblest science?)" (*Prose Works 1892*, 2:396–97).

If in place of motherhood Whitman had routinely used the word "parentage," perhaps no one today would have a problem with Whitman's images of women. Parentage, mentioned most often by Whitman as motherhood, performed in the personal realm the role that the Union did in the public. Parentage and the Union provided the seedbed, so to speak. Though the metaphor is ill chosen in terms of women, the seedbed for Whitman meant parentage, not only gestation. Whitman thought of the Union as the seedbed for the individual citizen. The more nourishing the seedbed, the more nourished, Whitman believed, the individual citizen: "Underneath the fluctuations of the expressions of society . . . , we see steadily pressing ahead and strengthening itself . . . this image of completeness in separatism, of individual personal dignity, of a single person, either male or female, characterized in the main, not from extrinsic acquirements or position, but in the pride of himself or herself alone. . . . it is mainly or altogether to serve independent separatism that we favor a strong generalization, consolidation. As it is to give the best vitality and freedom to the rights of the States . . . that we insist on the identity of the Union at all hazards" (*Prose Works 1892*, 2:374).

I have argued that the first three editions of *Leaves of Grass* represent "woman under the new dispensation" more than do the last three editions. The last three shifted the emphasis from representing the individual woman to the Mother of All, as Whitman sought to revise *Leaves* in order to strengthen images that represented union. In Whitman's ideal world, however, shifting the image from the activist woman to the Mother of All was not a demotion.

The point that Whitman stresses more than any other in "Democratic Vistas" is the need to inscribe into the culture of the United States that which is not there—the democratic ideology that the words of the Declaration of Independence and the Bill of Rights guarantee but that is not yet a political, actual fact. He saw literature as the medium most suited to accomplish the reification of national ideals into a national life. He felt literature to be the art form most accessible to the masses. He demonstrated the need for a new kind of representation to fit the new political facts when he offered four brief portraits of the New Woman in "Democratic Vistas." The four portraits were intended to serve as a suggestion of the ways in which literature could inscribe images of women in a democratic country. Whitman is doing here what Price, Davis, and Rose called for in their speeches.

Two of these four portraits differ from the images of women in Whitman's poetry. The tensions in Whitman between what he knew and was comfortable with and what he knew was consistent with his theory of democracy surface in instructive ways in these four images of the democratic woman. Judged by today's standards, these images seem bland. Carefully read in their historical context, however, they show Whitman imaging women's space as expansive, yet they show as well the poet's concern that such expansion would paradoxically not result in constriction. They show Whitman moving back and forth between possibilities at odds with the notion that women's innate qualities dictate their place in society. In so doing, he challenged prevailing concepts of the "nature" of "woman."

Is subjectivity a matter of biology, as present-day cultural feminists argue? Or is it a matter of positioning and language, a stance that poststructuralists take? In the nineteenth century, women's rights activists who argued on the basis of women's innate moral superiority sound much like today's cultural feminists, while women who argued for equal rights based on "natural" rights used rationales that align them with present-day poststructuralists. Nineteenth-century activists moved relatively unproblematically between these two views, using each to make their points. Whitman moved between them as well.

Here are Whitman's four portraits:

> I have seen a young American woman, one of a large family of
> daughters, who, some years since, migrated from her meagre coun-
> try home to one of the northern cities, to gain her own support. She
> soon became an expert seamstress, but finding the employment too
> confining for health and comfort, she went boldly to work for others,
> to house-keep, cook, clean, &c. After trying several places, she fell
> upon one where she was suited. She has told me that she finds noth-
> ing degrading in her position; it is not inconsistent with personal

dignity, self-respect, and the respect of others. She confers benefits and receives them. She has good health; her presence itself is healthy and bracing; her character is unstain'd; she has made herself understood, and preserves her independence, and has been able to help her parents, and educate and get places for her sisters; and her course of life is not without opportunities for mental improvement, and of much quiet, uncosting happiness and love.

I have seen another woman who, from taste and necessity conjoin'd, has gone into practical affairs, carries on a mechanical business, partly works at it herself, dashes out more and more into real hardy life, is not abash'd by the coarseness of the contact, knows how to be firm and silent at the same time, holds her own with unvarying coolness and decorum, and will compare, any day, with superior carpenters, farmers, and even boatmen and drivers. For all that, she has not lost the charm of the womanly nature, but preserves and bears it fully, though through such rugged presentation.

Then there is the wife of a mechanic, mother of two children, a woman of merely passable English education, but of fine wit, with all her sex's grace and intuitions, who exhibits, indeed, such a noble female personality, that I am fain to record it here. Never abnegating her own proper independence, but always genially preserving it, and what belongs to it—cooking, washing, child-nursing, house-tending—she beams sunshine out of all these duties, and makes them illustrious. Physiologically sweet and sound, loving work, practical, she yet knows that there are intervals, however few, devoted to recreation, music, leisure, hospitality—and affords such intervals. Whatever she does, and wherever she is, that charm, that indescribable perfume of genuine womanhood attends her, goes with her, exhales from her, which belongs of right to all the sex, and is, or ought to be, the invariable atmosphere and common aureola of old as well as young.

My dear mother once described to me a resplendent person, down on Long Island, whom she knew in early days. She was known by the name of the Peacemaker. She was well toward eighty years old, of happy and sunny temperament, had always lived on a farm, and was very neighborly, sensible and discreet, an invariable and welcom'd favorite, especially with young married women. She had numerous children and grandchildren. She was uneducated, but possess'd a native dignity. She had come to be a shepherdess, and reconciler in the land. She was a sight to draw near and look upon, with her large figure, her profuse snow-white hair, (uncoif'd by any head-dress or cap,) dark eyes, clear complexion, sweet breath, and peculiar personal magnetism. [*Prose Works 1892*, 2:400–1]

The woman in the first sketch takes on significance as she defies the conventional role of nineteenth-century white middle-class women, a role we now call the "Cult of True Womanhood." (If one subscribed to the belief in the moral superiority of women, it followed that one would also support the social division of domestic space from workspace; the woman would find her place, "naturally," at home protecting the morals.) The role of the True Woman bound the woman to the home and required her to exhibit piety, purity, and subservience; preferably she was married and had many children. The woman in Whitman's first sketch, however, defies this convention by being a single working woman supporting herself but still reaching beyond herself to help educate her sisters. An important point here in light of my discussions of Price, Rose, and Davis is that for this woman, education and marriage are not mentioned in a cause/effect relationship. In fact, marriage is not mentioned at all.

The woman works in the two respectable occupations open to women at the time—sewing and domestic service. She leaves the first because it is ruining her health; then she "boldly" tries one position after another as a domestic worker until she finds one that suits her. This position gives her independence, time, and opportunity for personal "mental improvement"; it gives her a sense of self-dignity. Whitman addresses in a positive way the very things so problematic for working women—the closed-shop nature of the workplace (the lack of options available for women who wanted and had to work), the stigma that domestic employment held for many working women, and the lack of time it gave them for self-improvement. By boldly pursuing the job market, Whitman says, a woman could get a job she could accept. By treating the two approved professions open to women, he works within conventional possibilities. The single most important message, however, is that this woman lives on her own, without the prop of marriage; she acts boldly, not submissively. She is not a woman who reflects the Cult of True Womanhood.

The sketch is interesting when placed next to another piece that Whitman wrote on working women, an unpublished manuscript called "Wants":

Our daily papers, in New York, show that the "wants" of the human race, hereabout, are by no means those few which philosophers have long been in the habit of recommending.—Every morning, there they appear—stretched columns of them—of one general character, and stereotyped phrase—but still with a certain variety that marks the difference of nation, taste, or circumstance.—

Life, to both poor and rich, in great cities, is an excitement and a struggle!—Those of our readers, in the country, who jog along their solid, easy way, and are not in danger of falling on slippery places, know very little of the shifts and frequent desperations of the existence of the poor in cities—which go far to counterbalance the supreme advantages that, (reasoners may say what they like,) make the city so attractive and fascinating.

These "wants" in the news papers are illustrative of the precarious nature of employment and existence here.—

The vast majority of those who have to do with the "Wants" department, are, domestic servants who need places and mistresses who need "help."[9]

In this sketch, Whitman states that in employment offices, "You will notice . . . hardly any Americans; probably none.—At the places we have beheld in our daily walks, we do not yet remember seeing a single American, of either sex."

There are striking differences between the description of the women in the "Wants" manuscript and the portrait in "Democratic Vistas." The obvious difference is that the woman in "Democratic Vistas" is a "young American woman" who has migrated from the country to the city, rather than from Europe to the United States. Another telling point is the amount of control on which the woman who takes the job in domestic service insists in "Democratic Vistas," control that Whitman carefully incorporates into the sketch. The women that Whitman depicts in the "Wants" article are not in a position to choose, but the young woman in "Democratic Vistas" chooses to leave her job as a seamstress because it is unhealthy and then tries out several positions as domestic servant, choosing and rejecting until she finds one that pleases her. In this context, it is fitting to recall Paulina Wright Davis's point—that it was important for women to choose their work and not to take a job purely on the grounds of survival, that until women could choose they were not truly exercising economic independence. Though the young woman in "Democratic Vistas" had virtually no choice in the *kind* of job she took, and thus did not meet Davis's criteria, she did choose her employer, and Whitman takes extreme care in emphasizing that her job is respectable and respected. In the "Democratic Vistas" sketch, Whitman avoids even the hint that this young woman is in servitude. Rather, he insists that *she* sets the limits: "She has made herself understood, and preserves her independence" (*Prose Works 1892*, 2:400).

Since the positions of seamstress and domestic worker were the two jobs most available to working women, in this portrait Whitman seems to be trying to work within the actualities of his time while suggesting that these actualities could be reformed. Whitman appears to accept these positions and perhaps even idealize them, but he also offers an image of a woman who resists conditions in order to create, within the range of her possibilities, a life better for herself than she would have had if she hadn't resisted, if she hadn't "boldly" tried different positions until she found one that gave her not only self-respect, money, and beneficial work but also time to improve herself. The job that this woman eventually finds does not fit the picture that Christine Stansell paints of domestic help in the nineteenth century; but then, Whitman is making images not of elements actually present in his culture but of elements he wanted to find there.

The woman in Whitman's second sketch even more overtly challenges the principles of the Cult of True Womanhood, as he uses activists' terms to sketch the new dispensation woman. Here we have another woman who is single. This woman, however, does not work for somebody else; she runs her own business. She "dashes out more and more into real hardy life, is not abash'd by the coarseness of the contact . . . , and will compare, any day, with superior carpenters, farmers, and even boatmen and drivers," all positions that Whitman admires. Her engagement outside the home circle is precisely what Abby Price called for. Note, however, that this woman does not lose "the charm of the womanly nature" as a result of her moving out of the home circle. Here Whitman reassures his society (and himself) that women, are, after all, women, thus suggesting a notion of essentialism. The woman in the second sketch has rejected cultural encoding and launched herself successfully into a business. This kind of representation of women rarely appears in Whitman's poetry, though the qualities she possesses appear. This sketch is the one that most radically crosses gender lines in depicting possibilities for women and work.

The third sketch appears innocuous to the contemporary reader if it is read ahistorically, but after it has been placed in its cultural context, it shows Whitman once more resisting his own culture's mainstream ideology. The woman in the third sketch is the wife of a mechanic; she does not herself carry on "a mechanical business," as does the woman in the second sketch. She resists the prescribed role of wife in two ways, however: she takes time away from domesticity (duty to and for others) for herself, and even more out of character, she has only two children. What makes this image of a mother with only two children especially significant in the context of *Leaves of Grass* is that it modifies the widespread notion of Whitman as the poet of fecundity, echoing his culture's obsession with eugenics. What would have made the image of this woman especially significant to the women reading it in 1871 is this implicit message of birth control, of the woman's control, at least to some degree, over her body. It is important for readers today to recognize this point.

Though Whitman was working against the grain of his culture in these respects, he nonetheless still voiced his culture's values. Here in the third sketch, the language is much more eloquent about this woman's joy in her "genuine womanhood" than in the previous two. The language voices the attractiveness the domestic role held for Whitman. Alternatively, though this possibility seems to me unlikely, he was following the lead of nineteenth-century women activists themselves, who rarely omitted paying some degree of homage to domesticity, no matter how passionately they sought change.

While Whitman saw the inevitability and logic of "woman under the new dispensation"—that is, of the need for women to move out of the home to work in the public sphere—he also feared the change. For one thing, the change in priorities would be disruptive. But I think too that Whitman feared the consequences of the new dispensation woman because he feared that she would lose the inclusive vision that he felt many women had and most men did not— the ability to see beyond the confines of self and to see the importance of community, defined as family, town, or, for Whitman, nation. The inclusiveness, cohesion, and nurturance that he saw in his mother and other women became qualities increasingly difficult to find in his culture following the Civil War as the United States moved into the Gilded Age. Whitman believed that citizens must exercise these communal qualities in order for his concept of democracy to work. He kept saying that males had to catch up—"The great chastity of paternity, to match the great chastity of maternity." I do not believe that he meant, ultimately, that these qualities were gender-bound, though he frequently spoke in these terms, nor did he mean that they occurred only in heterosexual, homosexual, or parental relationships: in a democracy, such qualities would have to infuse all human relationships.

The fourth and last sketch in "Democratic Vistas" portrays the Mother of All. In it we see an eighty-year-old woman whom Whitman called the Peacemaker, a mother and grandmother of many children—the Republican Mother. The same qualities she has shown in her life as "domestic regulator, judge, settler of difficulties . . . reconciler in the land" are those that America needed to bind the states into a Union. Whitman, as noted earlier, spoke of his own mother as the Peacemaker, and more than once he called her as "the greatest patriot of them all." Whitman said he learned about this peacemaker from his mother, but she could have been modeled on Louisa Whitman herself. In addition to resembling Louisa Van Velsor, this Peacemaker as physically described sounds much like press accounts of Lucretia Mott, whom Whitman said he knew "just a little: she was a gracious, superb character."[10] In reporting on the 1852 National Woman's Rights Convention, the *Syracuse Standard* wrote of Lucretia Mott: "It was a singular spectacle to see this gray-haired matron presiding over a Convention with an ease, dignity, and grace that might be envied by the most experienced legislator in the country."[11]

Following the four portraits, Whitman comments on images of women in literature current at the time: "The foregoing portraits, I admit, are frightfully out of line from these imported models of womanly personality—the stock feminine characters of the current novelists, or of the foreign court poems, (Ophelias, Enids, princesses, or ladies of one thing or another,) which fill the envying dreams of so many poor girls, and are accepted by our men, too, as supreme ideals of feminine excellence to be sought after. But I present mine just for a change" (*Prose Works 1892*, 2:401). What Whitman says here Lucretia Mott said in 1849 when she responded to a series of lectures given that year by Richard Henry Dana. He had censured American women for their new demands and "eulogized

Shakespeare's women, especially Desdemona, Ophelia, and Juliet, and recommended them to his dissatisfied countrywomen as models of innocence, tenderness, and confiding love in man, for their study and imitation."[12] In place of Shakespeare's female characters, Mott offered Elizabeth Fry and Dorothea Dix as positive role models.

Years later, Whitman and Traubel had a conversation about a performance of *Othello,* which Traubel had attended. Whitman questioned Traubel in detail about the performance. He asked him about a Mrs. Bowers, whom he had known when they both were younger and who had played Emilia, Iago's wife.[13] Whitman inquired about Bowers's "vigor, port, voice—how all had lasted." He commented: "I saw her Emilia long ago. Emilia is not a great part. I think anyhow, if Shakespeare had any weakness, it was in his women. All his women are fashioned so: in King John, in Richard—everywhere—the product of feudalism—daintily, delicately fashioned. Yet I suppose all right, occupying a fit position—in themselves a reflex of their times, though to us, to our eyes, open to criticism."[14] The women Whitman presents in his four portraits are no Desdemonas, Juliets, nor Ophelias. Though each one of Whitman's four representations of women in his "Democratic Vistas" portraits is bounded by conventions, each suggests new possibilities. To varying degrees, each actively works to create her own life circumstances.

At the tenth National Woman's Rights Convention, held at Cooper Institute in New York City on 10 and 11 May 1860, Susan B. Anthony mentioned, in passing, the role that literary women had played in the woman's rights movement: "Who of our literary women has yet ventured one word of praise or recognition of the heroic enunciators of the great idea of woman's equality—of Mary Woolstonecraft [*sic*], Frances Wright, Ernestine L. Rose, Lucretia Mott, Elizabeth Cady Stanton?"[15] Whitman's third edition of *Leaves of Grass,* which went on sale just days after Anthony spoke these words, recognized—though not by name—female "heroic enunciators" in poems like "Vocalism," "Mediums," "Song of the Broadaxe," "Our Old Feuillage," and others. His insistence that democracy demanded a new kind of hero recurs in the following passage: "Of course, in these States, for both man and woman we must entirely recast the types of highest personality from what the oriental, feudal, ecclesiastical worlds bequeath us, and which yet possess the imaginative and esthetic fields of the United States, pictorial and melodramatic, not without use as studies, but making sad work, and forming a strange anachronism upon the scenes and exigencies around us. Of course, the old undying elements remain. The task is, to successfully adjust them to new combinations, our own days" (*Prose Works 1892*, 2:401–2).

Reflecting on the direction being taken by the new women he had presented as possible models for his ideal democratic society, Whitman said: "Then there are mutterings, (we will not now stop to heed them here, but they must be heeded,) of something more revolutionary. The day is coming when the deep questions of woman's entrance amid the arenas of practical life, politics, the suffrage, &c., will not only be argued all around us, but may be put to decision, and real experiment" (*Prose Works 1892*, 2:401). It is helpful to remember that this passage was written in the heat of the debate over the Fourteenth and Fifteenth Amendments when the woman's movement was splintering over the very issues Whitman mentions here. Though this statement about women's participation in public and political life is not so bold a statement as Whitman made in his unpublished "Primer of Words" (*An American Primer*), written in 1856, it takes a bold stand, given its context, and it confirms that what Whitman learned from Price, Davis, and Rose did not vanish with the Civil War.

This book began in chapter 1 with letters to Walt Whitman from his mother. It will also end with letters to Whitman but not, this time, from his mother. Rather, the letters come from women who wrote to Whitman from the 1880s and until his death in 1892, women who admired him and his work.

The Charles Feinberg–Walt Whitman Collection, in the Manuscript Division of the Library of Congress, includes letters written to Whitman during these last years. Many responded to newspaper reports of Whitman's failing health. I have collected those that were written by women. One of these letters, from Helen Wilmans, is representative. In it she told Whitman that *Leaves of Grass* had educated her, that it had "done more to raise me from a poor working woman to a splendid position on one of the best papers ever published, than all the other influences in my life."[16] The Thomas B. Harned Collection of Walt Whitman's Papers, in the Library of Congress, includes a clipping dated 25 November 1882, from the first issue of a newspaper edited (and for the most part written) by Helen Wilmans, titled *The Woman's World*. Apparently Wilmans moved from working on a newspaper to publishing and editing one of her own.

Wilmans is an outspoken woman whose politics were radical for her day, certainly, and for our day as well. The first article, occurring in the first column of the paper, is titled "I." The first sentence reads: "To arouse the manhood of men and the womanhood of women,—this is the great necessity." She calls on people to respect themselves, to love themselves, to project ideal selves, and to grow toward these ideals. She then quotes Whitman and goes on to say, "It is the 'I' that I like in Walt Whitman's works. The honesty of the self-assertion; the frank confession of egotism. Doubt of one's self begets chronic distrust of one's own manhood or womanhood." Her words recall Juliette Beach's when she says about *Leaves of Grass:* "Its egotism delights me—that defiant ever recurring 'I,' is so irresistibly strong and good."[17]

Wilmans maintained her connection with Whitman after his death. The Horace L. and Anne Montgomerie Traubel Collection, at the Library of Congress, includes a letter from Charles F. Burman, Wilmans's business manager, and one from Wilmans as well, written to Horace Traubel and dated September 1902. Wilmans had moved to Florida and was now publishing a paper called *Freedom*. She had written an article in the 3 September issue of *Freedom* praising Traubel's own paper, the *Conservator.* Helen Wilman represents one of those women to whom Whitman referred when he spoke of women whose names do not appear in history: "It was in them to do actions as grand—to say as beautiful thoughts—to set examples for their race.—But in each one the book was not opened.—It lay in its place ready."[18]

It seems fitting to close with a selection of women's letters from the Feinberg-Whitman Collection, a chorus of women's voices replying to Whitman. He must have sat at his second-story window in his modest home on Mickle Street, in Camden, New Jersey, with the Delaware River barely in view, as he read these letters. The letters must have helped to fill that "terrible, irrepressible yearning, (surely more or less down underneath in most human souls)—this never-satisfied appetite for sympathy, and this boundless offering of sympathy—this universal democratic comradeship" of which Whitman spoke as one of the forces that motivated him to write *Leaves.* Just as Louisa's letters were filled with her expressions of love and gratitude toward her son Walt, so too are these women's words.

I often think about you, and you have written so many lines for me that I wish to say a word back. When I read I say, 'Yes, I am she' . . . , and sometimes I think I must put out my hand for you; and I am sure that we have gone together down that brown road a great many times; and perhaps it was my pulse that you heard.
 Eleanor Lawncy. Louisville, Kentucky. 5-11-84

Through the year just gone, I have come to count you my dear friend. It grows to be a need for me to let you know how much joy and strength you have given me—and through me to others who did not know you till I took you to them. You are in the world with me and it seems ungrateful to take so much in silence. I want you to know that you have helped another human, who returns your love for the help and thanks you beyond expressing.
 Elizabeth Coffin. Brooklyn. 1-1-91

I have known you for years through your poems and although I am a perfect stranger to you yet you can never be a stranger to me. . . . I have looked into your heart, that heart large enough to call all men your brothers, all women sisters! Hence I consider myself one of your sisters—
 Jennie Wren. New York City. 3-19-91

I have written sometimes what seemed poetry to me but when I tried to put it in regular harmonious order hoop it round like a barrel, as it were, the poetry was all choked out and it fell flat and insipid from my hands. [My poem] is only a harmless conceit of a working woman. . . . My husband was a southern soldier and is dead; it seemed as if it would be a sort of satisfaction to me if I could think in my mind, 'Walt Whitman has read my attempt at poetry.' I do not believe you will misunderstand my sentiment.
 Theresa Brown. Waco, Texas. 5-8-91.

For a long time you have been a friend to me through your poems, and I am very very grateful to you for what you have written so nobly and fearlessly and for the wider thoughts, and greater aims, that have come to me in reading and learning what you write. [Having your name in my copy of *Leaves*] will seem to me while I treasure it as a handclasp from someone that I love and reverence and honor.
 Josephine Webling. New York City. 11-11-91.

[Your words] open up Vistas. . . . I know that things that troubled me formerly will have power to vex me no longer, I will be at ease, with you for my friend, I will commune with you more frequently. . . . If I could I would clasp your hand and tell you that I felt your physical weakness and suffering.
Isabel Brown. Ottawa. 1-5-92.

Though unknown to you I cannot forbear in this way to take you by the hand and tell you that I am glad to call myself your friend. I want to thank you for [*Leaves of Grass*]. . . . It has helped me to see and understand more the beauty and truth that is in the world, and given me a broader sympathy for all mankind—and an insight into the reality of life. Please pardon the familiarity of my writing, this letter is just for you alone and is from the heart of a friend.
Mrs. J. L. Pittman. Brooklyn. 1-6-92.

I am only what I think in America you call a "school marm" and of no "eminence," but I expect it's the average intellect you most want to touch as they form the bulk of the living beings. [*Leaves of Grass* and *Specimen Days*] are both moral tonics in their joyous healthiness and seem to me just the antidote that is needed to all the morbid self-analysis and sickly sentimentality of the present age. I never read them without feeling more strongly than ever what a beautiful sane thing human life is. I wish, as I am a woman, you had told us more of your views about us. I wonder what your ideal of woman is.
Jessie Taylor. Maryborough, Australia. 8-7-88.

Since reading [your poems], I have felt conscious of a new vista opening before me. . . . I wish I could explain to you in what way they touched as with a magnet some latent chord. And yet I feel there is no need to explain anything. . . . I have already reached across the water and clasped your hand. I think you will understand all I would convey. The little picture of your home life in Specimen Days has so much interested me. Now I feel as if I knew you in the flesh as well as in the spirit.
Louisa Snowdon. London. 8-2-87.

No man ever lived whom I have so desired to take by the hand as you. I read Leaves of Grass, and got new conceptions of the dignity and beauty of my own body and of the bodies of other people; and life became more valuable as a consequence. Always carrying you in my thoughts—holding imaginary conversations with you. . . . I am proud of my feeling for you. It has educated me; it has done more to raise me from a poor working woman to a splendid position on one of the best papers ever published, than all the other influences of my life.

Helen Wilmans. Chicago. 5-21-82.

Notes

Introduction

1. Traubel, *With Walt Whitman in Camden*, 4:188.

2. Alys married Bertrand Russell in 1894, but by 1902 Russell had fallen "completely out of love with her." See *Mary Berenson: A Self-Portrait from Her Letters & Diaries*, ed. Barbara Strachey and Jayne Samuels (New York: W. W. Norton, 1983), 106. Barbara Strachey was Mary's first grandchild, the daughter of Ray Costelloe Strachey and Oliver Strachey.

3. In 1891 Mary left her husband to live with the Italian art connoisseur Bernard Berenson, and she married him in 1900 after Costelloe died. Frank and Mary Costelloe had two daughters, Ray and Karin. Ray, who married Oliver Strachey, became an activist for women's rights and a writer. Her most significant book is *The Cause: A Short History of the Women's Movement in Great Britain* (1929).

4. Traubel, *With Walt Whitman in Camden*, 3:313.

5. Traubel, *With Walt Whitman in Camden*, 4:188.

6. Walt Whitman, *Manuscripts, Autograph Letters*, 82.

7. Folsom, "Prospects," 4, 9.

8. Walt Whitman, *Daybooks and Notebooks*, 3:772–73.

9. Killingsworth, "Tropes of Selfhood," 41.

10. Allen, *The Solitary Singer*, 202.

11. Price, "Letter from Helen Price," 28.

12. Price, "Reminiscences of Walt Whitman," *New York Evening Post*, May 31, 1912, p. 2.

13. Allen, *The Solitary Singer*, 125.

14. Folsom, " 'Scattering it freely forever,' " 139–40.

15. Walt Whitman, "To William D. O'Connor," 6 January 1865 (letter 149), in *The Correspondence*, 1:247.

16. Traubel, *With Walt Whitman in Camden*, 2:331.

1. Louisa Van Velsor Whitman

1. Louisa Van Velsor Whitman to Walt Whitman, 12 January 1872 and 19 January 1872, Trent Collection, Special Collections Library, Duke University, Durham, N.C. Whitman material in Special Collections at Duke University is hereafter cited as "Trent Collection." The transcript bears the date 1873, but the context leads me to date it to the preceding year. All of Louisa Van Velsor Whitman's letters to Walt Whitman on which I draw in this chapter are transcripts of the original letters in this collection. The dating of the transcripts is often conjectural. Except where I note otherwise, I have used the dates that appear on the transcripts.

2. Walt Whitman, 1855 Preface, in *Prose Works 1892*, 2:443.

3. Walt Whitman, "As at Thy Portals Also Death," *Leaves of Grass*, Comprehensive Reader's Edition, 497.

4. Traubel, *With Walt Whitman in Camden*, 2:113–14.

5. Gohdes and Silver, *Faint Clews*, 183.

6. Miller, *Walt Whitman's Poetry*.

7. Cavitch, *My Soul and I*. A shortened version of Cavitch's argument, "The Lament in 'Song of the Broad-Axe,'" appears in Krieg, *Walt Whitman: Here and Now*, 125–35.

8. December 1863, Trent Collection, transcript dated March 1863.

9. My study is a revisionary interpretation based on extensive examination of the 143 letters from Louisa to Walt in the Trent Collection at the Duke University Library; Louisa's letters to Walt in the Hanley Collection in the Harry Ransom Humanities Research Center in Austin; Louisa's letters to Helen Price in the Pierpont Morgan Library in New York City; Helen's letters (and one from her mother, Abby, to Louisa) in the Trent Collection; and letters to her from various friends and relatives in the Charles Feinberg–Walt Whitman Collection in the Manuscript Division at the Library of Congress in Washington, D.C. I also have Whitman's letters to her, collected in *The Correspondence*, as further contextualization. For theoretical grounding I am indebted to feminist theory in general. Feminist historians have been invaluable in all of my work.

10. Whitman visited his mother in the fall of 1863, a year after he left

Brooklyn to live in Washington. He commented in a letter he wrote to his soldier friends in the Armory Square hospital: "[My mother] is cheerful & hearty, & still does all her light housework & cooking—She never tires of hearing about the soldiers, & I sometimes think she is the greatest patriot I ever met, one of the old stock—I believe she would cheerfully give her life for the Union, if it would avail any thing—and the last mouthful in the house to any union soldier that needed it" (Walt Whitman, "To Lewis K. Brown," 8–9 November 1863 [letter 94], in *The Correspondence*, 1:179).

11. 21 April 1873, Trent Collection.

12. About 1 November 1863, Trent Collection.

13. Stansell, *City of Women*, 45.

14. 25 June 1868, 19 November 1867, 18 January 1866, Trent Collection.

15. 23 June 1869, Trent Collection.

16. 13 June 1871, Trent Collection.

17. 19 December 1865, Trent Collection.

18. Stansell says, "Household work involved [urban working women] constantly with the milieu outside their own four walls; lodgers, neighbors, peddlers and shopkeepers figured as prominently in their domestic routines and dramas as did husbands and children. It was in the urban neighborhoods, not the home, that the identity of working-class wives and mothers was rooted" (*City of Women*, 41). Certainly Louisa Van Velsor Whitman's circle extended beyond her brownstone floor, but she also guarded her own space and feared for its loss.

19. Walt Whitman, "To Louisa Van Velsor Whitman," 28 March [1848] (letter 5), in *The Correspondence*, 1:33.

20. 3 May 1867, Trent Collection. Note Louisa's use of the words "comfort" and "contented." These words recur frequently in Louisa's letters.

21. Walt Whitman, *The Correspondence*, 1:326.

22. About 20 April 1869, Trent Collection.

23. 31 March 1869, Trent Collection.

24. 14 April 1869, Trent Collection. Mattie's willingness to take action in contrast to Hannah's unwillingness is illustrated in the following vignette, which Louisa included in a letter to Walt. The vignette also illustrates the seemingly good relationship between Mattie and Jeff, and it illustrates a practice that was common at the time: women took in piecework in order to support themselves or, in Mattie's case, to make supplemental income. The letter is dated 29 August 1865. Louisa writes: "martha has very much to doo she has been foolish enoughf to take 2 or 300 dozens of shirt fronts and she cant get them stiched every girl is full of work so she and

Jeff has set up every night till midnight to work i think she will be perfectly satisfied when she gets this lot done to not take any more." Louisa was worried that Mattie had taken on too much, because Mattie's health was poor. Mattie died at thirty-seven from tuberculosis.

25. Walt Whitman, *Manuscripts, Autograph Letters,* 82.

26. November 1863, Trent Collection.

27. 27 February 1865, Trent Collection.

28. 20 June 1867, Trent Collection.

29. Walt Whitman, *"Leaves of Grass": A Textual Variorum,* 245 (hereafter cited as *Variorum*).

30. 1 July 1868, Trent Collection.

31. 11 September 1865, Trent Collection.

32. 7 June 1866, Trent Collection.

33. 12 February 1868, Trent Collection.

34. November 1863, Trent Collection.

35. 25 February 1868, Trent Collection.

36. 13 March 1868, 7 April 1868, 5 May 1868, Trent Collection.

37. 24 March 1869, Trent Collection.

38. Walt Whitman, *The Correspondence,* 1:151.

39. 9 February 1871, Trent Collection.

40. 24 March 1868, Trent Collection.

41. Walt and Louisa also mention in their letters the books he sent to his sisters Mary and Hannah and to his friend Helen Price. He sent his niece Hattie at least one copy of the *Graphic.*

42. 17 February 1868, Trent Collection.

43. 11 March 1868, Trent Collection.

44. 30 November 1870, Trent Collection.

45. 5 May 1868, Trent Collection.

46. 27 February 1867, Trent Collection.

47. 12 February 1868, Trent Collection.

48. 21 February 1867, Trent Collection.

49. 28 December 1868, Trent Collection.

50. 31 March 1868, Trent Collection.

51. 14 November 1865, Trent Collection.

52. Helen E. Price, "Reminiscences of Walt Whitman," *[New York] Evening Post,* 31 May 1919.

53. 27 April 1867, Trent Collection. The interchange of newspapers between the two was an ongoing process. In a letter dated 3 December 1865, she asked Whitman whether he had received the *Union* that she had asked Jeff to send. In a letter dated 3 March 1867, she told him she was

sending along a piece about him that she had cut out of the *Williamsburg Times*. On 19 November 1867 she remarked, "George got the Broadway he thought the piece was very good they say the december galaxy will be out about the 26th." On 20 April (?) 1869 she said that she was enclosing a compliment from the *Philadelphia Bulletin*.

54. Louisa Van Velsor Whitman to Walt Whitman, 25 November 1865, Trent Collection. *Drum-Taps* had been printed in May. Thomas and James Rome ran a printing shop in Brooklyn, on the corner of Fulton and Cranberry, and printed Whitman's 1855 *Leaves of Grass*.

55. 1 August 1867, Trent Collection.

56. 25 February 1868, Trent Collection.

57. See Freedman, *William Douglas O'Connor,* 204–5.

58. Allen, *The Solitary Singer,* 416. See also Marion Walker Alcaro's *Walt Whitman's Mrs. G.*

59. Allen, *The Solitary Singer,* 420.

60. About August 1870, Trent Collection.

61. Helen Price to Maurice Bucke, 7 May 1881, Charles E. Feinberg–Walt Whitman Collection, Manuscript Division, Library of Congress.

62. Mid-March 1873, Trent Collection. Lou's home fit the perfectly engineered model introduced to the United States in the 1840s by works such as Catharine Beecher's *Treatise on Domestic Economy* and Andrew Jackson Downing's *Cottage Residences.* See Kathryn Kish Sklar, *Catharine Beecher: A Study in American Domesticity* (New York: Norton, 1973), xi.

63. Walt Whitman, *Variorum,* 1:82.

64. Louisa Van Velsor to Helen Price, October 1872, MA 918, Pierpont Morgan Library (hereafter cited as "Morgan"), New York City.

65. 26 November 1872, Morgan.

66. 9 January 1873, February 1873, 13 March 1873, Morgan. The numerous occurrences of these words in Louisa's letters to Walt and Helen Price indicate to me how difficult it was for Louisa to maintain composure and to find contentment and comfort.

67. Lou wanted her aunt there ostensibly to take care of her, since Lou believed that she was pregnant. As a consequence of the "rest-cure"—a cure devised by S. Weir Mitchell that made women in essence invalids—she stayed in bed; George even carried her up and down stairs.

68. Quoted in Traubel, *With Walt Whitman in Camden,* 4:514.

69. Walt Whitman, *The Correspondence,* 2:187, n. 42.

70. Walt Whitman, *The Correspondence,* 2:200–1, n. 25.

71. Walt Whitman, *The Correspondence,* 2:208–9, n. 47.

72. Walt Whitman, *The Correspondence,* 2:223, n. 91.

73. Walt Whitman, *The Correspondence,* 2:240.
74. Walt Whitman, *The Correspondence,* 2:245.
75. Walt Whitman, *The Correspondence,* 2:248.
76. Walt Whitman, *The Correspondence,* 3:69.
77. Quoted in Traubel, *With Walt Whitman in Camden,* 5:95.
78. Morgan, 18 April 1873.
79. Morgan, October [1872].
80. Martha Mitchell Whitman, *Mattie.*
81. Quoted in Barrus, *Whitman and Burroughs,* 57 and 254.
82. Ellen O'Connor, "Walt Whitman." This version of O'Connor's article was lent to me by Gay Wilson Allen. I appreciate his generosity.
83. Quoted in Traubel, *With Walt Whitman in Camden,* 1:78.
84. Walt Whitman, *The Correspondence,* 1:110.
85. Walt Whitman, *The Correspondence,* 1:183.
86. Walt Whitman, *The Correspondence,* 1:185.
87. Walt Whitman, *The Correspondence,* 1:186.
88. Quoted in Traubel, *With Walt Whitman in Camden,* 1:11.
89. Traubel, *With Walt Whitman in Camden,* 3:500.
90. Quoted in Traubel, *With Walt Whitman in Camden,* 2:280.
91. Walt Whitman, *Notebooks,* 1:435.
92. Tanenbaum, "Sisterhood," 18.
93. Quoted in Barrus, *Whitman and Burroughs,* 339.
94. Walt Whitman, *Notebooks,* 1:81–82.
95. Quoted in Traubel, *With Walt Whitman in Camden,* 3:581.
96. Michael, "Woman and Freedom in Whitman," 220.
97. Erkkila, "The Federal Mother," 427.
98. Erkkila, *Whitman the Political Poet,* 316–17. For a negative view of Whitman and motherhood, see Wrobel, "Noble American Motherhood," 7–25. For a discussion of Whitman and motherhood that looks at the cultural perception of motherhood, see Killingsworth's "Whitman and Motherhood," 28–43.
99. Walt Whitman, *The Correspondence,* 1:59.
100. Walt Whitman, *Variorum,* 2:480–81.
101. Walt Whitman, *The Correspondence,* 1:203. For a gay critical approach to Whitman's relationship with Civil War soldiers, see Shively's *Drum Beats.*
102. Walt Whitman, *The Correspondence,* 1:205.
103. Walt Whitman, *The Correspondence,* 1:230.
104. Walt Whitman, *The Correspondence,* 1:81–82.

105. In this respect, the activists used mainstream ideology subversively—to achieve ends that patriarchy denied them.

106. Walt Whitman, *Variorum,* 1:157.

107. Walt Whitman, *Variorum,* 2:374.

108. Walt Whitman, *Variorum,* 2:526–27.

109. Walt Whitman, *Variorum,* 2:556.

110. Walt Whitman, *The Correspondence,* 1:114–15.

111. Walt Whitman, *The Correspondence,* 1:203.

112. Walt Whitman, *The Correspondence,* 1:204.

113. Walt Whitman, *Variorum,* 3:639.

114. Walt Whitman, *Prose Works 1892,* 2:381.

115. Walt Whitman, *Variorum,* 3:671.

116. Walt Whitman, *Variorum,* 3:694.

117. Helen E. Price, "Reminiscences of Walt Whitman."

118. Walt Whitman, *Variorum,* 2:552.

119. Walt Whitman, *Variorum,* 2:553.

120. Walt Whitman, *Variorum,* 2:556.

121. Walt Whitman, *Variorum,* 2:542.

2. Abby Hills Price

1. Quoted in Campbell, *Man Cannot Speak for Her,* 1:68.

2. For a recent discussion of Pfaff's, see Christine Stansell's "Whitman at Pfaff's," 107–26.

3. Sokolow, "Culture and Utopia," 96.

4. Sokolow, "Culture and Utopia," 93.

5. For a recent discussion of Whitman and science, see Robert J. Scholnick, " 'The Password Primeval.' "

6. Mary Wright Johnson, letter to [Ellen Wright], 20 May 1857, Garrison Family Papers, Sophia Smith Collection, Smith College, Northampton, Mass. Ellen Wright was Martha Coffin Wright's daughter and Lucretia Mott's niece.

7. Lydia and George B. Arnold had three children—John, Abby, and George G. Arnold. George G. Arnold studied art before becoming a writer. Abby Spring Arnold married Benjamin Urner, a printer. George B. Arnold has been misidentified by Whitman scholars. Edwin H. Miller, in *The Correspondence,* and Gay Wilson Allen, in *The Solitary Singer,* among others, mis-

takenly call him John; John was his older son. John O. Holzhueter, at the State Historical Society of Wisconsin, generously shared with me his research on Arnold (including Arnold's will) for Walter Donald Kring's *Liberals Among the Orthodox* (1974).

8. Holloway and Schwarz erroneously date "Health Among Females" to October 17. The correct date is December 17; there was no October 17 issue of the *Times*.

9. Greenspan, *Walt Whitman and the American Reader,* 184–85.

10. Walt Whitman, "To Charles M. Skinner," 19 January 1885 (letter 1309), in *The Correspondence,* 3:385–86. Note that Allen does not choose the 1856 date, however.

11. Walt Whitman, *Specimen Days,* in *Prose Works 1892,* 1:288.

12. Walt Whitman, 1876 Preface, in *Leaves of Grass,* Comprehensive Reader's Edition, 750.

13. Walt Whitman, "To Ellen O'Connor," 11 February [1874] (letter 580), in *The Correspondence,* 2:276.

14. Walt Whitman, "To Ellen O'Connor," 23 November [1874] (letter 641), in *The Correspondence,* 2:315.

15. Walt Whitman, "To Abby M. Price," 29 March [1860], in *The Correspondence,* 1:49–50. Walt Whitman, "To Abby Price," 11–15 October 1863 (letter 86), in *The Correspondence,* 1:161.

16. Abby Price to Walt Whitman, [25 March 1867], Yale Collection of American Literature, Beinecke Rare Book and Manuscript Library, Yale University Library, New Haven, Conn. The trustees of the firm were willing to pay Whitman $1,000 for his efforts. As it turned out the ruffles were not taxed, and as far as is known, Whitman did not receive pay from Price's firm. In a letter dated 14 July 1870, Louisa told Walt that Abby's business was much more efficiently managed than previously and that Abby would begin receiving $500 twice a year as a result of changes in personnel. The business used one of George B. Arnold's inventions to make ruffles for clothing. City directories in the Brooklyn Historical Society contain listings for this business. *The Report of the [U.S.] Commissioner of Patents for the Year 1860* cites Patent No. 28,139: "George B. Arnold, of New York, N.Y.—Improvement in Sewing Machines. Patent dated May 8, 1860."

17. Allen, *The Solitary Singer,* 381.

18. William D. O'Connor to Abby Hills Price, 11 January 1866, Yale Collection of American Literature, Beinecke Rare Book and Manuscript Library, Yale University Library, New Haven, Conn.

19. Walt Whitman, *Notebooks,* 6:2032.

20. Harold Aspiz's chapter "The Body Electric" in his *Walt Whitman*

and the Body Beautiful demonstrates the influence on Whitman's poetry of the active spiritualist movement in the 1850s. Aspiz notes that Whitman "reprinted a favorable review of the first edition of his poems from the *Christian Spiritualist* (1856), one of about twenty spiritualist periodicals then published in the United States" (164). In a 20 June 1857 letter to Sarah Tyndale (Price's associationist and woman's rights activist friend), Whitman mentions discussing with Arnold the spiritualist Cora L. V. Hatch. Helen Price also speaks of Whitman's and Arnold's discussions of spiritualism. Price's home provided Whitman with a forum for discussing this intriguing and widespread cultural movement. Price wrote several articles on spiritualism for the *Practical Christian*. Adin Ballou, Hopedale's founder, became a believer in spiritualism. Price, however, remained skeptical and rejected the idea that the dead spoke through the body of a living person.

Helen Price said that at times when Whitman would say things "at variance with what he had written, Mr. A. would remark to him, half jokingly, 'Why, Walt, you ought to read *Leaves of Grass*.' " Helen Price, "Letter from Helen Price," 31.

Arnold's will lists the scientific instruments he left to his daughter Abby Urner: compound microscopes, dissecting instruments; cabinet with mounted objects; and three-inch telescope. Helen Price, in a letter that she wrote to Louisa Van Velsor on New Year's Day, 1873, says, "Mr Arnold has just had an observatory built on the roof of the house for his telescope and he is up there at all hours of the night." On 31 January 1873, she wrote, "Mr Arnold was up in his observatory almost all last night. He has had so few clear nights since it was built that he makes the most of them" (Helen Price to Louisa Van Velsor Whitman, [1 January] 1873 and 31 January 1873, Trent Collection).

21. *New York Times,* 3 February 1889.

22. Justin Kaplan, *Walt Whitman: A Life,* 246.

23. Louisa Van Velsor Whitman to Walt Whitman, 7 December 1869, Trent Collection.

24. Louisa Van Velsor Whitman to Walt Whitman, M 30 evening, Hanley Collection, Harry Ransom Humanities Research Center, University of Texas at Austin.

25. Parry, *Garrets and Pretenders,* 47.

26. Helen E. Price, "Letter from Helen Price," 29.

27. Helen E. Price, "Reminiscences of Walt Whitman."

28. Walt Whitman, "To Abby Price," 10 April 68 (letter 285), in *The Correspondence,* 2:26.

29. Price, "Letter from Helen Price," 29.

30. Walt Whitman, "To William D. and Ellen O'Connor," 27 September 1868 (letter 306), in *The Correspondence*, 2:49.

31. Walt Whitman, *Notebooks*, 1:147.

32. Price, "Letter from Helen Price."

33. Walt Whitman, "To Abby M. Price," 29 March [1860] (letter 18), in *The Correspondence*, 1:50; "To Abby H. Price," 11–15 October 1863 (letter 86), in *The Correspondence*, 1:162; "To Abby H. Price," 16 July 1869 (letter 345), in *The Correspondence*, 2:83.

34. Walt Whitman, "To Abby H. Price," 21 April 1871 (letter 386), in *The Correspondence*, 2:120.

35. Spann, *Hopedale*, xiii.

36. Walt Whitman, *Variorum*, 22.

37. Thomas, *The Lunar Light of Whitman's Poetry*, 77.

38. "In Memoriam: Mrs. Abby H. Price," *Woman's Journal*, 25 May 1878.

39. Walt Whitman, *Leaves of Grass*, Comprehensive Reader's Edition, 351.

40. Ballou, *History of the Town of Milford, Worcester County*, 979.

41. Edmund Quincy to Caroline Weston, 17 September 1844, Anti-Slavery Papers, Boston Public Library, Boston, Mass.

42. Abby Hills Price to Abby Kelley Foster, [7 August] 1844, Abigail Kelley Foster Papers, American Antiquarian Society, Worcester, Mass.

43. See Spann, *Hopedale*, for more on George Stacy, especially 38–39.

44. Abby Hills Price, "To the Friends in Hopedale," *Practical Christian*, 7 February 1846.

45. Spann, *Hopedale*, 70–71.

46. Walt Whitman, *Manuscripts, Autograph Letters*, 82; *Notes and Fragments*, 34.

47. Abby Price was greatly indebted to Sarah Grimké, who articulated these points in her *Letters on the Equality of the Sexes* (1838). Grimké, in turn, owed much to Mary Wollstonecraft. Price often used passages from Grimké verbatim.

48. Abby Price, "Address," 1.

49. Abby Price, "Address."

50. Abby Price, "Does the Woman's Rights' Convention Need a Paper," *Practical Christian*, 12 February 1853.

51. Abby Price, "Reasons," 11; Price, "Committee on Industrial Avocations," 21–22.

52. Abby Price, "Committee on Industrial Avocations," 19–20.

53. Abby Price, "Address."

54. Abby Price, "Reasons," 10–11.

55. Abby Price, "Reasons," 10–11.

56. Abby Price, "Address."

57. Abby Price, "Reasons," 10.

58. Linda Gordon in *Woman's Body, Woman's Right* discusses eugenics and its role in women's rights. Harold Aspiz's chapter "The Stale Cadaver Blocks Up the Passage" in *Walt Whitman and the Body Beautiful* focuses on the significance of the eugenics program for Whitman.

59. See Susan E. Cayleff's *Wash and Be Healed* and G. Barker-Benfield, *The Horrors of the Half-Known Life.*

60. Abby Price, "Committee on Industrial Avocations," 25.

61. Quoted in Allen, *The Solitary Singer,* 202.

62. Abby Price, "The Bloomer Costume—Again." In a letter to Susan B. Anthony dated 19 February 1854, Elizabeth Cady Stanton echoed Abby Price's argument, advising Anthony to stop wearing the bloomer: "We put the dress on for greater freedom, but what is physical freedom compared with mental bondage? . . . It is not wise, Susan, to use up so much energy and feeling that way. You can put them to better use. I speak from experience" (quoted in Eleanor Flexner, *Century of Struggle,* 84).

63. Abby Price, "Committee on Industrial Avocations," 26.

64. Abby Price, "National Woman's Rights Convention."

65. Abby Price, "Woman's Right to Suffrage."

66. Abby Price, "The Constitutional Convention."

67. Walt Whitman, *Notebooks,* 1:262.

68. Martha Coffin Wright to David Wright, 26 October 1856, Garrison Family Papers, Sophia Smith Collection, Smith College, Northampton, Mass.

69. Walt Whitman, *Notebooks,* 1:369.

70. Elizabeth Cady Stanton to Paulina Wright Davis, 6 December [1852], in *Papers of Elizabeth Cady Stanton and Susan B. Anthony.*

71. Spann, *Hopedale,* 39.

72. Abby Price, "Things at Home."

73. Abby Price, "Things at Home."

74. Abby Price, "Things at Home."

75. Spann, *Hopedale,* 129.

76. Abby Price, "Inquiry and Explanation."

77. "To Whom It May Concern."

78. Abby Hills Price to Samuel May, [5 or 6 July] 1853, Samuel May Papers, Anti Slavery Collections, Boston Public Library, Boston, Mass.

79. Samuel May to Richard D. Webb, 24 September 1858, Samuel May Papers, Anti Slavery Collections, Boston Public Library, Boston, Mass.

80. *Proceedings of the Woman's Rights Convention, 1853,* p. 34.

81. Abby Price, "Co-Operative Industry," 123.

82. Guarneri, *The Utopian Alternative,* 324.

83. Guarneri, *The Utopian Alternative,* 326.

84. Stovall, *The Foreground of "Leaves of Grass,"* 157.

85. Whitman, 1876 Preface, in *Prose Works 1892,* 2:471.

86. Lynch, " 'Here Is Adhesiveness,' " 67–96 (quotation on p. 72).

87. Smith-Rosenberg, "The Female World of Love and Ritual," 53–76 (quotation on p. 74).

88. Sarah Grimké, *Letters on the Equality of the Sexes.* Nancy Cott's *The Bonds of Womanhood* remains a helpful source for understanding the implications of Grimké's phrase: "thine in the bonds of womanhood," as does Carroll Smith-Rosenberg's *Disorderly Conduct.*

89. Smith-Rosenberg, "The Female World of Love and Ritual."

90. Thomas, *The Lunar Light of Whitman's Poetry,* 147.

91. Thomas, *The Lunar Light of Whitman's Poetry,* 145.

92. Walt Whitman, *Variorum,* 1:176–89.

93. See also Harold Aspiz, "An Early Feminist Tribute to Whitman," 404–9.

94. Helen Price, "Letter from Helen Price," 27.

95. Lewis, "Farnham, Eliza Wood Burhans," 599.

96. Black, *Whitman's Journeys into Chaos,* 156.

97. Cavitch, *My Soul and I,* 96.

98. Rosenfeld, "The Eagle and the Axe," 357.

99. Rosenfeld, "The Eagle and the Axe," 363.

100. Rosenfeld, "The Eagle and the Axe," 368.

101. Thomas, *The Lunar Light of Whitman's Poetry,* 143.

102. Gregory, "The Celebration of Nativity," 7.

103. Erkkila, *Whitman the Political Poet,* 140–41.

104. Abby Price, "The Annual Meeting."

105. Walt Whitman, *An American Primer,* 13.

106. Louisa Van Velsor Whitman to Walt Whitman, 6 March 1868, Trent Collection.

107. Henry S. Saunders, an important figure in Whitman scholarship, especially for his success in collecting photographs taken of Whitman, wrote to Augusta Larned in 1915. She told Saunders she was sorry that she had not written anything at "any time of much length on Whitman." She had, she said, "a peculiar & I may say almost sacred admiration for Whitman" and kept "his book always at hand" where she could "refresh" herself "by reading him in certain moods." She then spoke of meeting Whitman.

It must have been at the Prices' home. Larned knew Abby Price through the woman's movement. "Many years ago when I was young . . . I spent an evening with Mr. Whitman, or I may say in the same room with him. He generally stopped while in New York with some friends of mine, & on a certain occasion I was invited to meet him at their house. He was engaged with other people, & I had no opportunity to converse with him, but I know I was surprised to find that the quiet, conventionally dressed gentleman was Walt Whitman." Larned's letter is in the Brown University Library, Providence, R.I. See Augusta Larnet to Henry Scholey Saunders, 4 November 1915, Henry Scholey Saunders Collection, MS. 81.5, Brown University Library.

108. We also learn more about George B. Arnold and his interest in science in Helen's letters as well as other family information.

109. See Paulina Wright Davis, *A History of the National Woman's Rights Movement,* 41. The manuscript copy of "Decade Meeting" is in the Paulina Kellogg Wright Davis Papers, Special Collections, Vassar College Libraries, Poughkeepsie, N.Y.

110. Abby Hills Price to Louisa Van Velsor Whitman, probable date 13 October 1872, Trent Collection.

111. Louisa Van Velsor Whitman to Walt Whitman, 12 April 1872, Trent Collection.

112. Walt Whitman, "To Abby H. and Helen Price," [11 January (?) 1874] (letter 569), in *The Correspondence,* 2:267.

113. Walt Whitman, "To Abby H. Price," 3 March [1874] (letter 588), in *The Correspondence,* 2:281.

114. Walt Whitman, "To Helen and Abby H. Price," 6 October 1876 (letter 771), in *The Correspondence,* 3:62.

3. Paulina Wright Davis

1. *Water-Cure Journal* 7 (June 1849):192.

2. "Biography: Paulina Wright Davis, Phrenological Character," *American Phrenological Journal* 18 (1853):11.

3. Ryan, *Cradle of the Middle Class,* 228.

4. Walt Whitman, *Notebooks,* 1:304.

5. Elder, "Mrs. Wright's Lectures," 11.

6. Cayleff, *Wash and Be Healed,* 6.

7. *Water-Cure Journal* 6 (September 1848):83.

8. Davis, "The Providence Physiological Society," 41.

9. Providence Physiological Society Records, Rhode Island Historical Society Library, Providence, R.I.

10. See Brodie's *Contraception and Abortion in Nineteenth-Century America*.

11. Erkkila, *Whitman the Political Poet*, 125.

12. Mary S. Gove Nichols to Paulina Wright Davis, 29 June 1875, Paulina Kellogg Wright Davis Papers, Vassar College Libraries, Poughkeepsie, N.Y.

13. Ryan, *Cradle of the Middle Class*, 227.

14. Paulina S. Wright to Sidney Howard Gay, 4 April 1845, Sidney Howard Gay Papers, Rare Book and Manuscript Library, Columbia University, New York. Gay was editor of the *Anti-Slavery Standard* at this time and was managing editor of the *New York Tribune* during the Civil War.

15. Paulina Wright Davis to Caroline Healey Dall, 25 September 1855, Caroline Healey Dall Papers, 1811–1917, Library of Congress.

16. Elder, "Mrs. Wright's Lectures," 11.

17. Elder, "Mrs. Wright's Lectures," 12.

18. Wyman and Wyman, *Elizabeth Buffum Chace, 1806–1899*, 115.

19. Providence Physiological Society Records, 1850–53.

20. "Woman's Rights Convention."

21. Paulina Wright Davis to Caroline Healey Dall, 17 November 1854, Dall Papers.

22. Paulina Wright Davis to Caroline Healey Dall, about 1 October 1855, Dall Papers.

23. Paulina Wright Davis to Caroline Healey Dall, 20 June 1855, Dall Papers.

24. Paulina Wright Davis to Caroline Healey Dall, 1 June 1853, Dall Papers.

25. Paulina Wright Davis to Caroline Healey Dall, 20 June 1855, Dall Papers.

26. Paulina Wright Davis to Caroline Healey Dall, 21 June 1855, Dall Papers.

27. Paulina Wright Davis to Caroline Healey Dall, 20 June 1855, Dall Papers.

28. Paulina Wright Davis to Caroline Healey Dall, 21 June 1855, Dall Papers.

29. Paulina Wright Davis to Caroline Healey Dall, date uncertain (probably late June or early July 1855), Dall Papers.

30. Davis, "To Our Readers," 376.

31. Jane Knapp to Paulina Wright Davis, *Una* 2 (December 1854):374. Sounding like Beecher, Caroline Dall's brother, George W. Healey, wrote much the same thing to Dall in a letter dated 11 November 1851. He had heard Elizabeth Oakes Smith lecture and commented: "Although some parts of her lecture were fine and the whole was well written I could not help thinking how I should feel if you were in her place as you have often threatened. For gods sake do anything but that. I would rather see you (much as I dislike the doings and actings of the Abolition party) the most violent of them, than to see or hear of you speaking on the stage. It is perfectly disgusting, although there could be no fault found with regard to the deportment of Mrs S. on the stage and I allowed the lecture was fine, still when I got home I said it was disgusting" (Dall Papers).

32. Paulina Wright Davis to Caroline Healey Dall, 29 January 1853, Dall Papers.

33. Paulina Wright Davis to Caroline Healey Dall, 28 October 1855, Dall Papers.

34. Davis, "On the Renting of a Hall for Woman's Rights Meetings," Paulina Kellogg Wright Davis Papers, Special Collections, Vassar Library, Poughkeepsie, New York (unpaginated).

35. Kerber, "The Republican Mother," in *Women of the Republic,* 283.

36. Davis, "Address," 6–7.

37. Davis, "Address," 10. Anna E. Green, reviewing Ellen Carol DuBois's *Feminism and Suffrage,* says of Davis and the decade of the 1850s: "The breadth and vitality of the debate within the movement at this time, with Paulina Wright Davis concluding that woman's wrongs called for 'the radical, thorough re-organization of society,' was not to be equaled until the 1960s." Anna E. Green, review of Ellen Carol DuBois's *Feminism and Suffrage.*

38. Jimmie Killingsworth mentions the "relative lack of critical attention" paid to "Poem of Women," saying that perhaps critics have glossed over it because after the 1856 edition, the poem was "decentralized and buried"; he also speculates that the poem's "ideological qualities" may have caused critics to ignore the poem. True, in the 1860 and 1867 editions of *Leaves,* it was placed in the "Leaves of Grass" sections. In 1871, however, it returned to a prominent position, following "Inscriptions," "The Ship Starting," and "To You." In the 1881 edition, it became part of "Two Rivulets," where it stayed. My sense is that the lack of attention overall given to women in Whitman's life accounts for the neglect. *Whitman's Poetry of the Body,* 62.

39. My reading disagrees with Jimmie Killingsworth's reading of the editions. Killingsworth says: "Beginning in 1856 we come to associate

woman with a sense of unfulfilled potential, with a *lack,* in *Leaves of Grass"* (*Whitman's Poetry of the Body,* 73).

40. Walt Whitman, "Whitman to Emerson, 1856," in *Leaves of Grass,* Comprehensive Reader's Edition, 737. Betsy Erkkila, in her 1989 *Whitman the Political Poet,* sees the poem as "a female creation myth that radically rewrites the Victorian glorification of the female reproductive capacity" (135). She also sees the poem as the poetic equivalent of the 1856 letter to Emerson that was included in the 1856 *Leaves of Grass.* As Erkkila says, "writing the body and sex was, in Whitman's view, part of the process of liberating the individual from the political tyranny of the past, and thus part of the democratic creation of America" (135).

41. Walt Whitman, "Unfolded Out of the Folds," in *Variorum,* 1:160–61. Harold Aspiz's article "Unfolding the Folds," published in the December 1966 *Walt Whitman Review,* remains to date the most extensive discussion of the poem. Aspiz praises "Unfolded," calling it "a richly-textured poem, whose several levels of intelligibility combine to reveal its profound meaning" (81). Aspiz's familiarity with the major phrenological texts read by Whitman (and by the culture in general) allows him to formulate numerous connections between phrenology (and the firm of Fowler and Wells) and Whitman. He cites four different contexts in which the poem can be placed: spiritual evolution; glorification of sex and parenthood; the context of eugenics, physiology, and phrenology as understood in the 1850s; and an autobiographical context. He does not, however, include the woman's rights movement as a context. Aspiz notes the kinship of the word "unfolded" to the word "evolved," which Jimmie Killingsworth also mentions as he discusses the poem in *Whitman's Poetry of the Body.* Aspiz critiques the poem, and in the notes, he creates another text as he carefully documents the occurrence in other poems of the unfolding trope, thus weaving his own web of interconnections. In one of his notes, he points out that the line "Unfolded only out of the inimitable poems of woman can come the poems of man, (only thence have my poems come)" originally read "the inimitable poem of the woman," this earlier reading half suggesting a "female organ of Poetry" (86). Killingsworth develops this point as well—that in "Unfolded" we have the vagina as poem, rather than the penis, as in "Spontaneous Me" (64). Aspiz's last sentence reads: "In the perspective of all the *Leaves,* these unfoldings can be seen as the prelude to an endless series of unfoldings of the spirit through eternity" (87).

42. See Harold Aspiz's "Walt Whitman: The Spermatic Imagination," 379–95. In this article, Aspiz speaks of the link Whitman makes between the "persona's phallicism and his vocalism . . . , the basic element of the

spermatic trope" (384). The link exists between female genitalia and vocalism as well. Aspiz himself notes this link in passing when he speaks of "By Blue Ontario's Shore": "The 'embouchure' imagery is ambiguously oral and vulval" (388).

43. We hear the cultural inscription of woman as passive and long-suffering from the 15 April 1852 minutes of the Providence Physiological Society describing a lecture that Orson Fowler presented to the society. The secretary states his topic: the improvement or perfection of woman. "He treated the subject in a very familiar and pleasant way, & tho much of it was to us like household words it was none the less necessary or important on that account." Fowler insists on the cultural inscriptions that Whitman wished to deconstruct, as evidenced in the notebook entry "Lect. (To Women." and in the poem "Unfolded out of the Folds." Fowler: "Man is endowed with strength, but woman eminently with devotion. He has power, and she has love. He can dare, but she can endure. His nature is adapted to the rougher, harsher, combative scenes of life, hers to accomplish by the force of that principle which is stronger than death, and which if persevered in never fails." In Whitman's poem, "woman" has power.

44. See Green, "A Note," 23–28. Judith Kent Green makes a convincing claim for the influence of Robert Chambers's *Vestiges of Creation* on Whitman, yet she also reminds us of Whitman's eclecticism. Robert J. Scholnick also credits Chambers as a major influence on Whitman's understanding of science, as well as his contemporary Edward Livingston Youmans (" 'The Password Primeval,' " 385–425). Other scholars trace Whitman's understanding of evolutionary ideas to Lamarck. Harry Gershenowitz, in "Two Lamarckians," 35–39, links Lamarck, Carpenter, and Whitman. See also the following: Emmanuel, "Whitman's Fusion of Science and Poetry," 73–82; Gershenowitz, "Whitman and Lamarck Revisited," 121–23; Leonard, "Lamarckian Evolution," 21–28; Millhauser, "The Literary Impact," 213–26; Pfeifer, "The Theory of Evolution," 31–35; Tanner, "The Lamarckian Theory of Progress," 3–11; Tanner, "Walt Whitman: Poet of Evolution."

45. For example, see Abby Price: "Place an infant in a dungeon, shut entirely away from all the active scenes of life, and he comes out a Casper Hauser. So, to a great extent, is it with Woman" ("Committee on Industrial Avocations," 21). See also Harriet Fosby to Caroline Dall, 18 September 1850: "Many [women] too are weak and incapable. They have within them a self, which, like Caspar Hauser, has been kept in prison and darkness; and this self must be so long and carefully cherished, and taught, and developed, before it can do justice to its nature." See, too, the ending of chapter 2 of Melville's *Billy Budd*. For a recent, brief account of the Caspar Hauser

story, see chapter 1, "Who Was Kaspar Hauser?—The Historical Facts," in Ursula Sampath's *Kaspar Hauser,* 9–13.

46. By crediting the organism with *sentiment intérieur,* Lamarck left room for Davis (and others) to use a scientific explanation of process and change in a more or less mystical way that was not, I think, what Lamarck meant. It was important to Davis that there was an opportunity for "mysticism," however, for her purposes would never have been served, given her audience, by a strictly materialistic argument for change. And she herself could not have accepted a completely material and chemical view of evolution. She came to believe more and more strongly in spiritualism, like so many other nineteenth-century reformers.

47. Davis, "Address," 11.

48. Davis, "Report on the Education of Females," 361.

49. Davis, "Letter from Paulina Wright Davis," 832.

50. Davis, "Intellect of the Sexes," 121.

51. Davis, "Inequality of Women in Marriage," 214. To make the point another way, in the January 1855 *Una,* the following short, wry note appeared: "UNHAPPY MARRIAGES—An English paper, descanting relative to the various qualities of connubial bliss, states that in the city of London the official record for the last year stands thus: Runaway wives, 1,132; runaway husbands, 2,348; married persons legally divorced, 4,175; living in open warfare, 17,345; living in private misunderstanding, 13,279; mutually indifferent, 55,340; regarded as happy, 3,175; nearly happy, 127; perfectly happy, 13" (6).

52. Walt Whitman, *Notebooks,* 1:341.

53. Quoted in Stanton, Anthony, and Gage, *History of Woman Suffrage,* 1:534–35.

54. Paulina Wright Davis, "Reply to Mrs. Dall," *Liberator* 29 October 1852.

55. Davis, "Inequality of Women in Marriage," 214–15.

56. Davis, "Intellect of the Sexes," 120.

57. Stephen J. Gould's chapter "Measuring Heads: Paul Broca and the Heyday of Craniology," in his *The Mismeasure of Man,* exposes Broca's racism and sexism. Gould quotes Broca: "We might ask if the small size of the female brain depends exclusively upon the small size of her body. Tiedemann has proposed this explanation. But we must not forget that women are, on the average, a little less intelligent than men, a difference which we should not exaggerate but which is, nonetheless, real. We are therefore permitted to suppose that the relatively small size of the female brain depends

in part upon her physical inferiority and in part upon her intellectual inferiority" (104).

58. Davis, "Pecuniary Independence of Women," 200.

59. Whitman, *Leaves of Grass,* Comprehensive Reader's Edition, 42.

60. Walt Whitman, *The Correspondence,* 1:43.

61. [Paulina Wright Davis], "Female Compositors, and Opposition of Interests," 152.

62. She subscribed to the theory of Dianaism, which advocated "free sexual contact of all sorts except intercourse" (Gordon, *Woman's Body, Woman's Right,* 106). Linda Gordon quotes from one of Elmina Slenker's articles: "We want the sexes to love more than they do; we want them to love openly, frankly, earnestly; to enjoy the caress, the embrace, the glance, the voice, the presence & the very step of the beloved. We oppose no form or act of love between any man & woman. Fill the world as full of genuine sex love as you can . . . but forbear to rush in where generations yet unborn may suffer for your unthinking, uncaring, unheeding actions." Gordon comments on this passage: "The definition of sex in terms of heterosexual intercourse has been one of the oldest and most universal cultural norms. Slenker's alienation from existing sexual possibilities led her to explore alternatives with a bravery and a freedom from religious and psychological taboos extraordinary for a nineteenth-century Quaker reformer" (106–7).

63. Sears, *The Sex Radicals,* 217.

64. Elmina Slenker to Walt Whitman, 3 August 1888, Charles E. Feinberg–Walt Whitman Collection, Manuscript Division, Library of Congress.

65. For a thorough discussion of the 1882 banning controversy, see Loving, *Walt Whitman's Champion,* 123–38.

66. Providence Physiological Society Records, 16 December 1851 (unpaginated). The minutes also record the condescension toward the women when they first started inviting physicians, most of whom were male, to lecture to them: "A report from the committee, appointed to see if any of our Physicians in Providence would lecture before the Society, was not remarkably cheering, no encouragement being given, to comply with the request. Fears were entertained by some, to whom application was made, with regard to the object of the society, had in view; and no doubt, kindly advised, to continue in our social way, among ourselves, doing as little harm as possible. Notwithstanding this advice, it was resolved to have a course of lectures on Physiology, including five, or six in the course, & Mrs. Davis, at the earnest request of the Society, consented to give the first lecture" (11 July 1850).

67. Years later, Whitman told Horace Traubel much the same thing: "The women will take care of sex things—make them what they choose: man has very little to do with it except to conform." Traubel, *With Walt Whitman in Camden*, 3:439. Davis is quoted from Providence Physiological Society Records, 1850–1862 (unpaginated).

68. No doubt Esther Shephard, author of *Walt Whitman's Pose*, is right—that Whitman got the idea for "O Hymen! O Hymenee!" from George Sand's *The Countess of Rudolstadt* (*Walt Whitman's Pose*, 179). Shephard is angry about this; I think that Davis and Price would not be. The exchange of texts was very much a part of the nineteenth-century woman's movement. Abby Price, for example, used phrases from Sarah Grimké, who borrowed verbatim from Mary Wollstonecraft.

69. Ryan, *Cradle of the Middle Class*, 157.

70. Noah Webster, *An American Dictionary of the English Language* (Springfield: George and Charles Merriam, 1845); Joseph E. Worcester, *An Elementary Dictionary of the English Language* (Boston: Brewer and Tileston, 1860).

71. Showalter, *Alternative Alcott*, xxxv.

72. Walt Whitman, *Variorum*, 1:240. The sexuality imaged in "A Woman Waits for Me," however, posed a threat to mainstream society. For example, in 1897 in Sellwood, Oregon, Henry Addis was arrested for mailing obscene matter. Addis wrote to Horace Traubel in Traubel's capacity as editor of the *Conservator* and champion of Whitman to get Traubel's help. The evidence used against Addis was his inclusion of Whitman's "A Woman Waits for Me" in his paper, the *Firebrand*. Whitman's poem was "the objectionable part of the contents"—objectionable because it depicted women as sexual beings. Horace L. and Anne Montgomerie Traubel Collection, Library of Congress, Washington, D.C.

73. Stanton, *Elizabeth Cady Stanton*, 210.

74. Stanton, "Letter from Elizabeth Cady Stanton," 815.

75. Nichols, *Esoteric Anthropology*, 111–12.

76. Killingsworth, *Whitman's Poetry of the Body*, 61.

77. Walt Whitman, *The Correspondence*, 2:60.

78. Walt Whitman, *The Correspondence*, 2:60.

79. Jeannie Channing was Ellen Tarr O'Connor's sister. William Francis Channing was the only son of the Reverend William Ellery Channing.

80. Walt Whitman, *The Correspondence*, 2:61.

81. Walt Whitman, *The Correspondence*, 2:193.

82. Walt Whitman, *The Correspondence*, 2:64. Sarah Helen Whitman was herself a poet whose collection of poems—called *Hours of Life*—appeared

two years before *Leaves of Grass.* Edgar Allen Poe's poem "To Helen" was addressed to her. Nora Perry's article on Whitman appeared in *Appleton's Journal* in 1876.

83. Walt Whitman, *The Correspondence,* 2:66.
84. Walt Whitman, *The Correspondence,* 2:66.
85. Quoted in Allen, *The Solitary Singer,* 370.
86. Quoted in Traubel, *With Walt Whitman in Camden,* 3:35.
87. Davis, *A History of the National Woman's Rights Movement.*
88. Walt Whitman, *The Correspondence,* 2:281.
89. Walt Whitman, *The Correspondence,* 2:315.

4. Ernestine L. Rose

1. Walt Whitman, "To Richard Maurice Bucke," 8 November 1890 (letter 2351), in *The Correspondence,* 5:115.
2. Quoted in Traubel, *With Walt Whitman in Camden,* 6:322–23.
3. Walt Whitman, *Variorum,* 2:421. Interestingly, two women who wrote about Whitman at the turn of the century quoted these lines from "France" in their articles. Both women wrote about *Leaves* and its ability to inscribe freedom for women. See Helena Born, "Poets of Revolt," in *Whitman's Ideal Democracy,* and Helen Michael, "Woman and Freedom in Whitman," 232.
4. Walt Whitman, *Prose Works 1892,* 1:268.
5. Suhl, *Ernestine Rose and the Battle for Human Rights,* 66.
6. Suhl, *Ernestine Rose and the Battle for Human Rights,* 48.
7. Wilentz, *Chants Democratic,* 154.
8. Quoted in Traubel, *With Walt Whitman in Camden,* 2:208.
9. Walt Whitman, *Prose Works 1892,* 1:140–42. Quoted in Traubel, *With Walt Whitman in Camden,* 1:79–80.
10. "Women and the Tariff," *New York Tribune,* 15 October 1853.
11. Traubel, *With Walt Whitman in Camden,* 1:149; 3:5; 5:20. The seven volumes of Traubel, *With Walt Whitman in Camden,* include many other instances in which Whitman consistently maintained his stance on the tariff.
12. Stanton, Anthony, and Gage, *History of Woman Suffrage,* 3:120.
13. Schappes, "To Be Included."
14. Schappes "To Be Included."
15. Stanton, Anthony, and Gage, *History of Woman Suffrage,* 1:98.
16. Clare, "Thoughts and Things."

17. Stanton, Anthony, and Gage, *History of Woman Suffrage*, 1:693.

18. Stanton, Anthony, and Gage, *History of Woman Suffrage*, 1:692–93.

19. Walt Whitman, *Prose Works 1892*, 2:369.

20. Stanton, Anthony, and Gage, *History of Woman Suffrage*, 1:692.

21. Wilentz, *Chants Democratic*, 177.

22. Quoted in Stanton, Anthony, and Gage, *History of Woman Suffrage*, 1:606.

23. Traubel, *With Walt Whitman in Camden*, 1:80.

24. Traubel, *With Walt Whitman in Camden*, 2:205.

25. Traubel, *With Walt Whitman in Camden*, 2:445.

26. Traubel, *With Walt Whitman in Camden*, 2:499.

27. Traubel, *With Walt Whitman in Camden*, 2:500.

28. Stanton, Anthony, and Gage, *History of Woman Suffrage*, 1:52.

29. Walt Whitman, *Notebooks*, 1:344.

30. Walt Whitman, *Notebooks*, 1:248 and 1:453; 2:839.

31. Stanton, Anthony, and Gage, *History of Woman Suffrage*, 1:633–34.

32. Stanton, Anthony, and Gage, *History of Woman Suffrage*, 1:541.

33. Stanton, Anthony, and Gage, *History of Woman Suffrage*, 1:540–41.

34. In the *Proceedings* of the third National Woman's Rights Convention (1852), held in Syracuse, there is a page-long announcement of publications available for purchase: "Woman's Rights Tracts." Number 8 is entitled: " 'No need of a permanent organization': A Letter from Mrs. Angelina Grimké Weld to the Convention at Syracuse. Single copy, 4 cts.; by the hundred, $2.00."

35. Stanton, Anthony, and Gage, *History of Woman Suffrage*, 1:624.

36. Walt Whitman, *The Correspondence*, 2:189.

37. Walt Whitman, *Daybooks and Notebooks*, 669.

38. Walt Whitman, *Daybooks and Notebooks*, 3:712.

39. Walt Whitman, *Daybooks and Notebooks*, 3:666.

40. Walt Whitman, *Daybooks and Notebooks*, 3:686.

41. [Fifth National Woman's Rights Convention, Second Day], *Lily*, 1 November 1854.

42. Walt Whitman, *Leaves of Grass*, Facsimile Edition of the 1860 Text, 418–20.

43. Walt Whitman, *Notebooks*, 1:234.

44. Walt Whitman, *Notebooks*, 1:303.

45. Stanton, Anthony, and Gage, *History of Woman Suffrage*, 1:593.

46. Stanton, Anthony, and Gage, *History of Woman Suffrage*, 1:376.

47. Stanton, Anthony, and Gage, *History of Woman Suffrage*, 1:693.

48. Walt Whitman, *The Eighteenth Presidency*, 35.

49. Schappes, "Ernestine L. Rose," 344–55.

50. Folsom, *Walt Whitman's Native Representations*, 106.

51. Walt Whitman, *An American Primer*, 9.

52. Walt Whitman, *Leaves of Grass*, Comprehensive Reader's Edition, 737.

53. Walt Whitman, *Variorum*, 2:425.

54. Pease, *Visionary Compacts*, 113.

55. Walt Whitman, *Eighteenth Presidency*, 19–20.

56. Carroll Hollis's *Language and Style in "Leaves of Grass"* authoritatively documents the influence of oratory.

57. Stanton, Anthony, and Gage, *History of Woman Suffrage*, 1:537.

58. "Woman's Rights Convention [Rochester, November 30, 1853]," *Una* 2 (January 1854):196.

59. "Mrs. Rose's Lecture in Washington," *Una* 2 (May 1854):269.

60. Stanton, Anthony, and Gage, *History of Woman Suffrage*, 1:133.

61. Stanton, Anthony, and Gage, *History of Woman Suffrage*, 1:536.

62. Stanton, Anthony, and Gage, *History of Woman Suffrage*, 1:717.

63. Stanton, Anthony, and Gage, *History of Woman Suffrage*, 1:594.

64. Stanton, Anthony, and Gage, *History of Woman Suffrage*, 1:525.

65. Stanton, Anthony, and Gage, *History of Woman Suffrage*, 1:134.

66. Walt Whitman, *Variorum*, 2:297.

67. Walt Whitman, *Variorum*, 2:308.

68. Holland and Gordon, *Papers of Elizabeth Cady Stanton and Susan B. Anthony*.

69. Paulina Wright Davis to Caroline Healey Dall, 23 August 1853, Caroline Healey Dall Papers, 1811–1917, Library of Congress, Washington, D.C.

70. Suhl, *Ernestine Rose and the Battle for Human Rights*, 216.

71. Suhl, *Ernestine Rose and the Battle for Human Rights*, 217.

72. Suhl, *Ernestine Rose and the Battle for Human Rights*, 218.

73. Suhl, *Ernestine Rose and the Battle for Human Rights*, 226.

74. Suhl, *Ernestine Rose and the Battle for Human Rights*, 227.

75. Suhl, *Ernestine Rose and the Battle for Human Rights*, 228.

76. Stanton, Anthony, and Gage, *History of Woman Suffrage*, 2:209.

77. Suhl, *Ernestine Rose and the Battle for Human Rights*, 240.

78. Suhl, *Ernestine Rose and the Battle for Human Rights*, 246.

79. Morris Schappes's private file. Schappes notes: "Beginning about 1880, Mrs. Rose was listed among the officers of the National Woman's Suffrage Association as one of the Honorary Vice-Presidents 2nd from the top; with Lucretia Mott as 1st Honorary Vice-Pres."

80. Schappes, "Queen of the Platform," 7.
81. Schappes, "Queen of the Platform," 7.

5. Responses of Some 19th-Century Women to the 1860 *Leaves of Grass*

1. Erkkila, *Whitman the Political Poet*, 314.
2. Coultrap-McQuin, *Doing Literary Business*, 174.
3. Harris, " 'But Is It Any Good?' " 47.
4. Blatt, *Free Love and Anarchism*, 142–44.
5. Quoted in Traubel, *With Walt Whitman in Camden*, 3:438–39.
6. Stanton, Anthony, and Gage, *History of Woman Suffrage*, 1:716–17.
7. Stanton, Anthony, and Gage, *History of Woman Suffrage*, 1:719.
8. Stanton, Anthony, and Gage, *History of Woman Suffrage*, 1:720.
9. Stanton, Anthony, and Gage, *History of Woman Suffrage*, 1:722.
10. Stanton, Anthony, and Gage, *History of Woman Suffrage*, 1:723 (quotation of Blackwell), 729 (quotation of Rose).
11. Stanton, Anthony, and Gage, *History of Woman Suffrage*, 1:730–31.
12. Stanton, Anthony, and Gage, *History of Woman Suffrage*, 1:732.
13. Stanton, Anthony, and Gage, *History of Woman Suffrage*, 1:840–41.
14. Elizabeth Cady Stanton to Susan B. Anthony, 1 March [1853], in *Papers of Elizabeth Cady Stanton and Susan B. Anthony*, ed. Holland and Gordon.
15. DuBois, "On Labor and Free Love," 263–64.
16. Quoted in Traubel, *With Walt Whitman in Camden*, 1:237. For background information on Clapp and the *Saturday Press*, see M. Jimmie Killingsworth, "The Saturday Press," 357–64.
17. Walt Whitman, *Daybooks and Notebooks*, 1:100, 3:788, and 3:834; Walt Whitman, *Notebooks*, 1:248 and 1:248n. Neither Grier nor White correctly identifies Chilton.
18. Macdonald, *Fifty Years of Freethought*, 1:384–85.
19. See Kenneth Price's "Whitman, Free Love, and the *Social Revolutionist*," 70–82.
20. Macdonald, *Fifty Years of Freethought*, 1:450.
21. Chilton, "Suffrage."
22. Spurlock's *Free Love, Marriage and Middle-Class Radicalism in America, 1825–1860*, provides a helpful discussion of Josiah Warren (1798–

1873), whose principles Spurlock summarizes: "The happiness of society could be insured by giving each person sovereignty over his or her own person and property, an equal share of natural wealth, and an equivalent whenever property was exchanged" (108).

23. Stoehr, *Free Love in America*, 432.

24. Conway, "Modern Times, New York," *Fortnightly Review* 6 (1 July 1865):427. The account of Conway's visit also appeared in his *Autobiography*, 1:264–68.

25. Macdonald, *Fifty Years of Freethought*, 451.

26. "Prospectus," *Social Revolutionist* (January 1856):4.

27. Spurlock, *Free Love*, 2.

28. Overton, "Horrors of Slavery," 162.

29. Whitman, *Leaves of Grass*, Comprehensive Reader's Edition, 157–58.

30. Chilton, "Do We Need Marriage?" *Social Revolutionist* (June 1857):172.

31. Whitman, *Leaves of Grass*, Comprehensive Reader's Edition, 151.

32. Walt Whitman, *Leaves of Grass*, 1855, 127.

33. Chilton, "Sexual Purity," 5.

34. Walt Whitman, *Leaves of Grass*, 1860, 314.

35. Faderman, *Surpassing the Love of Men*, 275.

36. Charles Warren Stoddard quoted Reade, taking the information from Reade's memoir. Stoddard, "La Belle Menken," 478.

37. In addition, in the 14 January 1860 issue of the *Saturday Press*, Ada Clare, a regular weekly columnist for the *Press*, criticized her friend William Winter's poem "Song of the Ruined Man" and praised Whitman's "Child's Reminiscence."

38. Faderman, *Surpassing the Love of Men*, 18.

39. Dickinson, *Selected Letters*, 173. Ezra Greenspan pointed out this connection to me.

40. Allen, *The Solitary Singer*, 261; Kaplan, *Walt Whitman: A Life*, 242; Erkkila, *Whitman the Political Poet*, 311–12.

41. Quoted in Traubel, *With Walt Whitman in Camden*, 2:375.

42. Quoted in Traubel, *With Walt Whitman in Camden*, 4:196.

43. Burroughs, "Walt Whitman and His 'Drum Taps,' " 608.

44. Barrus, *The Life and Letters of John Burroughs*, 1:120.

45. Freedman, *William Douglas O'Connor*, 317.

46. Freedman, *William Douglas O'Connor*, 57.

47. "Woman's Rights Convention in Boston," *Una* 3 (October

1855):153. For the year 1886, Ernestine L. Rose appears first in a long list of honorary vice presidents for the National Woman Suffrage Association; Ellen O'Connor is listed tenth.

48. Algeo, "Equal Suffrage Notes."

49. Calder, "Personal Recollections of Walt Whitman," 829.

50. Walt Whitman, "Letter to Abby H. Price," 10 December 1866 (letter 207), in *The Correspondence*, 1:301.

51. Gay Wilson Allen lent me Clifton Furness's Ledger, in which Furness had copied Ellen O'Connor Calder's original draft of the article that appeared in the 1907 *Atlantic*. The section on Beach did not appear in the published article.

52. Walt Whitman, "Democratic Vistas," *Prose Works 1892*, 2:424–25. Whitman reiterated this point eighteen years later: "I round and finish little, if anything; and could not, consistently with my scheme. The reader will always have his or her part to do, just as much as I have had mine. I seek less to state or display any theme or thought, and more to bring you, reader, into the atmosphere of the theme or thought—there to pursue your own flight." Walt Whitman, "A Backward Glance O'er Travel'd Roads," in *Leaves of Grass*, Comprehensive Reader's Edition, 570.

53. Whitman, "Democratic Vistas," in *Prose Works 1892*, 2:425. A Woman [Juliette Beach], "Walt Whitman," *Saturday Press*, 23 June 1860.

54. Walt Whitman, 1876 Preface, in *Leaves of Grass*, Comprehensive Reader's Edition, 754. See also Whitman, "Backward Glance," in ibid., 565, ll. 135–41.

55. Beach to Clapp, 7 June 1860 and 13 August 1860, Charles Feinberg–Walt Whitman Collection, Manuscript Division, Library of Congress, Washington, D.C.

56. Beach to Clapp, 7 June 1860 and 13 August 1860.

57. Whitman said of Ada Clare right after her death in a letter to Ellen O'Connor: "Poor, poor, Ada Clare—I have been inexpressibly shocked by the horrible & sudden close of her gay, easy, sunny free, loose, but *not ungood life*—I suppose you have seen about it, but I cut the enclosed from the Herald in case you have not." *The Correspondence*, 2:285. Clare died from rabies on 4 March 1874 as a result of a dog bite five weeks earlier. Clare, Whitman, and Adah Isaacs Menken frequented the same circle of "Bohemians" at Pfaff's beer cellar.

58. C.C.P., "Walt Whitman's New Volume," *Saturday Press*, 23 June 1860.

59. Walt Whitman, "A Memorandum at a Venture," *Prose Works 1892*, 2:491.

60. Walt Whitman, "A Memorandum at a Venture," 2:493–94.

61. Campbell, *Man Cannot Speak for Her,* 122.

62. Whitman, *Leaves of Grass,* Comprehensive Reader's Edition, 594.

63. *Leaves of Grass,* 1860, 309. The "smut" in line 11 was of course not what the writer of the *Springfield Republican* had in mind when he entitled his article "Leaves of Grass:—Smut in Them."

64. For a discussion of "sentiment intérieur," see Burlingame, "Lamarck," 591.

65. Whitman, *Leaves of Grass,* Comprehensive Reader's Edition, 107–8.

66. Aspiz, *Walt Whitman and the Body Beautiful,* 147.

67. Walt Whitman, *Variorum,* 1:239.

68. Aspiz, *Walt Whitman and the Body Beautiful,* 148.

69. Whitman, *Leaves of Grass,* Comprehensive Reader's Edition, 108.

70. Hollis, in *Language and Style in "Leaves of Grass,"* discusses Whitman's use of the personal pronoun "you," 94–95, 97–100, 101–2, 107–11, 116–23. Also see Greenspan's *Walt Whitman and the American Reader,* especially the last chapter.

71. Charles Eldridge, "Walt Whitman as a Conservative," *New York Times,* 7 June 1902. Eldridge's letter makes up most of this article.

72. Traubel, *With Walt Whitman in Camden,* 5:347.

Conclusion

1. Walt Whitman, "Democratic Vistas," in *Prose Works 1892,* 2:414.

2. Walt Whitman, "To Rudolf Schmidt," 16 January 1872 (letter 421), in *The Correspondence,* 2:154; "To Edward Dowden," 18 January 1872 (letter 422), in *The Correspondence,* 2:154.

3. Bleier, *Science and Gender,* 132–33. See also Nancy Tanner and Adrienne Zihlman, "Women in Evolution, Part I," 585–608.

4. Walt Whitman, "America," in *Leaves of Grass,* Comprehensive Reader's Edition, 511. A recording of Whitman reading this poem, discovered by Larry D. Griffin, can be purchased from *Walt Whitman Quarterly Review.* See "Walt Whitman's Voice."

5. Erkkila, *Whitman the Political Poet,* 259.

6. Abby H. Price, "Reasons Why," 10.

7. See Traubel, *With Walt Whitman in Camden,* 6:279.

8. Quoted in Traubel, *With Walt Whitman in Camden,* 1:149.

9. Walt Whitman, *Notebooks*, 1:88–89. "Wants" was the heading that daily papers used. Edward Grier says that this manuscript was "obviously a piece of journalism destined for an unknown paper" (1:88).

10. Quoted in Traubel, *With Walt Whitman in Camden*, 2:19.

11. Stanton, Anthony, and Gage, *History of Woman Suffrage*, 1:520.

12. Stanton, Anthony, and Gage, *History of Woman Suffrage*, 1:367. In 1852, Ernestine L. Rose sharply rebutted Horace Mann's lectures in an article entitled "Hints to a Young Woman." Mann didn't want women to vote, hold a public office, or enter into politics. See Suhl's biography, *Ernestine Rose and the Battle for Human Rights*, 125–27, for a concise report on Rose's handling of Mann's repressive stand.

13. Mrs. Bowers was Elizabeth Bowers (Mrs. D. P. Bowers), a sister to Sarah G. Crocker (Mrs. Frederick B. Conway). Both were professional actors.

14. Quoted in Traubel, *With Walt Whitman in Camden*, 6:175.

15. Stanton, Anthony, and Gage, *History of Woman Suffrage*, 1:690.

16. Wilmans to Whitman, 21 May 1882, Charles Feinberg–Walt Whitman Collection, Manuscript Division, Library of Congress.

17. Ibid.

18. Whitman, *Daybooks and Notebooks*, 3:773.

Bibliography

Alcaro, Marion Walker. *Walt Whitman's Mrs. G: A Biography of Anne Gilchrist*. Rutherford, N.J.: Fairleigh Dickinson University Press, 1991.

Algeo, Sara M. "Equal Suffrage Notes." *Sunday Journal* [Providence]. 23 July 1911.

Allen, Gay Wilson. *The Solitary Singer: A Critical Biography of Walt Whitman*. Chicago: University of Chicago Press, 1985.

Aspiz, Harold. "An Early Feminist Tribute to Whitman." *American Literature* 51 (November 1979):404–9.

——. "Unfolding the Folds." *Walt Whitman Review* 12 (December 1966):81–87.

——. *Walt Whitman and the Body Beautiful*. Urbana: University of Illinois Press, 1980.

——. "Walt Whitman: The Spermatic Imagination." *American Literature* 56 (October 1984):379–95.

Ballou, Adin. *History of the Town of Milford, Worcester County*. 1882. Boston: Reed, Avery, 1882.

Barker-Benfield, G. *The Horrors of the Half-Known Life: Male Attitudes Toward Women and Sexuality in Nineteenth Century America*. New York: Harper and Row, 1976.

Barrus, Clara. *The Life and Letters of John Burroughs*. Vol. 1. New York: Houghton Mifflin, 1925.

——. *Whitman and Burroughs: Comrades*. Boston: Houghton Mifflin, 1931.

"Biography: Paulina Wright Davis, Phrenological Character." *American Phrenological Journal* 18 (1853):11–13.

Black, Stephen A. *Whitman's Journeys into Chaos: A Psychoanalytic Study of the Poetic Process*. Princeton: Princeton University Press, 1975.

Blatt, Martin Henry. *Free Love and Anarchism: The Biography of Ezra Heywood*. Urbana: University of Illinois Press, 1989.

Bleier, Ruth. *Science and Gender: A Critique of Biology and Its Theories on Women*. Athene Series. New York: Pergamon Press, 1984.

Born, Helena. *Whitman's Ideal Democracy*. Boston: Everett Press, 1902.

Brodie, Janet Farrell. *Contraception and Abortion in Nineteenth-Century America*. Ithaca: Cornell University Press, 1994.

Bucke, Richard Maurice. *Walt Whitman*. Philadelphia: David McKay, 1883.

Burlingame, Leslie J. "Lamarck." In *Dictionary of Scientific Biography*, edited by Charles Coulston Gillispie. Vol. 7. New York: Scribner's, 1973.

Burroughs, John. "Walt Whitman and His 'Drum Taps.' " *Galaxy* 2 (Fall 1866):606–15.

Calder, Ellen M. "Personal Recollections of Walt Whitman." *Atlantic Monthly* 99 (June 1907):823–29.

Campbell, Karlyn Kohrs. *Man Cannot Speak for Her: A Critical Study of Early Feminist Rhetoric*. Vol. 1. New York: Praeger, 1989.

Cavitch, David. *My Soul and I: The Inner Life of Walt Whitman*. Boston: Beacon Press, 1985.

Cayleff, Susan. *Wash and Be Healed: The Water-Cure Movement and Women's Health*. Philadelphia: Temple University Press, 1987.

Chilton, Mary A. "Sexual Purity." *Social Revolutionist* (July 1857):5–6.

———. "Suffrage." *Revolution*, 22 July 1869.

Clare, Ada. "Thoughts and Things." *Saturday Press*, 19 May 1860.

Conway, Moncure. *Autobiography: Memories and Experiences*. Vol. 1. Boston: Houghton Mifflin, 1904.

———. "Modern Times, New York." *Fortnightly Review* 6 (1 July 1865):421–34.

Cott, Nancy. *The Bonds of Womanhood: "Woman's Sphere" in New England, 1780–1835*. New Haven: Yale University Press, 1977.

Coultrap-McQuin, Susan. *Doing Literary Business: American Women Writers in the Nineteenth Century*. Chapel Hill: University of North Carolina Press, 1990.

Dall, Caroline H., Papers, 1811–1917. Library of Congress, Washington, D.C. (Microfilm edition; original manuscripts are held at the Massachusetts Historical Society, Boston, Mass.)

Davis, Paulina Wright. "Address." *Proceedings of the [First National] Woman's Rights Convention, Held at Worcester, October 23rd and 24th, 1850*. Boston: Prentiss and Sawyer, 1851.

——. "Female Compositors, and Opposition of Interests." *Una* 1 (October 1853):152.

——. *A History of the National Woman's Rights Movement, for Twenty Years.* New York: Journeymen Printers' Co-Operative Association, 1871.

——. "Inequality of Women in Marriage." *Una* 2 (February 1854):214–15.

——. "Intellect of the Sexes." *Una* 1 (August 1853):120–21.

——. "Letter from Paulina Wright Davis." In *The History of Woman Suffrage,* edited by Elizabeth Cady Stanton, Susan B. Anthony, and Matilda Joslyn Gage. Vol. 1. Rochester, N.Y.: Charles Mann, 1887.

——. "Pecuniary Independence of Women." *Una* 2 (January 1854):200–1.

——. "The Providence Physiological Society." *Water-Cure Journal* 12 (August 1851):41.

——. "Reply to Mrs. Dall." *Liberator,* 29 October 1852.

——. "Report on the Education of Females, Given at the Convention in Worcester, Mass., October 15, 1851." *Una* 2 (November 1854):360–62.

——. "To Our Readers." *Una* 2 (December 1854):376–77.

Dickinson, Emily. *Selected Letters.* Edited by Thomas H. Johnson. Cambridge, Mass.: Harvard University Press, 1986.

DuBois, Ellen. "On Labor and Free Love: Two Unpublished Speeches of Elizabeth Cady Stanton." *Signs* 1 (Autumn 1975):263–64.

Elder, William. "Mrs. Wright's Lectures to Ladies on Anatomy, Physiology, and Health." *Water-Cure Journal* 2 (June 1846):11.

Eldridge, Charles. "Walt Whitman as a Conservative." *New York Times,* 7 June 1902.

Emmanuel, Lenny. "Whitman's Fusion of Science and Poetry." *Walt Whitman Review* 17 (September 1971):73–82.

Erkkila, Betsy. "The Federal Mother: Whitman as Revolutionary Son." *Prospects* 10 (1985):423–41.

——. *Whitman the Political Poet.* New York: Oxford University Press, 1989.

Faderman, Lillian. *Surpassing the Love of Men: Romantic Friendship and Love Between Women from the Renaissance to the Present.* New York: William Morrow, 1981.

[Fifth National Woman's Rights Convention, Second Day]. *The Lily* 1 (November 1854). In *Papers of Elizabeth Cady Stanton and Susan B. Anthony.* Edited by Patricia G. Holland and Ann D. Gordon. Wilmington, Del.: Scholarly Resources, 1989. (Microfilm, series 3, reel 8.)

Flexner, Eleanor. *Century of Struggle*. Cambridge, Mass.: Harvard University Press, 1975.

Folsom, Ed. "Prospects for the Study of Walt Whitman." *Resources for American Literary Study* 20 (1994):1–15.

———. " 'Scattering it freely forever': Whitman in a Seminar on Nineteenth-Century American Culture." In *Approaches to Teaching Whitman's "Leaves of Grass."* Approaches to Teaching World Literature, 32. Edited by Donald D. Kummings. New York: Modern Language Association, 1990.

———. *Walt Whitman's Native Representations*. New York: Cambridge University Press, 1994.

Freedman, Florence Bernstein. *William Douglas O'Connor: Walt Whitman's Chosen Knight*. Athens: Ohio University Press, 1985.

Gershenowitz, Harry. "Two Lamarckians: Walt Whitman and Edward Carpenter." *Walt Whitman Quarterly Review* 2 (Summer 1984):35–39.

———. "Whitman and Lamarck Revisited." *Walt Whitman Review* 25 (September 1979):121–23.

Gohdes, Clarence, and Rollo G. Silver, eds. *Faint Clews and Indirections: Manuscripts of Walt Whitman and His Family*. Durham, N.C.: Duke University Press, 1949.

Gordon, Linda. *Woman's Body, Woman's Right: A Social History of Birth Control in America*. New York: Penguin, 1977.

Gould, Stephen J. *The Mismeasure of Man*. New York: W. W. Norton, 1981.

Green, Anna E. Review of *Feminism and Suffrage: The Emergence of an Independent Women's Movement in America, 1848–1869* by Ellen Carol DuBois. *Signs* 5 (Autumn 1979):176.

Green, Judith Kent. "A Note on Walt Whitman's Probable Reading of Robert Chambers." *Walt Whitman Quarterly Review* 3 (Winter 1986):23–28.

Greenspan, Ezra. *Walt Whitman and the American Reader*. New York: Cambridge University Press, 1990.

Gregory, Dorothy M-T. "The Celebration of Nativity: 'Broad-Axe Poem.' " *Walt Whitman Quarterly Review* 2 (Summer 1984):1–11.

Griffin, Larry D. "Walt Whitman's Voice." *Walt Whitman Quarterly Review* 9 (Winter 1992):125–33.

Grimké, Sarah. *Letters on the Equality of the Sexes and Other Essays*. Edited by Elizabeth Ann Bartlett. New Haven: Yale University Press, 1988.

Guarneri, Carl. *The Utopian Alternative: Fourierism in Nineteenth-Century America*. Ithaca: Cornell University Press, 1991.

Harris, Susan K. " 'But Is It Any Good?': Evaluating Nineteenth-Century American Women's Fiction." *American Literature* 63 (March 1991):43–61.

Hollis, C. Carroll. *Language and Style in "Leaves of Grass."* Baton Rouge: Louisiana State University Press, 1983.

"In Memoriam: Mrs. Abby H. Price." *Woman's Journal,* 25 May 1878.

Johnson, Mary Wright. Letter to [Ellen Wright]. 20 May 1857. Garrison Family Papers. Sophia Smith Collection. Smith College, Northampton, Mass.

Kaplan, Justin. *Walt Whitman: A Life.* New York: Bantam, 1980.

Kerber, Linda. *Women of the Republic: Intellect and Ideology in Revolutionary America.* New York: W. W. Norton, 1980.

Killingsworth, M. Jimmie. "The Saturday Press." In *American Literary Magazines: The Eighteenth and Nineteenth Centuries,* edited by Edward E. Chielens. Westport, Conn.: Greenwood Press, 1986.

———. "Tropes of Selfhood: Whitman's 'Expressive Individualism.' " In *The Continuing Presence of Walt Whitman,* edited by Robert K. Martin. Iowa City: University of Iowa Press, 1992.

———. "Whitman and Motherhood: A Historical View." *American Literature* 54 (1982):28–43.

———. *Whitman's Poetry of the Body: Sexuality, Politics, and the Text.* Chapel Hill: University of North Carolina Press, 1989.

Knapp, Jane. [Letter from Jane Knapp to Paulina Wright Davis]. *Una* 2 (December 1854):374.

Krieg, Joann P., ed. *Walt Whitman: Here and Now.* Westport, Conn.: Greenwood Press, 1985.

Kummings, Donald D., ed. *Approaches to Teaching Whitman's "Leaves of Grass."* New York: Modern Language Association, 1990.

Leonard, David Charles. "Lamarckian Evolution in Whitman's 'Song of Myself.' " *Walt Whitman Review* 24 (March 1979):21–28.

Lewis, David. "Farnham, Eliza Wood Burhans." In *Notable American Women, 1607–1950,* edited by Edward T. James, Janet Wilson James, and Paul S. Boyer. Cambridge, Mass.: Harvard University Press, 1971.

Loving, Jerome. *Walt Whitman's Champion: William Douglas O'Connor.* College Station: Texas A & M University Press, 1978.

Lynch, Michael. " 'Here Is Adhesiveness': From Friendship to Homosexuality." *Victorian Studies* 29 (Autumn 1985):67–96.

Macdonald, George E. *Fifty Years of Freethought.* Vol. 1. New York: Truth Seeker, 1929.

Martin, Robert K., ed. *The Continuing Presence of Walt Whitman: The Life After the Life.* Iowa City: University of Iowa Press, 1992.

Michael, Helen. "Woman and Freedom in Whitman." *Poet-Lore* 9 (1897):216–37.

Miller, Edwin Haviland. *Walt Whitman's Poetry: A Psychological Journey.* New York: Houghton Mifflin, 1968.

Millhauser, Milton. "The Literary Impact of *Vestiges of Creation.*" *Modern Language Quarterly* 17 (September 1956):213–26.

"Mrs. Rose's Lecture in Washington." *Una* 2 (May 1854):269.

Nichols, Thomas Low. *Esoteric Anthropology.* London: T. L. Nichols, 1854.

Overton, C. M. "Horrors of Slavery." *Social Revolutionist* 4 (December 1857):162–64.

Parry, Albert. *Garrets and Pretenders: A History of Bohemianism in America.* New York: Covici-Friede, 1933.

Pease, Donald E. *Visionary Compacts: American Renaissance Writings in Cultural Context.* Madison: University of Wisconsin Press, 1987.

Perry, Nora. "A Few Words About Walt Whitman." *Appleton's Journal* 15 (January-June 1876):531–37.

Pfeifer, Edward J. "The Theory of Evolution and Whitman's 'Passage to India.' " *ESQ* 42 (1966):31–35.

Price, Abby H. "Address: Read to the 'Woman's Rights Convention' at Worcester, by Mrs. Abby H. Price of Hopedale." *Practical Christian,* 15 February 1851 and 1 March 1851.

——. "The Annual Meeting." *Practical Christian,* 18 December 1852.

——. "The Bloomer Costume—Again." *Practical Christian,* 9 October 1852.

——. "The Constitutional Convention." *Practical Christian,* 18 June 1853.

——. "Co-Operative Industry." *Una* 1 (July 1853):122–23.

——. "Does the Woman's Rights' Convention Need a Paper." *Practical Christian,* 12 February 1853.

——. "Inquiry and Explanation." *Practical Christian,* 2 July 1853.

——. Letter to Walt Whitman. [25 March 1867]. Yale Collection of American Literature. Beinecke Rare Book and Manuscript Library. Yale University Library, New Haven, Conn.

——. "National Woman's Rights Convention at Syracuse." *Liberator,* 8 October 1852.

——. "Reasons Why Woman Should Define Her Own Sphere." *Una* 1 (February 1853):10–11.

——. "[Report on the Behalf of the] Committee on Industrial Avocations." In *Proceedings of the [Second National] Woman's Rights Convention, Held at Worcester, October 15th and 16th, 1851*. New York: Fowlers and Wells, 1852.

———. "Things at Home." *Practical Christian,* 17 July 1852.

———. "Things at Home." *Practical Christian,* 31 July 1852.

———. "To the Friends in Hopedale." *Practical Christian,* 7 February 1846.

———. "To Whom It May Concern." *Practical Christian,* 30 July 1853.

———. "Woman's Right to Suffrage." *Practical Christian,* 15 January 1853.

Price, Helen E. "Reminiscences of Walt Whitman." *New York Evening Post,* 31 May 1919.

Price, Kenneth. "Whitman, Free Love, and the *Social Revolutionist.*" *American Periodicals* 1 (Fall 1991):70–82.

Proceedings, Second National Woman's Rights Convention. New York: Fowlers and Wells, 1852.

Proceedings of the Woman's Rights Convention. Broadway Tabernacle, 6 and 7 September 1853. New York: Fowlers and Wells, 1853.

"Prospectus." *Social Revolutionist* 1 (January 1856):4.

Providence Physiological Society Records. Minutes, 1850–53. Rhode Island Historical Society Library, Providence, R.I.

Quincy, Edmund. Letter to Caroline Weston. 17 September 1844. Anti-Slavery Collection. Boston Public Library, Boston, Mass.

The Report of the [U.S.] Commissioner of Patents for the Year 1860. Patent No. 28,139: "George B. Arnold, of New York, N.Y.—Improvement in Sewing Machines. Patent dated May 8, 1860." Washington, D.C.: U.S. Government Printing Office, 1860.

Rosenfeld, Alvin H. "The Eagle and the Axe: A Study of Whitman's 'Song of the Broad-Axe.' " *American Imago* 25 (Winter 1968):354–70.

Ryan, Mary P. *Cradle of the Middle Class: The Family in Oneida County, New York, 1790–1865.* Cambridge: Cambridge University Press, 1981.

Sampath, Ursula. "Who Was Kaspar Hauser?—The Historical Facts." *Kaspar Hauser: A Modern Metaphor.* Columbia, S.C.: Camden House, 1991.

Schappes, Morris U. "Ernestine L. Rose: Her Address on the Anniversary of West Indian Emancipation." *Journal of Negro History* 34 (July 1949):344–55.

———. "Ernestine Rose, Queen of the Platform." *Jewish Life,* March 1949, pp. 7–10.

———. "To Be Included." *Morning Freiheit,* 13 March 1948, n.p.

Scholnick, Robert J. " 'The Password Primeval': Whitman's Use of Science in 'Song of Myself.' " In *Studies in the American Renaissance, 1986,* edited by Joel Myerson. Charlottesville: University of Virginia Press, 1986.

Sears, Hal D. *The Sex Radicals: Free Love in High Victorian America.* Lawrence: Regents Press of Kansas, 1977.

Shephard, Esther. *Walt Whitman's Pose.* New York: Harcourt, Brace, 1938.

Shively, Charley. *Drum Beats: Walt Whitman's Civil War Boy Lovers.* San Francisco: Gay Sunshine Press, 1989.

Showalter, Elaine. *Alternative Alcott.* New Brunswick: Rutgers University Press, 1988.

Smith-Rosenberg, Carroll. "The Female World of Love and Ritual: Relations Between Women in Nineteenth-Century America." In *Disorderly Conduct: Visions of Gender in Victorian America.* New York: Oxford University Press, 1985.

Sokolow, Jayme A. "Culture and Utopia: The Raritan Bay Union." *New Jersey History* 94 (Summer 1976):96.

Spann, Edward K. *Hopedale: From Commune to Company Town, 1840–1920.* Columbus: Ohio State University Press, 1992.

Spurlock, John C. *Free Love, Marriage, and Middle-Class Radicalism in America, 1825–1860.* New York: New York University Press, 1988.

Stansell, Christine. *City of Women: Sex and Class in New York, 1789–1860.* Urbana: University of Illinois Press, 1987.

——. "Whitman at Pfaff's: Commercial Culture, Literary Life, and New York Bohemia at Mid-Century." *Walt Whitman Quarterly Review* 10 (Fall 1992):107–26.

Stanton, Elizabeth Cady. *Elizabeth Cady Stanton, As Revealed in Her Letters, Diary, and Reminiscences.* Edited by Theodore Stanton and Harriot Stanton Blatch. New York: Harper and Brothers, 1922.

——. "Letter from Elizabeth Cady Stanton." In *History of Woman Suffrage,* edited by Elizabeth Cady Stanton, Susan B. Anthony, and Matilda Joslyn Gage. Vol. 1. Rochester: Charles Mann, 1887.

——. Letter to Paulina Wright Davis. 6 December [1852]. In *Papers of Elizabeth Cady Stanton and Susan B. Anthony,* edited by Patricia G. Holland and Ann D. Gordon. Wilmington, Del.: Scholarly Resources, 1989. (Microfilm, series 3, reel 7.)

——. Letter to Susan B. Anthony. 1 March [1853]. In *Papers of Elizabeth Cady Stanton and Susan B. Anthony,* edited by Patricia G. Holland and Ann D. Gordon. Wilmington, Del.: Scholarly Resources, 1989. (Microfilm, series 3, reel 7.)

Stanton, Elizabeth Cady, and Susan B. Anthony. *Papers of Elizabeth Cady Stanton and Susan B. Anthony.* Edited by Patricia G. Holland and Ann D. Gordon. Wilmington, Del.: Scholarly Resources, 1989. Microfilm.

Stoddard, Charles Warren. "La Belle Menken." *National Magazine* 21 (February 1905):477–88.

Stoehr, Taylor. *Free Love in America: A Documentary History.* New York: AMS Press, 1979.

Stovall, Floyd. *The Foreground of* Leaves of Grass. Charlottesville: University Press of Virginia, 1974.

Suhl, Yuri. *Ernestine Rose and the Battle for Human Rights.* New York: Reynal, 1959.

Tanenbaum, Leora. "Sisterhood, For and Against." *Women's Review of Books* 10 (May 1993):18.

Tanner, James T. F. "The Lamarckian Theory of Progress in *Leaves of Grass.*" *Walt Whitman Review* 9 (March 1963):3–11.

———. "Walt Whitman: Poet of Evolution." Ph.D. Dissertation, Texas Tech University, 1965.

Tanner, Nancy, and Adrienne Zihlman. "Women in Evolution, Part I: Innovation and Selection in Human Origins." *Signs* 2 (1976):585–608.

Thomas, M. Wynn. *The Lunar Light of Whitman's Poetry.* Cambridge, Mass.: Harvard University Press, 1987.

Traubel, Horace. *With Walt Whitman in Camden.* Vols. 1–3. New York: Rowman and Littlefield, 1961.

———. *With Walt Whitman in Camden.* Edited by Sculley Bradley. Vol. 4. Philadelphia: University of Pennsylvania Press, 1953.

———. *With Walt Whitman in Camden.* Edited by Gertrude Traubel. Vol. 5. Carbondale: Southern Illinois University Press, 1964.

———. *With Walt Whitman in Camden.* Edited by Gertrude Traubel and William White. Vol. 6. Carbondale: Southern Illinois University Press, 1982.

Whitman, Louisa Van Velsor. Letters to Helen Price. MA 918. Pierpont Morgan Library, New York.

———. Letters to Walt Whitman. Trent Collection. Special Collections Library. Duke University, Durham, N.C.

———. Letters to Walt Whitman. Hanley Collection. Harry Ranson Humanities Research Center, Austin, Texas.

Whitman, Martha Mitchell. *Mattie: The Letters of Martha Mitchell Whitman.* Edited by Randall H. Waldron. New York: New York University Press, 1977.

Whitman, Walt. *An American Primer.* Stevens Point, Wis.: Holy Cow Press, 1987.

———. *The Collected Writings of Walt Whitman.* Edited by Gay Wilson Allen and Sculley Bradley. 22 vols. New York: New York University Press.

———. *The Correspondence.* Edited by Edwin Haviland Miller. 6 vols. Collected Writings of Walt Whitman. New York: New York University Press, 1961–77.

———. *Daybooks and Notebooks.* Edited by William White. 3 vols. Collected Writings of Walt Whitman. New York: New York University Press, 1978.

———. *The Early Poems and Fiction.* Edited by Thomas L. Brasher. Collected Writings of Walt Whitman. New York: New York University Press, 1963.

———. *The Eighteenth Presidency.* Edited by Edward F. Grier. Lawrence: University of Kansas Press, 1956.

———. *Leaves of Grass.* Comprehensive Reader's Edition. Edited by Harold W. Blodgett and Sculley Bradley. Collected Writings of Walt Whitman. New York: New York University Press, 1965.

———. *Leaves of Grass.* 1855 ed. Edited by Malcolm Cowley. New York: Penguin, 1985.

———. *Leaves of Grass.* Facsimile ed. of the 1860 text. Introduction by Roy Harvey Pearce. Ithaca: Cornell University Press, 1984.

———. *"Leaves of Grass": A Textual Variorum of the Printed Poems.* Edited by Sculley Bradley, Harold W. Blodgett, Arthur Golden, and William White. 3 vols. Collected Writings of Walt Whitman. New York: New York University Press, 1980.

———. *Manuscripts, Autograph Letters, First Editions, and Portraits of Walt Whitman Formerly the Property of the Late Dr. Richard Maurice Bucke.* Edited by E. F. Hannaburgh and Jacob Schwarz. New York: American Art Association, 1936.

———. *Notebooks and Unpublished Prose Manuscripts.* Edited by Edward F. Grier. 6 vols. Collected Writings of Walt Whitman. New York: New York University Press, 1984.

———. *Notes and Fragments: Left by Walt Whitman.* Edited by Richard Maurice Bucke. London, Ontario: A. Talbot, 1899.

———. *Prose Works 1892.* Edited by Floyd Stovall. 2 vols. Collected Writings of Walt Whitman. New York: New York University Press, 1964.

Wilentz, Sean. *Chants Democratic: New York City and the Rise of the American Working Class, 1788–1850.* New York: Oxford University Press, 1984.

"Woman's Rights Convention." *Practical Christian,* 27 September 1851.

"Woman's Rights Convention [Rochester, November 30, 1853]." *Una* (January 1854):196.

"Woman's Rights Convention in Boston." *Una* 3 (October 1855):153.

"Women and the Tariff." *New York Tribune,* 15 October 1853.

Wrobel, Arthur. "Noble American Motherhood: Whitman, Women, and the Ideal Democracy." *American Studies* 21 (1980):7–25.

Wyman, Lillie Buffum Chace, and Arthur Crawford Wyman. *Elizabeth Buffum Chace, 1806–1899: Her Life and Its Environment.* Vol. 2. Boston: W. B. Clarke, 1914.

Index

About the Author

Sherry Ceniza, Associate Professor of English at Texas Tech University, Lubbock, received the Feinberg Award in recognition of the most significant contribution to Whitman scholarship to have appeared in the *Walt Whitman Quarterly Review* (1989–90). In addition to journal publications, she has essays in *Approaches to Teaching Whitman's "Leaves of Grass,"* edited by Donald D. Kummings, and *The Cambridge Companion to Walt Whitman*, edited by Ezra Greenspan. She also has entries in the forthcoming *Walt Whitman Encyclopedia*.